Lecture Notes in Computer Science 12512

More information about this series at http://www.springer.com/series/7410

George Hatzivasilis · Sotiris Ioannidis (Eds.)

Model-driven Simulation and Training Environments for Cybersecurity

Second International Workshop, MSTEC 2020
Guildford, UK, September 14–18, 2020
Revised Selected Papers

 Springer

Editors
George Hatzivasilis (iD)
Foundation for Research
and Technology - Hellas
Heraklion, Greece

Sotiris Ioannidis
Technical University of Crete
Chania, Greece

ISSN 0302-9743   ISSN 1611-3349   (electronic)
Lecture Notes in Computer Science
ISBN 978-3-030-62432-3   ISBN 978-3-030-62433-0   (eBook)
https://doi.org/10.1007/978-3-030-62433-0

LNCS Sublibrary: SL4 – Security and Cryptology

This Springer imprint is published by the registered company Springer Nature Switzerland AG
The registered company address is: Gewerbestrasse 11, 6330 Cham, Switzerland

Preface

This volume contains the papers presented at the Second Workshop on Model-driven Simulation and Training Environments for Cybersecurity (MSTEC 2020), held virtually on September 17, 2020, under the ESORICS 2020 conference.

The MSTEC 2020 workshop addressed recent advances in the field of cyber modeling and simulation. It aimed to provide a forum of practitioners and researchers to discuss cyber modeling and simulation (M&S) as well as its application to the development of cyber-security training scenarios and courses of action (COAs). Specifically, it focused on the verification and validation (V&V) process, which provides the operational community with confidence in knowing that cyber models represent the real world, and discusses how defense training may benefit from cyber models. It also investigates advances in emulators, simulators, and their potential combination. The papers presented at MSTEC 2020 took a holistic approach to the overall system assurance process, presenting advances in the simulation of people, policies, processes, and technologies currently available in the field. The workshop aimed to connect the multiple threads that currently compose M&S into a coherent view of what is usable in order to train experts and non-computer-savvy users towards an assured operation of critical systems.

There were 20 submissions. Each submission was reviewed by at least three Program Committee members. The committee decided to accept 10 papers.

The main sponsorship was provided by the European Union Horizon's 2020 research and innovation program THREAT-ARREST (www.threat-arrest.eu) under the grant agreements No. 786890.

We would like to thank the committee members and the reviewers for their voluntary effort as well as all the authors of the submitted papers for their contributions.

September 2020
George Hatzivasilis
Sotiris Ioannidis

Organization

Program Committee Chair

Sotiris Ioannidis   Technical University of Crete, Greece

General Chairs

Ernesto Damiani   University of Milan, Italy
Vassilis Prevelakis   Technical University of Braunschweig, Germany
George Spanoudakis   Sphynx Technology Solutions AG, Switzerland
Michael Vinov   IBM, Israel

Technical Committee

George Hatzivasilis   FORTH, Greece
Fulvio Frati   University of Milan, Italy
Marinos Tsantekidis   Technical University of Braunschweig, Germany
Kostantinos Fysarakis   Sphynx Technology Solutions AG, Switzerland
Ludger Goeke   Social-Engineering Academy, Germany
Hristo Koshutanski   ATOS, Spain
George Leftheriotis   TUV Hellas, Greece
George Tsakirakis   ITML, Greece

Additional Reviewers

Othonas Soultatos   Iason Somarakis
Eftychia Lakka   Manos Michalodimitrakis
Georeg Leftheriotis   Manos Chatzimpyrros
Torsten Hildebrandt   Dirk Wortmann
Stelvio Cimato   Chiara Braghin
George Bravos   Vina Rompoti
Robert Bordianu   Menelaos Ioannidis
Oleg Blinder   Maria Crociani
Fotis Oikonomou   Takis Varelas
Giovanni Gorgoni   Libor Manda

Contents

Cyber Security Training Modelling

Cyber Taxi: A Taxonomy of Interactive Cyber Training and Education
Systems.. 3
    Marcus Knüpfer, Tore Bierwirth, Lars Stiemert, Matthias Schopp,
    Sebastian Seeber, Daniela Pöhn, and Peter Hillmann

Cyber Range Training Programme Specification Through Cyber Threat
and Training Preparation Models.................................... 22
    Michail Smyrlis, Konstantinos Fysarakis, George Spanoudakis,
    and George Hatzivasilis

Serious Games

A Pond Full of Phishing Games - Analysis of Learning Games
for Anti-Phishing Education....................................... 41
    Rene Roepke, Klemens Koehler, Vincent Drury, Ulrik Schroeder,
    Martin R. Wolf, and Ulrike Meyer

Conceptualization of a CyberSecurity Awareness Quiz................ 61
    Sebastian Pape, Ludger Goeke, Alejandro Quintanar,
    and Kristian Beckers

Emulation and Simulation Studies

Towards the Monitoring and Evaluation of Trainees' Activities
in Cyber Ranges.. 79
    Chiara Braghin, Stelvio Cimato, Ernesto Damiani, Fulvio Frati,
    Elvinia Riccobene, and Sadegh Astaneh

Automatically Protecting Network Communities
by Malware Epidemiology... 92
    Xiao-Si Wang, Jessica Welding, and Tek Kan Chung

Attacks

Chasing Botnets: A Real Security Incident Investigation 111
    George Hatzivasilis and Martin Kunc

Software System Exploration Using Library Call Analysis 125
    Marinos Tsantekidis and Vassilis Prevelakis

Security Policies

A Pattern–Driven Adaptation in IoT Orchestrations to Guarantee SPDI
Properties.. 143
  Papoutsakis Manos, Fysarakis Konstantinos,
  Michalodimitrakis Emmanouil, Lakka Eftychia, Petroulakis Nikolaos,
  Spanoudakis George, and Ioannidis Sotiris

Password Management: How Secure Is Your Login Process?............ 157
  George Hatzivasilis

Author Index 179

Cyber Security Training Modelling

Cyber Taxi: A Taxonomy of Interactive Cyber Training and Education Systems

Marcus Knüpfer[1(✉)], Tore Bierwirth[1,2], Lars Stiemert[1,2], Matthias Schopp[1,2],
Sebastian Seeber[1,2], Daniela Pöhn[1,2], and Peter Hillmann[1]

[1] Universität der Bundeswehr München, 85577 Neubiberg, Germany
{marcus.knuepfer,peter.hillmann}@unibw.de
[2] Team localos, Munich, Germany
{tore.bierwirth,lars.stiemert,matthias.schopp,sebastian.seeber,
daniela.poehn}@localos.io

Abstract. The lack of guided exercises and practical opportunities to learn about cybersecurity in a practical way makes it difficult for security experts to improve their proficiency. Capture the Flag events and Cyber Ranges are ideal for cybersecurity training. Thereby, the participants usually compete in teams against each other, or have to defend themselves in a specific scenario. As organizers of yearly events, we present a taxonomy for interactive cyber training and education. The proposed taxonomy includes different factors of the technical setup, audience, training environment, and training setup. By the comprehensive taxonomy, different aspects of interactive training are considered. This can help trainings to improve and to be established successfully. The provided taxonomy is extendable and can be used in further application areas as research on new security technologies.

Keywords: Capture the flag · Cyber range · Cybersecurity · Cyber defence · Cyber education

1 Introduction

With increasing digitalization and the integration of computers into the daily life, the number of threats is also rising. The amount of sophisticated attacks is increasing every year and poses a challenge in terms of efficient detection and countermeasures. At the same time, the required technical knowledge of an intruder decreases with the development of more automated tools [6,27]. The defence against these attacks is based on the continuous use and monitoring of security tools. Well-trained personnel is required for this. However, current statistics show a global shortage of approximately four million information security professionals [17]. In recent years, many different training systems have been developed with focus on cybersecurity. Companies have emerged offering new certifications and universities are developing cybersecurity degree programs. Interactive training systems are further approaches that follow our motivation

© Springer Nature Switzerland AG 2020
G. Hatzivasilis and S. Ioannidis (Eds.): MSTEC 2020, LNCS 12512, pp. 3–21, 2020.
https://doi.org/10.1007/978-3-030-62433-0_1

as cybersecurity trainers: Theoretical knowledge is good, practical proficiency is better. These systems utilize gamification and playful scenarios to train participants in specific topics [1].

Interactive training systems offer the opportunity of real-time feedback and specific education. The focus is on instructing the participants with an efficient method and the desirable knowledge. These systems create awareness for security threats and the resulting impact in real life. In order to provide an overview of a large range of practical possibilities, we present a taxonomy to structure interactive cyber training and education. This overview allows universities, companies, and other institutions to

- identify gaps in their training system.
- improve existing training systems and intensify the training.
- provide a guideline for establishing new training possibilities.

The taxonomy includes surrounding aspects, e.g., training of teamwork, communication capabilities as well as reporting processes. As far as we know, there is no holistic taxonomy for practical and interactive cyber training and education. Such a taxonomy is mandatory to support education, structure the entire area, and accelerate further research. It enables a comprehensive evaluation of interactive training systems and the visualization of the requirements gap.

The paper is structured as follows: Section 2 establishes the requirements for a taxonomy. In the following section, we briefly discuss related approaches with their advantages and disadvantages. In Sect. 4, we describe our taxonomy in detail. Afterwards, we classify other examples with our taxonomy and show the practical benefit. Beside this, we discuss the presented aspects on our case study. Finally, we conclude the paper and give future directions.

2   Definition of Terms and Requirements

We define *Interactive Cyber Training and Education* (ICTE) as follows:

Definition: ICTE is a comprehensive set of hands-on approaches in a secure and observable environment that enables participants to become engaged in learning and practice their cyber skills and to acquire new skills.

For a better understanding of the following taxonomy, a common basis of definition is mandatory. In general, a taxonomy structures a knowledge field to provide an overview about a specific area and its possibilities. It divides the topic hierarchical into main groups and subcategories. A taxonomy should focus on the following, ideal properties [24, 26]:

- The categories have to be mutually exclusive, i.e., no overlapping between the categories.
- Clear and unambiguous classification criteria.
- Comprehensible and useful as well as comply with established terminology.

Beside the requirements for the taxonomy of ICTE, there are the following demands on systems:

- What are the optimal approaches and motivation for developing new cyber skills?
- What skills and competencies in security are required to move to a more proactive position?
- Which kind of training system requires which functionalities and possibilities?
- What changes in terms of process, technology, and staff are required in the operational environment to support new abilities?
- What are the business objectives and strategic goals of an organization from a security point of view?

Furthermore, there are the following assessment criteria to further evaluate a classified training system. These criteria follow the National Institute of Standards and Technology (NIST) [31], which developed the cybersecurity workforce framework for the National Initiative for Cybersecurity Education (NICE). The requirements are tantamount to the ISO/IEC 25010 [19] and ISO 9126 [18] standards, which focus more on system and software quality properties. These are also valid to our scenario.

- **Functional Completeness:** The degree of realization to cover all the specified tasks and user objectives.
- **Functional Correctness:** The degree to which the cyber training system provides the correct and reproducible results with the needed degree of precision.
- **Learnability:** Efficiency to achieve the specified goal of learning individual and as cooperative team.
- **Operability:** The difficulty to run the training.
- **Accessibility:** Amount of expertise to be successful in a scenario.
- **Adaptability:** The degree to customize the scenarios to the expertise of the participants.
- **Portability:** The degree to transfer scenarios from an education system to another.
- **Maintainability:** Difficulty to operate the system and to fulfill a training session.
- **Modularity:** Possibility to adapt and extend the system to current needs.

3   Related Work

Several different taxonomies were developed, e.g., taxonomies for *Computer System Attack Classification* [2,14,23,29,32,47,51]. These list a comprehensive set of attacks and focus on a structural overview of attacks. Jouini et al. [21] classify security threats in information systems by threat source, agent, motivation, intention, and impact. Easttom and Butler [12] describe a taxonomy of cyber attacks based on a modified McCumber cubes. Amongst others, they classify the categories transmission, storage, technology, policy and practices, education, training, and awareness. Simmons et al. [39] propose a taxonomy of cyber attacks called AVOIDIT, classifying attack vector, operational impact, defence, informational impact, and target. All these taxonomies can be used to develop security challenges, such that a wide spectrum of knowledge is necessary to solve them.

Different approaches focus on *Cyber Range Training*. ECSO explains cyber ranges in their WG5 Paper [13], but neither a definition nor a taxonomy is given. Priyadarshini [34] analyses and classifies existing cyber ranges based on infrastructure association, cloud usage, teams, and deployment. Other aspects are left out. Yamin et al. [52] build a taxonomy based on literature review. The taxonomy includes scenarios, monitoring, learning, management, teaming, and environment. Based on the taxonomy the authors describe several tools used within cyber ranges. The taxonomy is specific for cyber ranges and does not take target audience, proficiency level, and scoring, amongst others, into account.

Several papers describe *Cybersecurity Exercises*. INCIBE [11] analyses cyber exercises and builds a short taxonomy based on the factors focus, model, vertical sector, scope for participation, and dissemination of results. It has a rough structure and a high level focus. The perspective is only for coverage of subject areas and educational view. Beyer and Brummel [4] describe different factors for effective cybersecurity training. Kick [22] depicts playbooks in detail. Others analyze different environments for cyber training [3,28,42,44,48]. Different papers relate to aspects of gamification, serious games, and education [20,25,43,45]. As a result, a holistic taxonomy for the management and organization of ICTE is missing.

4   Taxonomy

Within this Section, our taxonomy for ICTE and its components is described in detail. Figure 1 provides an overview about the taxonomy. During the design, attention was paid to the complete coverage of all necessary capabilities with regard to the cyber exercise life cycle [22] and training competencies [31].

4.1   Technical Setup

The technical setup consists of environment structure, deployment, and orchestration. These are described in detail in the following.

Environment Structure: The environment structure refers to the basic characteristic of the event. This characteristic is composed of the following sub-characteristics:

– **Tabletop Style:** A session that involves the movement of counters or other objects round a board or on a flat surface.

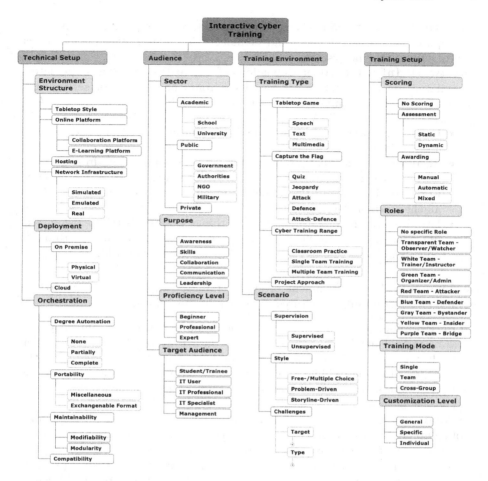

Fig. 1. Taxonomy of interactive cyber training and education systems

– **Online Platform:** The digital service describes a wide range of interactive possibilities available on the internet including marketplaces, search engines, social media, creative content outlets, app stores, communications services, payment systems, services comprising the collaborative economy.
  • **Collaboration Platform:** The environment allows organizations to incorporate real-time communication capabilities and providing remote access to other systems. This includes the exchange of files and messages in text, audio, and video formats between different computers or users.
  • **E-Learning Platform:** A software application for the administration, documentation, tracking, reporting, and delivery of educational courses, training programs, or learning and development programs.

- **Hosting:** A cyber training based on single hosts uses primarily a personal computer to providing tasks and challenges for a user. It allows a direct interaction with the systems.
- **Network Infrastructure:** Dependent of the realization type - simulated, emulated, or real - a network-based environment consists of servers and clients, which are connected to each other in a local area network (LAN) or wide area network (WAN).
  - **Real:** Physical components are used to connect the systems and to setup a scenario.
  - **Simulated:** A simulation copies the network components from the real world into a virtual environment. It provides an idea about how something works. It simulates the basic behavior but does not necessarily abide to all the rules of the real systems.
  - **Emulated:** An emulator duplicates things exactly as they exist in real life. The emulation is effectively a complete imitation of the real thing. It operates in a virtual environment instead of the real world.

Deployment: The environment of cyber training can either be deployed on premise or on cloud infrastructures, as shown in the following.

- **On Premise:** The environment for the training can either run on physical or virtual machines. Either way, the data is stored locally and not on cloud; nor is a third party involved. The benefit of virtual machines is the maximum of configurability. The advantages of on premise solutions are the physical accessibility, which makes it possible to use the complete range of cyber challenges.
- **Cloud:** A training setup deployed in the cloud has on-demand availability of computer system resources, especially data storage and computing power, without direct active management by the user. In contrast to on premise setups, cloud solutions are rapid elastic on request. So the training can be adapted flexible on a large amount of users and is easily usable world wide.

Orchestration: We understand orchestration as the composition of parts and components of a pool of tasks. The goal is to setup a holistic scenario and integrate cyber training session. Furthermore, it includes a declarative description of the overall process in the form of a composite and harmonic collaboration. A system typically exists of functions, processes, and data. It provides a common service embedded in an environment for the specified purpose. Beside this, orchestration has also a strong relation to the deployment strategy and the customization possibilities. Well known approaches are tools like Chef [7], Puppet [35], Ansible [37], and SaltStack [38].

A flexible concept for orchestration and maintainability is important for the administration of the cyber training system. Especially, the possibility of a fast troubleshooting in case of live events is mandatory. Nevertheless, it also has an impact on the participants in relation to user experience and quality of service in providing a training with adequate atmosphere.

The criterion orchestration is further divided in the degree of process automation, portability, maintainability, and compatibility.

- **Automation:** It specifies the automation of processes and the amount of human interaction with the system to maintain and administrate, especially for repetitive exercise. Subclasses for automation are non-automation, partially-automation, and full-automation.
- **Portability:** The possibility to exchange data, challenges, or entire scenarios to other environments or locations. The portability can be separated in miscellaneous approaches and the usage of common data format for exchange like YAML, Extensible Markup Language (XML), and JavaScript Object Notation (JSON) [16,41]. The objective of future research direction is an exchange format for entire cyber scenarios to flexible deploy these in different environments and locations.
- **Maintainability:** Maintainability represents effectiveness and efficiency with which a session can be modified or adapted to changes. A modular concept has advantages in reusability and combinability.
- **Compatibility:** The Compatibility deals with the technical interaction possibilities via interfaces to other applications, data, and protocols.

4.2 Audience

The target of cyber training and education is the audience, which is further characterized in the following. The audience has the characteristics sector, purpose, proficiency level, and target audience.

Sector: The sector from which the audience comes determines the nature of the training. The following categories can be distinguished [5,8].

- **Academic:** This includes universities and schools. The focus is on the principles underlying cybersecurity, ranging from theoretical to applied.
- **Private:** The private sector and industry focuses more on protecting its investments. The effectiveness of security mechanisms and people are more important than principles they embody.
- **Public:** This includes amongst others Government, NGO, and Military. Cybersecurity is seen as tool to protect the public interest. Hence, it emphasizes on developing policies and systems to implement laws and regulations.

Purpose: Purpose answered the question for which reason trainings should be used. Training can address different objectives which are listed in the following.

- **Awareness:** To raise the awareness in multiple and different security threats.
- **Skill:** To recognize the different skill levels of the participants so that can they be improved in a targeted manner.
- **Collaboration:** To improve the cooperation within a team or beyond.
- **Communication:** To increase the efficiency of internal and external communication in case of an incident.
- **Leadership:** To improve the management and coordination of the responsible entities.

Proficiency Level: Proficiency describes the knowledge of users and what they are able to do. The proficiency is grouped into three different levels.

– **Beginner:** The lowest level. Beginner are limited in abilities and knowledge. They have the possibility to use foundational conceptual and procedural knowledge in a controlled and limited environment. Beginners cannot solve critical tasks and need significant supervision. They are able to perform daily processing tasks. The focus is on learning.
– **Professional:** The mid level. Professionals have deeper knowledge and understanding in specific sectors. For these sectors they are able to complete tasks as requested. Sometimes supervision is needed but usually they perform independently. The focus is on enhancing and applying existing knowledge.
– **Expert:** The highest level. Experts have deeper knowledge and understanding in different sectors. They complete tasks self-dependent and have the possibilities to achieve goals in the most effective and efficient way. Experts have comprehensive understanding and abilities to lead and train others. The focus is on strategic action.

Target Audience: Target audience describes the audience, which is targeted by the training. This can be condensed to the following.

– **Student/Trainee:** Student and trainees have little to none practical knowledge. Training can be used for students and trainees, to enhance their knowledge and to practice theoretical courses, see [20,25,43,45].
– **IT User:** IT users use the IT but have little to none knowledge about IT security. Users can get trained to understand principles of IT security and to grow awareness.
– **IT Professional:** Professionals have little to medium knowledge about IT security. Their professional focus is in specific sectors, therefore, they receive IT security knowledge for their sectors.
– **IT Specialist:** Specialists already have a comprehensive knowledge in IT security. Therefore, the training is focussed on specific aspects.
– **Management:** Management has little knowledge about IT security, but a broad overview. By the training, management can understand changed settings better.

4.3   Training Environment

The training environment details the environment around the training, consisting of training type and scenario. Both characteristics are described in the following.

Training Type: Education in cybersecurity follows different approaches [53]. The level of interaction and hands-on experience distinguishes different types of training. For interactive cyber training, the following training types exist.

- **Table Top:** This type is a lightweight, but intellectually intense exercise. In this setting, the involved teams or participants focus on opposing missions. On a theoretical basis, the teams develop different strategies and countermeasures to explore the offensive cyber effects on operations. Table top trainings could be based on speech-only, text-only, or multimedia [22, 46].
- **Project Approach:** In this type of training, hands-on projects are to be completed during the training. Thereby, the participants learn and understand the basic concepts of security. During the projects, the teachers can intervene and control the learning process [53].
- **Capture the Flag:** Capture the Flag (CTF) is a well-known cybersecurity contest in which participants compete in real-time. Several distinct kinds of CTF have evolved in the recent years, including quiz, jeopardy, attack-only, defence-only, and attack-defence [9].
- **Cyber Training Range:** A cyber range provides an environment to practice network operation skills. It should represent real-world scenarios and offer isolation from other networks to contain malicious activity. In this training type, complex attacks take place in a simulated environment. The participants perform divers educational hands-on activities according to their role. Possible trainings are classroom practice, single team, and multiple team trainings. In these trainings the roles that are not covered by participants are simulated or covered by the instructors [10, 48].

Scenario: The scenario is a main component of cybersecurity training. Scenarios are needed to reach the goal of the training and are described by the following characteristics.

- **Supervision:** Either the training is supervised or unsupervised. Cyber range trainings are typically supervised, while jeopardy CTFs are unsupervised.
- **Style:** The style describes how the different challenges within the training are setup. Free-/Multi Choice can be the case with CTFs. Other directions are problem-driven and storyline-driven, if the challenges are arranged around a problem or a central storyline.
- **Challenges:** The challenges are the content of the training. These are defined by target and type. The target of the training can be a network, host, application, protocol, data, person, or physical. For solving the challenge types, foot-printing, scanning, enumeration, exploitation, pivoting, privilege escalation, covering tracks, and maintaining access may be needed. Souissi [40] and Lehto [25] use similar characterisations for attacks respectively competence areas.

4.4 Training Setup

The training setup further describes the training itself with the scoring, roles, the training mode as well as the customization level.

Scoring: Scoring is an important component of a cyber training. Depending on the purpose of the training, the scoring provides means to motivate the participants and a way to give feedback. It is also used to track the progress during a training. For competition-oriented trainings, like CTFs, a scoring is necessary. The scoring can be based, but is not limited to monitoring systems, defined objectives, or over-the-shoulder evaluation mechanisms.

- **Awarding:** In this variant of scoring, participants get awards for predefined actions or achievements. These awards can be granted both manually and automatically. Furthermore, a mixed approach is possible, e.g., by automatically giving awards for general objectives and manually giving awards for outstanding achievements. In general, awarding has a lower granularity than the detailed assessment and requires less administrative effort, but gives reasonable feedback and motivation for the participants.
- **Assessment:** This scoring variant is more complex than awarding and allows to assess participants and compare them to each other. The assessment scores can be assigned in different ways. One type is the static setting of different scores for tasks and objectives. In order to distinguish it from awarding, the degree of difficulty can be included here. Furthermore, the scores for different tasks can be set dynamically using mathematical functions. But also other dynamic methods, such as the Elo Rating System [33], are covered by this variant.
- **No Scoring:** Depending on the training, a scoring is not necessarily needed.

Roles: Participants in a training are split in different teams, according to their skills, role, and tasks during a training. For the identification, each team has a color assigned based on its role. The following teams are commonly used in cyber trainings and exercises [22,49].

- **Green Team:** The operators that are responsible for the exercise infrastructure build this team. Before a training, this team sets up and configures the environment and takes it down afterwards. During a training, it also monitors the environments health and handles problems that may arise.
- **White Team:** This team consists of instructors, referees, organizers, and training managers. They design the training scenario including objectives, rules, background story, and tasks. During the training, this team controls the progress and assigns tasks to the teams. These so-called *injects* also include simulated media, operation coordination, or law enforcement agencies. Giving hints for the training teams could also be part of this team.
- **Red Team:** This team consists of people authorized and organized to model security adversaries. They are responsible to identify and exploit potential vulnerabilities present in the training environment. Depending on the training environment, the tasks can follow a predefined attack path.
- **Blue Team:** The group of individuals that is responsible for defending the training environment. They deal with the red team's attacks and secure the compromised networks. Guidelines for that team are the training rules and local cyber law.

Additionally, there are further roles involved in training, which are summarized in the following teams [50, 52].

- **Transparent Team:** Members of this team observe the training. Usually, these people have a defined purpose, but have no influence on the training itself. Possible purposes are learning about the training topic and roles, studying strategies of participants, or supervising employees.
- **Yellow Team:** Members of this team perform not only tasks like generating legitimate network traffic and user behavior but also perform erroneous actions that lead to vulnerabilities and attacks. This team can also include the regular system builders, like programmers, developers, and software engineers and architects.
- **Purple Team:** In a training, this team is a bridge between red and blue teams that helps to improve the performance of both. Through joint red-blue activities it improves the scope of the training participants. Goals are to maximize the Blue Teams capability and the effectiveness of Red Teams activities.
- **Gray Team:** Bystanders of a training form this team. They do not necessarily have a specific intention or purpose, but an interest in the training event itself. It is also possible that this team interacts with participants and thereby unintentionally influences the training.
- **No specific role:** Individuals who do not fit into the defined teams can be assigned to this role.

According to [50], the orange team completes the so called Color Wheel. This team is of special importance in a holistic system development process.

Training Mode: Training mode defines the mode in which the training is accomplished. The training mode has three different alignments.

- **Single:** A single player plays against others. Others can be real persons, but also scripted opponents.
- **Team:** A team plays against others. In this alignments, each player can bring its expertise into the training, focussing on different aspects. Examples are Blue and Red Teams.
- **Group:** A group plays against others. In this setting, the group members might not know each other. Example are CTF competitions and training for the entire organization in a breach scenario.

Customization Level: Depending on the goal of the training, the training setup can be customized. A distinction is made here between three variants.

- **General:** A general purpose training setup is not, or only little customized. This variant is suited for an entry level training or to learn about general processes without regard to the underlying setup.

- **Specific:** The training setup can be customized for a specific training goal or target audience. Examples for this variant are specific trainings within the High School education [15] or for the health sector [36].
- **Individual:** The most tailored variant is an individual customization. Hereby, the training setup corresponds to a real environment in the best possible way. Exemplary uses of this variant are the training of teams in their environment or the training of new expert-level employees.

5   Examples and Case Studies of Cyber Training and Education Systems

A tailored modification of a CTF for educational purposes is described by [28], named Class CTF (CCTF). The idea behind this approach is to maximize the learning outcome and minimize the time spent for a CTF event. They observed a higher motivation of their students helping each other solving the challenges. Also much more interest in learning and practicing skills during hands-on exercises was noticed. This seems to be a usual behavior if changing the learning setup to more hands-on exercises. Nevertheless, this approach can be categorized in our taxonomy as follows: The training setup is based on Red and Blue team roles. To give all participants the same chances, the presented scoring is based on fixed solutions for every challenge and, therefore, static. CCTFs follow a team based approach and are designed for students in universities to improve their skills and foster communication and collaboration abilities. The proficiency level starts from beginner level and can evolve during a series of CCTFs.

The presented taxonomy progressed during our own Capture the Flag experiences. Whereas this taxonomy was very basic during the first phase of our initial CTF in 2015, it evolved further during the next events. Table 2 summarizes our past events with some details. In the next section, our CTFs are categorized based on the taxonomy. This is followed by our experiences during the organization of various CTF events.

Year	Title	Duration	Teams	Attendees	Challenges	Tracks
2015	The Beginning	9 h	11	31	34 + 1 Easteregg	Beginner, Advanced
2016	A New Hope	8 h	14	49	18 + 2 Eastereggs	Beginner, Advanced, Professional
2017	24: The Revolution	24 h	18	69	48 + 2 Eastereggs	Beginner, Advanced
2018	Dark Fiber	18 h	24	92	39 + 3 Eastereggs, 3 Scenarios/Maps	Jeopardy, Attack-Defence
2019	The 5th Element	18 h	29	129	50 + 2 Eastereggs	Jeopardy

Fig. 2. Overview of accomplished CTF events. Each session consisted of an additional Online-Qualifying over one week.

5.1   Application of the Taxonomy

Since our goal was to organize an event for the students of our university, we followed an approach to support their skills, their team spirit, and nevertheless fun during the event. That said we classify our CTFs based on our *taxonomy* as follows.

- **Audience**
  - **Target Audience:** Students and IT professionals.
  - **Sector:** Public (NGOs, government agencies), and academic.
  - **Proficiency Level:** Beginner up to expert level.
  - **Purpose:** Improve skills and collaboration abilities within the teams.
- **Training Environment**
  - **Training Type:** Capture the flag including quiz and jeopardy. In 2019, we also set up an attack-defence track.
  - **Scenario:** Storyline-driven including some free-/multiple choice questions.
- **Training Setup**
  - **Scoring:** Assessment, as it uses dynamic scoring.
  - **Roles:** No specific roles.
  - **Training Mode:** Team.
  - **Customization Level:** Individual, because the incentive is to provide an environment near to real world scenarios.
- **Technical Setup**
  - **Environment Structure:** Online platform in sense of E-Learning platform, and hosting.
  - **Deployment:** On-premise.
  - **Orchestration:** Partial degree of automation and modular approach for designing the services.

5.2   Phase 1: Organization and Development

In the first step, it starts with an idea to organize a CTF event. Meetings are scheduled and all participants are on a hype that the event will be a great success. But latest during the first crunch-time, the hype ends and all participants realize the hard work. Therefore, it is necessary to structure and organize the phases. Choose a project management that fits for the needs. It is important to have regular meetings, but also a ticketing system and version control for the challenges and underlying infrastructure.

During the first meetings, the audience for the event and the requirements need to be defined. We used our *taxonomy*, as shown in the previous section, to help ourselves. The classification of a planned event allows organizers to derive additional constraints, e.g., to support multiple proficiency levels based on categories or changing the level of difficulty based on successful solves of challenges. We followed an approach to support their skills, their team spirit, and nevertheless fun during the event. This includes a story-driven scenario including some free-/multiple choice questions, e.g., eastereggs. Thereby, we develop several challenges for beginner as well as experts. In order to provide equality and increase the motivation, we provide different tracks with separate scoring based on the proficiency level. We have learned from experience that dynamic scoring makes it easier to determine the individual difficulty of the various challenges. As a result, the training setup includes our own developed scoring system. We promote no specific roles in our setup, but in the last years some teams joined the event with observer participants.

As an advice from our own experiences during the development of an event, we recommend planning sufficient buffers for unexpected issues regarding challenges and infrastructure. This saves the organizers from excessive crunch-time. Our technical setup was complex so far. It includes real network infrastructure and on-premise hardware for hosting the environment. On top of these hardware machines, we setup a virtual environment consisting of virtual machines and virtual networking infrastructure comparable to a real data centre. To minimize the workload during the event, we tried to orchestrate availability checks and restarts of vital services.

5.3   Phase 2: Testing and Dry Run

The main part of the second phase is testing. During this phase, all challenges are checked by an individual or small team independent from the developers of a challenge. If the event is based on a story line, all transitions to following challenges and activations of challenges after a successful solve need to be checked. Furthermore, it is necessary to keep in mind that nothing is more frustrating for participants than investing a lot of time in solving a challenge that is buggy or not solvable. Therefore, testing is more than essential for a successful event. The testing phase is also a good point in time to check the overall progress in developing challenges. To support the participants during the event, walkthroughs should be developed and tested in parallel. If a hint system is planned for the main event, it should also be checked during this phase. Nevertheless, every hint system has its own pros and cons. We did not find a satisfactory hint system for all participants so far; except for providing no hints for a single team. Finally in this phase, check the infrastructure readiness for the number of planned participants.

5.4   Phase 3: Accomplishment

The accomplishment phase usually takes place at two points in time: (1) qualifying and (2) main event. During the qualifying event, it is possible to gain experiences for the main event. Are the challenges too easy to solve? Is it necessary to split the participants into different tracks based on their skills? Are infrastructure resources planned adequately? Did the challenges need a supervision or are they robust enough? Taking these possible questions into account, the setup can be adjusted where appropriate. In case of different categories based on proficiency level, the participants should decide which track to choose. Additionally, it is important to plan enough resources in infrastructure and staff for the main event. It is usual that not all challenges and storylines run as expected. Preparation should also include unforeseen events such as network and power failures, unavailable challenges or challenges that cannot be solved even if tested in advance.

The event should start with a short introduction about the "Do's and Don'ts" during the event. All participant need to understand that any attempt to break the infrastructure or manipulation of the scoring system leads to disqualification. Have a system in place to monitor such attempts. If photos are taken during the event or names of persons or teams are published afterwards, the participants have to be asked for consent. Consideration should be given in advance to where this information will be placed afterwards. This is necessary for the terms under which it is allowed to do so, keeping in mind regulatory requirements. Furthermore, a monitoring system should be in place to track the availability of all challenges and scoring systems. Necessary services should restart automatically in case of a failure as there is no time for manual troubleshooting during the event.

Regarding the IT security of the participants and infrastructure, the "Do's and Don'ts" are presented in the first step. Yet, various technical measures are feasible to prevent, e.g., manipulation of virtual machines, containers or network infrastructure. Virtual Machines (VMs) virtualize an underlying computer, whereas with containers the operating system is virtualized. Each way has consequences for the security, resources, reproducibility of exploits, and permissions. If a participant is able to break out of a docker container, other challenges could be manipulated in other containers or directly on the VM. Furthermore, if a participant is able to break out the virtual machine, also other VMs on the host or even the hypervisor can be manipulated. Therefore, it is vital to make even a short risk assessment of your infrastructure hosting the challenges. If a team is manipulating their own challenges and infrastructure, it might be acceptable to disqualify the whole team. However, if it cannot be determined who has manipulated a challenge or infrastructure, it may be necessary to cancel the entire event. That would be very frustrating for the other teams playing a fair game.

5.5   Phase 4: Cleanup and Maintenance

The last phase starts with the collection of evaluation sheets handed out during the event. The feedback of the participants is a good measure to improve the quality of a CTF and at the same time input for further events. Dependent on the feedback form and participants, it includes feedback about the difficulty of the challenges, the setup, but also about the fringe. The traffic and log files generated during the event are a good starting point for further analytics. Outcomes could include information on team strategies, toolsets used, and additional solutions to your challenges If desirable, initiate a call for write-ups and provide a platform for the teams to share their solutions. It can be inspiring to read write-up of different solutions. Furthermore, traffic collected during the event showing various kinds of attacks to provided services is very valuable for security research. To reuse the hosted challenges for further events, clean-up the provided machines afterwards. An easy solution is either using container or making a snapshot of all resources in advance. This enables the reset to this snapshot after the event. To keep the system save, shutdown all resources if they are not in use between events.

It must be ensured that all participants have given their consent for relevant information to be collected from evaluation sheets, log files, traffic, pictures, and team names. In case of collected data from a participant that did not gave the consent, these data need to be deleted immediately. Subsequently, the data should be prepared for publishing, depending on the needs. Additionally, sponsors definitely welcome a short report about the event. Further, if the event was a success, publishing the results gives the organization and development team a good standing in organizing cybersecurity events.

6   Conclusion and Future Work

Cyber training and education systems are an important aspect in education of different persons in each sector. Interactive training can help to improve the security knowledge in a practical way. The development of such systems as well as the extension and improvement can be hampered because of a missing general classification. This is especially the case for specific systems with focus on an individual use case.

To overcome this shortcoming, we developed a flexible taxonomy for ICTE systems. The taxonomy provides a detailed description of all components with a focus on technical realization. All phases of the exercise life cycle are covered within the taxonomy to obtain a holistic approach. It supports the education and training of different roles under consideration of the current skill level. This allows a targeted teaching in specific scenarios. In a next step, we showed examples of education and training systems, before we provided a case study based on conducted trainings. The trainings were categorized by our taxonomy. These examples further explain different training types.

In the future, we will conduct a survey about training systems, in order to apply the taxonomy to further systems. For example, we will show the fully compatibility and extensibility with the NIST NICE Framework [30]. This can help to enrich the taxonomy with more details. Further non-technical possibilities are ICTE in context of assurances and certification levels. Beside this, the taxonomy motivates the discussion and highlights the advantages of such systems. In order to improve the trainings, we will compare different types of scoring methodologies and provide a better suited one. As different scenarios are developed, a universal scenario description format or language helps to compare and exchange scenarios. This will be designed in addition.

References

1. Amorim, J.A., Hendrix, M., Andler, S.F., Gustavsson, P.M.: Gamified training for cyber defence: methods and automated tools for situation and threat assessment. Nato Modelling & Simulation Group (NMSG) Multi-Workshop, MSG-111 (2013)
2. Amoroso, E.: Fundamentals of Computer Security Technology. Prentice-Hall, Upper Saddle River (1994)
3. Beuran, R., Pham, C., Tang, D., Chinen, K.I., Tan, Y., Shinoda, Y.: Cybersecurity education and training support system: CyRIS. IEICE Trans. Inf. Syst. **E101.D**, 740–749 (2018)
4. Beyer, R.E., Brummel, B.: Implementing effective cyber security training for end users of computer networks. SHRM-SIOP Sci. HR Ser. Promoting Evid.-Based HR **3**(10), 2018 (2015)
5. Bishop, M.: What do we mean by "computer security education"? In: 22nd National Information Systems Security Conference (1999)
6. CERT Division: CERT Coordination Center - 2002 Annual Report. Technical report,Carnegie Mellon University, Software Engineering Institute (2003)
7. Chef Software Inc.: Chef (2020). https://www.chef.io. Accessed 28 Aug 2020
8. CONCORDIA: Courses and Trainings for Professionals (2020). https://www.concordia-h2020.eu/map-courses-cyber-professionals/. Accessed 28 Aug 2020
9. Davis, A., Leek, T., Zhivich, M., Gwinnup, K., Leonard, W.: The fun and future of CTF. In: 2014 USENIX Summit on Gaming, Games, and Gamification in Security Education (3GSE 14) (2014)
10. Davis, J., Magrath, S.: A survey of cyber ranges and testbeds. Technical report, Defence Science and Technology Organisation Edinburgh (Australia) Cyber and Electronic Warfare Div (2013)
11. Díez, E.G., Pereira, D.F., Merino, M.A.L., Suárez, H.R., Juan, D.B.: Cyber exercises taxonomy. INCIBE (2015). https://www.incibe.es/extfrontinteco/img/File/intecocert/EstudiosInformes/incibe_cyberexercises_taxonomy.pdf. Accessed 28 Aug 2020
12. Easttom, C., Butler, W.: A modified McCumber cube as a basis for a taxonomy of cyber attacks. In: 2019 IEEE 9th Annual Computing and Communication Workshop and Conference (CCWC), pp. 943–949 (2019)
13. European Cyber Security Organisation: WG5 Paper - Understanding Cyber Ranges: From Hype to Reality. Technical report (2020)
14. Hansman, S., Hunt, R.: A taxonomy of network and computer attacks. Comput. Secur. **24**, 31–43 (2005)
15. Hembroff, G., Hanson, L., Vanwagner, T., Wambold, S., Wang, X.: The Development of a computer & network security education interactive gaming architecture for high school age students. USENIX J. Educ. Syst. Adm. **25** (2015)
16. Howard, J.D., Longstaff, T.A.: A Common Language for Computer Security Incidents. Technical repo, Sandia National Laboratories (1998)
17. (ISC)2: Strategies for Building and Growing Strong Cybersecurity Teams. Cybersecurity Workforce Study (2019). https://www.isc2.org/-/media/ISC2/Research/2019-Cybersecurity-Workforce-Study/ISC2-Cybersecurity-Workforce-Study-2019.ashx. Accessed 28 Aug 2020
18. ISO/IEC: ISO/IEC 9126. Software engineering - Product quality. ISO/IEC (2001)
19. ISO/IEC 25010: ISO/IEC 25010:2011, Systems and software engineering - Systems and software Quality Requirements and Evaluation (SQuaRE) - System and software quality models. ISO/IEC (2011)

20. Jin, G., Tu, M., Kim, T.H., Heffron, J., White, J.: Game based cybersecurity training for high school students. In: Proceedings of the 49th ACM Technical Symposium on Computer Science Education, SIGCSE '18, pp. 68–73. Association for Computing Machinery, New York (2018)
21. Jouini, M., Rabai, L.B.A., Aissa, A.B.: Classification of security threats in information systems. In: The 5th International Conference on Ambient Systems, Networks and Technologies (ANT-2014), Procedia Computer Science, vol. 32, pp. 489–496 (2014)
22. Kick, J.: Cyber Exercise Playbook. MITRE (2014., https://www.mitre.org/sites/default/files/publications/pr_14-3929-cyber-exercise-playbook.pdf. Accessed 28 Aug 2020
23. Kumar, S.: Classification and Detection of Computer Intrusions. Ph.D. thesis, Purdue University, USA (1996)
24. Landwehr, C.E., Bull, A.R., McDermott, J.P., Choi, W.S.: A taxonomy of computer program security flaw. ACM Comput. Surv. **26**, 211–254 (1994)
25. Lehto, M.: Cyber security education and research in the Finland's Universities and universities of applied sciences. Int. J. Cyber Warfare Terrorism **6**, 15–31 (2016)
26. Lindqvist, U., Jonsson, E.: How to systematically classify computer security intrusions. In: IEEE Symposium Security and Privacy, pp. 154–163 (1997)
27. Lipson, H.F.: Tracking and tracing cyber-attacks: technical challenges and global policy issues. Software Engineering Institute, CERT CoordinationCenter (2002)
28. Mirkovic, J., Peterson, P.A.H.: Class capture-the-flag exercises. In: 2014 USENIX Summit on Gaming, Games, and Gamification in Security Education (3GSE 14). USENIX Association, San Diego (2014)
29. Neumann, P.G., Parker, D.B.: A summary of computer misuse techniques. In: 12th National Computer Security Conference, Baltimore, MD, pp. 396–406 (1989)
30. Newhouse, W., Keith, S., Scribner, B., Witte, G.: National initiative for cybersecurity education (nice) cybersecurity workforce framework. NISTSpecial Publication 800-181 (2017)
31. Newhouse, W., Keith, S., Scribner, B., Witte, G.: National Initiative for Cybersecurity Education (NICE), Cybersecurity Workforce Framework, NIST Special Publication 800–181. National Institute of Standards and Technology, US Department of Homeland Security, National Initiative for Cybersecurity Careers and Studies (NICCS) (2017)
32. Paulauskas, N., Garsva, E.: Computer system attack classification. IEEE Autom. Rob. **66**, 84–87 (2006)
33. Pelánek, R.: Applications of the Elo rating system in adaptive educational systems. Comput. Educ. **98**, 169–179 (2016)
34. Priyadarshini, I.: Features and Architecture of The Modern Cyber Range: A Qualitative Analysis and Survey. Ph.D. thesis, University of Delaware (2018)
35. Puppet Inc: puppet (2020). https://www.puppet.com. Accessed 28 Aug 2020
36. Rajamäki, J., Nevmerzhitskaya, J., Virág, C.: Cybersecurity education and training in hospitals: Proactive resilience educational framework (Prosilience EF). In: 2018 IEEE Global Engineering Education Conference (EDUCON), pp. 2042–2046. IEEE (2018)
37. Red Hat Inc: Red Hat Ansible (2020). https://www.ansible.com. Accessed 28 Aug 2020
38. SaltStack Inc: Saltstack (2020). https://www.saltstack.com. Accessed 28 Aug 2020
39. Simmons, C., Ellis, C., Shiva, S., Dasgupta, D., Wu, Q.: AVOIDIT: a cyber attack taxonomy. In: 9th Annual Symposium on Information Assurance (ASIA'14), pp. 2–12 (2014)

40. Souissi, S.: A novel response-oriented attack classification. In: 2015 International Conference on Protocol Engineering (ICPE) and International Conference on New Technologies of Distributed Systems (NTDS), pp. 1–6 (2015)

41. Steinberger, J., Sperotto, A., Golling, M., Baier, H.: How to exchange security events? Overview and evaluation of formats and protocols. In: Badonnel, R., Xiao, J., Ata, S., Turck, F.D., Groza, V., dos Santos, C.R.P. (eds.) IFIP/IEEE International Symposium on Integrated Network Management, IM 2015, pp. 261–269. IEEE (2015)

42. Subaşu, G., Roşu, L., Bădoi, I.: Modeling and simulation architecture for training in cyber defence education. In: 2017 9th International Conference on Electronics, Computers and Artificial Intelligence (ECAI), pp. 1–4 (2017)

43. Švábenský, V., Vykopal, J., Cermak, M., Laštovička, M.: Enhancing cybersecurity skills by creating serious games. In: Proceedings of the 23rd Annual ACM Conference on Innovation and Technology in Computer Science Education, ITiCSE 2018, pp. 194–199. Association for Computing Machinery, New York (2018)

44. Taylor, C., Arias, P., Klopchic, J., Matarazzo, C., Dube, E.: CTF: state-of-the-art and building the next generation. In: 2017 USENIX Workshop on Advances in Security Education (ASE 17). USENIX Association, Vancouver (2017)

45. Urias, V.E., Van Leeuwen, B., Stout, W.M.S., Lin, H.W.: Dynamic cybersecurity training environments for an evolving cyber workforce. In: 2017 IEEE International Symposium on Technologies for Homeland Security (HST), pp. 1–6 (2017)

46. US Department of Defense: The Department of Defense Cyber Table Top Guidebook (2018). https://www.dau.edu/cop/test/DAUSponsoredDocuments/TheDoDCyberTableTopGuidebookv1.pdf. Accessed 28 ug 2020

47. Valúšek, M.: Classification of Network Attacks and Detection Methods. Technical report, Masaryk University, Czech Republic (2016)

48. Vykopal, J., Ošlejšek, R., Celeda, P., Vizváry, M., Tovarňák, D.: KYPO cyber range: design and use cases. In: Proceedings of the 12th International Conference on Software Technologies, ICSOFT, vol. 1, pp. 310–321 (2017)

49. Vykopal, J., Vizváry, M., Ošlejšek, R., Celeda, P., Tovarňák, D.: Lessons learned from complex hands-on defence exercises in a cyber range. In: 2017 IEEE Frontiers in Education Conference (FIE), pp. 1–8. IEEE (2017)

50. Wright, A.C.: Orange is the new purple. Blackhat conference presentation (2017). https://www.blackhat.com/docs/us-17/wednesday/us-17-Wright-Orange-Is-The-New-Purple-wp.pdf. Accessed 28 Aug 2020

51. Wu, Z., Ou, Y., Liu, Y.: A taxonomy of network and computer attacks based on responses. In: 2011 International Conference of Information Technology, Computer Engineering and Management Sciences, vol. 1, pp. 26–29 (2011)

52. Yamin, M.M., Katt, B., Gkioulos, V.: Cyber ranges and security testbeds: scenarios, functions, tools architecture. Comput. Secur. **88**, 101636 (2020)

53. Yurcik, W., Doss, D.: Different approaches in the teaching of information systems security. In: Proceedings of the Information Systems Education Conference, pp. 32–33 (2001)

Cyber Range Training Programme Specification Through Cyber Threat and Training Preparation Models

Michail Smyrlis[1,2]([envelope]) [iD], Konstantinos Fysarakis[1] [iD], George Spanoudakis[1,2] [iD], and George Hatzivasilis[3] [iD]

[1] Sphynx Technology Solutions AG, Zug, Switzerland
{smyrlis,fysarakis,spanoudakis}@sphynx.ch
[2] Department of Computer Science, City, University of London, London, UK
{michail.smyrlis.2,g.e.spanoudakis}@city.ac.uk
[3] Institute of Computer Science Foundation for Research and Technology–Hellas
(FORTH) Heraklion, Crete, Greece
hatzivas@ics.forth.gr
https://www.sphynx.ch/
https://www.city.ac.uk/about/schools/
mathematics-computer-science-engineering/computer-science
https://www.ics.forth.gr/

Abstract. In light of the ever-increasing complexity and criticality of applications supported by ICT infrastructures, Cyber Ranges emerge as a promising solution to effectively train people within organisations on cyber-security aspects, thus providing an efficient mechanism to manage the associated risks. Motivated by this, the work presented herein introduces the model-driven approach of the THREAT-ARREST project for Cyber Range training, presenting in detail the Cyber Threat Training and Preparation (CTTP) models. These models, comprising sub-models catering for different aspects of the training, are used for specifying and generating the Training Programmes. As such, the paper also provides details on implementation aspects regarding the use of these models in the context of a usable cyber range training platform and two specific training scenarios.

Keywords: Cyber range · Cyber security · Security assurance · Training Programmes · CTTP Models · CTTP Programmes

1 Introduction

The increasing levels of complexity and inter-connectivity of ICT infrastructures, supporting a plethora of heterogeneous applications, have given rise to an increased number of perceived threats and cyber-attacks. Cyber criminals constantly improve their arsenal and launch impactful attacks that affected both organisations and individuals. This is exacerbated by the lack of security awareness, as users are not able to promptly identify and minimise the impact of a

© Springer Nature Switzerland AG 2020
G. Hatzivasilis and S. Ioannidis (Eds.): MSTEC 2020, LNCS 12512, pp. 22–37, 2020.
https://doi.org/10.1007/978-3-030-62433-0_2

cyber attacks, instead acting as enablers for the various threat actors to successfully deploy attacks [17]. According to PwC's Global Economic Crime and Fraud Survey 2020 [16], companies, on average, experienced 6 security incidents throughout the last 2 years whereas 47% of the interviewed had experienced fraud in the same period. The latter consists the 2nd highest report level of incidents in the past 20 years. According to Cybint Solutions [1], the average cost of a data breach in 2020 exceeds $150 million, while Gartner [11] estimated that the worldwide spending on cyber-security is forecasted to reach $133.7bn in 2022.

In this landscape, cyber-security training is becoming increasingly pertinent as an effective way of mitigating cyber risks. The need for not only more skilled cyber-security professionals but also well-trained individuals regardless of their security expertise is ever-increasing. Nevertheless, the cyber-security training should be implemented as a holistic approach and the gained knowledge should be validated. Part of a well-defined cyber security program, is the creation of information security awareness and training campaigns that would be able influence the adoption of an overall secure behaviour. To accomplish that, modern training strategies are not only limited to learning software and hardware skills, but also include training to understand actual cyber security threats along with resistance-training techniques [19]. However, cyber range training that does not have the capacity to fit the necessities of an organisation and to effortlessly adjust to the quickly developing scene, is deficient, and rapidly becomes obsolete [20].

Motivated by the above, this paper presents the Cyber Threat and Training Preparation (CTTP) Models and associated Training Programmes (CTTP Programmes) at the core of the model-driven Cyber Range Training approach developed under the H2020 THREAT-ARREST Project [21, 22]. The delivery of Cyber Range Training Programmes is based on these CTTP models which define the structure and automate the development of the training programmes by determining a number of different aspects, such as: (a) the assets of a cyber-system, their relations and the threats covered by the CTTP Programme, (b) the ways these assets will be emulated and simulated, (c) the evaluation of the trainees based on their actions and level of expertise and (d) the preparedness and effectiveness level that the trainees are expected to achieve based on the targeted training programme. The benefit of having a model for every different aspect of a Training Programme, is the connection of it with the actual cyber system and its assessment allowing the trainee to interact with an actual cyber system. As of today, a model-driven approach that incorporates emulation, simulation, serious gaming and visualisation techniques aiming at preparing individuals with different types of responsibilities and level of expertise in defending high-risk cyber systems and organisations to counter-advanced, known and knew cyber-attacks does not seems to exist.

The remainder of this paper is organised as follows: Sect. 2 presents an overview of the Background & Related work, Sect. 3 describes the CTTP Models, Sect. 4 describes two CTTP Programmes created in the context of the THREAT-ARREST Project and Sect. 5 provides the specification of one of these Training Programmes. Finally, Sect. 6 summarises the paper and sets future goals.

2   Background and Related Work

To the best of our knowledge, there are only a few model-driven approaches that allow the whole specification of a Cyber Range Training program. Russo et al. [18] propose a Scenario Definition Language (SDL) based on the OASIS topology and Orchestration Specification for Cloud Applications (TOSCA) used as a components specification language. SDL is similar to the CTTP Specification Language [5] used in THREAT-ARREST, that allow us to specify the different components of a cyber system. Erdogan et al. [10] introduce a training and evaluation approach based on the CORAS risk models [19] that specify cyber-risk models in order to facilitate real-time risk assessment and evaluation of trainees. Similarly, the definition of the CTTP Models will drive the training process, and align it (where possible) with operational cyber system security assurance mechanisms to ensure the relevance of training. Lastly, Braghin et al. [2] provide a model-driven engineering approach based on the creation of a subset of the CTTP model, namely the Emulation sub-model (see Table 2). The approach presented herein is based on the Security Assurance Model proposed by Somarakis et al. [20], extended to cover the needs of the Cyber Range training developed under the H2020 THREAT-ARREST project. According to Yamin et al. [23], existing model-driven cyber range approaches lack the ability to validate their models against real word scenarios. Contrariwise, the proposed approach is generic, thus it can be applied to both various domains and people with different levels of expertise and cyber-security knowledge. To demonstrate this, we have created a number of Training Programmes and applied them to three different pilots: shipping, healthcare and smart-energy [6].

3   Cyber Threat and Training Preparation Models

At the core of the model-driven approach to Cyber Range training proposed in this paper is the development of the CTTP Model. The creation of the latter consists of three main phases namely: (a) the Cyber System Analysis and creation of the Core Assurance Model, (b) the *Creation of CTTP sub-models* and (c) the *Training Programme definition*. Thus, a CTTP Model has (at a minimum) three compulsory parts namely: (a) the *Core Assurance Model*, (b) the *Training Model Generation and Delivery parameters* and (c) the *Emulation, Simulation, Gamification, Data Fabrication* sub-model or a combination of them. The corresponding sub-models will be analysed in the subsections that follow.   This process, as visualised in Fig. 1, is in line with expected stages in cyber range programme development and execution; as in the case of the THREAT-ARREST platform [4], such platforms need to incorporate emulation, simulation, serious gaming and data fabrication capabilities to be able to adequately prepare stakeholders with different types of responsibility and levels of expertise in realistic and customisable scenarios tailored to the intricacies of each organisation's cyber-systems and the most pertinent cyber-attack scenarios [22].

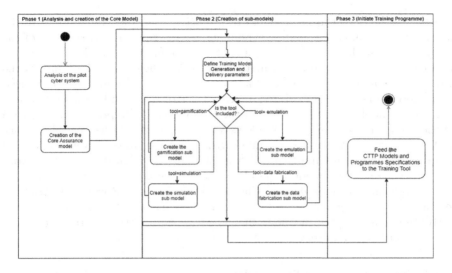

Fig. 1. Overall methodology for creating Training Programmes

Core Assurance Model. The Core Assurance model specifies the cyber system(s) that the Training Programme will be related to. More precisely, it determines the assets of the cyber system, their relations and their corresponding threats. An asset can be a software asset, hardware asset, physical infrastructure asset, data and person. Each asset has a number of required and optional fields. For instance, the required fields of a software asset include the *name, vendor* and *version*; these are also used in order to construct the Common Platform Enumeration (CPE) [3] (an industry standard that can also be used as part of the vulnerability analysis conducted from the assurance component of the THREAT-ARREST platform). Other required fields include *the type of asset* (e.g.. software or physical asset) and its *kind* (service or component). Optional fields include the *value* of the asset (in monetary terms), the *date that the asset will cease to exist* (if applicable) and a brief *description*. Each asset also comes with a flag value named *status* that allows the THREAT-ARREST platform to decide whether it will be part of the overall assessment. For instance, if the status is set to *draft*, the definition of the different fields is not yet finalised, thus it will not take part in the overall assessment. Lastly, the assets defined in the Core Assurance Model are utilised in order to define the emulation and simulation parts of the CTTP Programme.

Emulation Sub-model. The emulation sub-model includes the information of the emulated components that will be used as part of the Training and is intended to be being dynamically parsed by Emulation tool (e.g., virtual infrastructure management solutions based on OpenStack [15] or Kubernetes [13]). An emulation sub-model includes the: *Training Programme name*, the *status* (as described in Sect. 3), the *created and termination date* and one or more **module types**. An emulation module type includes: (a) the core information of the deployed Virtual Machine (VM), (b) its network configuration and (c) the scripts to be run at boot. The core information of the VM fields are: the *name* of the VM, the type of operating system, the specification of the connection to be used to remotely connect to the VM, the allocated size of RAM and disk, the name of the image to deploy, using as index in the OpenStack [15] repository along with the username and, in case of a Windows VM, the password, the virtual network the VM is connected to - accompanied with a fixed address, if applicable- and the id of the script module that will run at boot (if applicable). The network configuration module includes: the id that will be used as a reference point in the core information module, the Classless Inter Domain Routing (CIDR) - a method for allocating the IP address and IP routing- and the default gateway. Lastly, the script module includes the *script id* used as the reference point in the core information module- and the script to be run at boot.

Simulation Sub-model. The simulation sub-model includes the information of the simulated components that will be used as part of the Training phase and are intended to be dynamically parsed by simulation components (e.g., NS-3 [14]). A simulated sub-model includes: (a) the core information of the simulation environment (e.g. the *name* of the simulated tool, the *simulation template*, the *deployment mode*, the *initial execution time*, the *execution speed* etc.) and one or more simulation module types. A simulation module type includes one or more components. A component can be a *root* one, i.e. a component that has a one or more child components and is first in the component hierarchy, or a child. Each component has a number of fields such as: the *name* of the component container, the *id* of the Training Programme it will be involved, the *type* of the component (used as a descriptor of the internal java class of the simulation tool), one or more *component attributes* (i.e. values that hold a certain state of the simulation tools during the simulation phase), a flag value that describes whether this component is root or child and the *connections* between the different components.

Gamification Sub-model. The Gamification sub-model includes the information needed to create a Gamification environment integrated into the training platform; e.g.., in the case of THREAT-ARREST, this is provided by the Social Engineering Academy (SEA) gamification tools [7]. This sub-model consists of one or more *Game* modules. A *Game* module includes the following fields: (a) the type of the game (e.g.., AWARENESS QUEST [7] or PROTECT [12], as supported in THREAT-ARREST), (b) the difficulty level, (c) the overall game time, (d) one or more card deck id's and (e) whether this game needs any special practise.

Data Fabrication Sub-model. Lastly, the Data-Fabrication (DF) sub-model includes information intended to be provided to data fabrication tools, e.g. the

IBM Data Fabrication Platform developed by IBM Israel [9] that is integrated into THREAT-ARREST. The DF sub-model includes: (a) the core information of the Data-Fabrication tool (such as the *name, status, created and termination date*) and (b) the declaration of the *network-attached computers, switches* and other relevant hardware (structured as nodes). Each hardware node is augmented with properties and "installed" software applications and services.

Training Model Generation and Delivery Parameters. The Training Model Generation and Delivery parameters determine the way in which the Training Programme will be structured; in the case of THREAT-ARREST, this is parsed by the Training Tool developed by ITML [8]. The parameters are descriptors that allow the trainer, trainee and the Training Tool to understand the scope of a specific Training Programme as well as the tools involved in it. To be more precise, the parameters include: (a) a brief *description* of the Training Programme, (b) the *expected goal* of it, (c) the *difficulty*, (d) the *maximum score* that the trainee can achieve and (e) the *base score* that the trainee should achieve in order to successfully complete the programme, (f) the *examined actions* that trainees are expected to take against cyber-attacks covered by the programme (e.g., preparedness, incident detection and analysis, real time incident response, and post incident response), (g) the *role(s)* that the trainee will have (e.g. system administrator, end-user etc.), (h) the *owner* of the Training Programme and (i) *educational material* that will allow the trainee to better understand the scope of the Training Programme. The parameters also describe the *Training Session Specification* which define the number of screens that will be presented to the trainee, the *order* each screen will be presented, the *difficulty* of each screen, the *duration* this screen will stay available and the *tool* (e.g. Emulation, Simulation or Gamification) involved in each of these screens. A screen is also accompanied by a *hint*, that if the trainee chooses to use, will have a negative impact to its final score. Lastly, each screen comes with one or more *expected traces*. The latter tracks the progress of the user and has three different versions: (a) the *Evaluation Report* where the trainee is being assessed by answering questions regarding the deployed defence mechanisms, the potential threats etc., (b) the *Event Captors* which monitor if the correct configuration steps have been executed and (c) the *Gamification Report* which checks the total score as reported by the Gamification tool, the number of lost lives and the remaining time.

4   CTTP Programme Scenario Definition

The creation of a CTTP Programme is based on a CTTP Model with the purpose of specifying training scenarios, focusing on particular threats, cyber system components and assessment tools that are pertinent for the specific targeted environment (e.g., vertical domain or specific application), as defined in the model. This drives the execution of simulation, emulation and serious gaming processes, to realise within the cyber range the scenario environment and the steps implementing it.

As of today 13 such CTTP Training Programmes have been defined in the context of THREAT-ARREST, covering the domains of shipping, smart energy and healthcare. In this section, two of them will be presented: (i) the "Response & Mitigation" Programme of the smart-energy pilot in the context of smart home-/IoT environments, and; (ii) the "Navigation combo attack (phishing email and GPS spoofing)" in the context of Smart Shipping applications. Each programme includes a brief description, the progression steps and the Programme modelling.

4.1   Smart Home/IoT - Threat Response & Mitigation Training Programme

This Training Programme aims to train end-users with no security knowledge (as is typically the case for IoT/Smart Home consumers) on how to response to an abnormal behaviour and take immediate actions in order to mitigate the risk. The Programme involves the Emulation, Simulation and Gamification tool and is modelled based on Lightsources' cyber system (see Fig. 2).

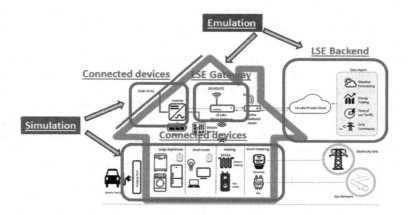

Fig. 2. Smart Energy pilot architecture and Virtual Lab deployment

Description. In this scenario, the trainee (user) is the owner of a smart plug, and the web based Lightsource application allows users to monitor its power consumption and/or its on/off behaviour. It also provides alerts of the system if an abnormal behaviour is detected. An intruder has gained access to the smart plug and executed a malicious application which stopped the smart plug from reporting its power consumption and turned a switch on and off at random time points. The user is notified by an alert, through the web application, that an abnormal behaviour was detected, and is asked to read the Lightsource guideline provided during the setup phase, in order to bring the device back to its expected behaviour.

Progression Steps. The individual steps comprising the scenario are as follows:

1. The trainer sets up the gateway and provides the log files and the database schema that contains the end users' credentials (in an encrypted form) and the IP of the smart plug. He also sets up the private cloud that provides the alerts to the web-based application of the trainee.
2. The trainee is informed about the security concerns surrounding smart devices and, upon installation of the edge device, receives an incident response and abnormal behaviour guideline.
3. The trainee receives an alert to its web-based application letting him/her know that the smart plug stopped reporting the power consumption and that the device connected to it reports abnormal on/off patterns. The trainee opens the web-based application to check if the alert was correct.
4. The trainee reads the guideline and, as instructed in the first step, resets the smart plug to its factory settings by pressing its button for 10 s. Then, he checks the graphs presented in the web application, but he observes that the abnormal behaviour is still there (i.e. no power consumption is presented).
5. The trainee then moves to the second step of the guideline and resets the device itself.
6. Finally, the trainee checks the graphs, and observers that both the smart plug started reporting its power consumption and the connected device was not reporting abnormal behaviour.

Training Programme Modelling. To realise this Training Programme, the following cyber range platform components are leveraged:

– The **Emulation tool** facilitates the following Virtual Machines:
  • The Gateway VM with a number of log files and the database schema pre-installed.
  • The VM that will involve the Simulation Tool.
  • The private cloud VM.
  • The trainee PC that includes a web browser allowing the trainee to open the Lightsource application.

– The **Simulation** and **Visualisation tool**:
  • Simulates the smart plug and a button for the device connected to it.
  • Three different phases are presented:
    * Normal Behaviour
    * Faulty/Compromised smart plug device
    * Compromised Device

– The **Gamification tool** presents a game for smart home security awareness

– The **Training Tool** includes:
  • A short course for security awareness in general
  • Lightsource' incident response guideline

4.2   Smart Shipping - Navigation Combo Attack (Phishing Email and GPS Spoofing)

This Training Programme aims to train the decision-making of end-users with moderate security knowledge. The Programme involves the Emulation, Simulation and Gamification tools and is based on DANAOS' cyber system (see Fig. 3).

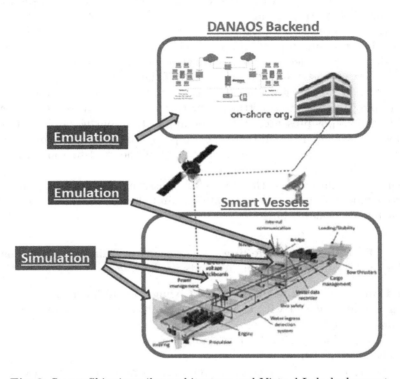

Fig. 3. Smart Shipping pilot architecture and Virtual Lab deployment

Description. In this scenario, the decision-making of trainee (captain) is being tested. More specifically, it consists of two different phases. During the first phase, a set of malicious/faulty/legitimate emails is being sent to the trainee in order to mislead him/her in performing requested actions. The second phase takes place after the ship has started its journey and consists of a GPS spoofing attack, where the trainee should identify it and perform a set of actions to ensure that the ship will safely arrive to its final destination.

Progression Steps. The individual steps comprising the scenario are as follows:

1. The trainee (captain) starts a journey from the port of Heraklion to the port of Piraeus (which will be designated by the back-end office via an email to the captain).
2. A faulty (but legitimate) email, commanding the trainee to go to Thessaloniki's port, is being sent. The email contains the details of another journey and was sent to the trainee by mistake.
   (a) The trainee identifies that this is a legitimate email.
   (b) Since the destination port was Thessaloniki, the trainee understands that this email was sent to him/her by mistake.
   (c) The trainee ignores the email and reports it back to the back-end office.
3. Then, the trainee receives a malicious (phishing) email, alerting him/her that a bad weather condition will take place, thus, he/she needs to go to another port to make a stop. The trainee needs to identify that this is a phishing email, ignore it and report it to the back-end office.
4. Lastly, the trainee receives a legitimate email with the weather forecast, denoting that the weather is good, and the destination is the Piraeus port.
5. During the trip, the trainee checks a **simulated** digital map that presents the current ship's position based on GPS data and the predetermined route (checkpoints) from Heraklion to Piraeus. The trainee realises that the ships' position on the digital map (receiving signal from a GPS receiver) is away from the designated way point and the ship is off course. The trainee should check if this is due to his/her own navigational orders or due to external factors (strong current streams) and should correct course by returning to the predetermined route or, if something is wrong, make use of the navigational monitor (digital map). The trainee proceeds with an order of actions to validate position from the GPS signal. The orders of actions are once again stem from the CTTP Model.
6. The trainee checks a magnetic compass and the marine paper map (Nautical Charts), in order to understand the actual position of the ship.
7. While checking the compass, he/she understands that it points towards a different direction to the ship course. Following, the trainee marks on the Nautical Charts, the position as depicted in the GPS (faulty coordinates). Then, the trainee is crosschecking objects (navigation aids, restrictions, bathymetry) mapped on charts with what he/she observes by looking outside the ship's bridge windows with his/her binoculars and with what he/she receives from other bridge equipment (e.g. bathymetry on the map against see depth from echo sounder). The trainee understands that the ship is navigating on different routes than those corresponding to the position given by GPS (faulty coordination).
8. Finally, the trainee understands that a GPS spoofing attack might have occurred, stops following the Digital Map Application (received signal from GPS receiver) and manually navigates the ship to its correct destination (by turning off the auto pilot).

Training Programme Modelling. To realise this Training Programme, the following cyber range platform components are leveraged:

- The **Emulation Tool** facilitates the following Virtual Machines:
  - The trainee operates the VM for the captain's PC.
  - The faulty/malicious and legitimate messages are being sent by the VM that includes the trainer's mail application.
  - The Simulation and visualisation VM.
- The **Simulation Tool** contains the simulated on-deck navigation equipment, i.e. the Digital Map (GPS Receiver), the magnetic compass and the Nautical Charts
- The **Gamification tool** presents a game for social engineering.
- The **Training tool** includes a short course for social engineering.

5   CTTP Programme Model Specification

The final step towards instantiating a Training Programme is the CTTP Programme Model Specification, i.e. encoding the training scenario parameters into an instance of the CTTP model that will be used to drive the actual training. For the sake of brevity, this section will only provide an example of this process for the Response & Mitigation Training Programme defined in Sect. 4.1. A similar process can be followed for any other scenario.

As previously mentioned, this Training Programme involves the Emulation, Simulation and Data Fabrication tools. Thus, three sub-model instances (along with the Core Assurance Model and the Training Model Generation and Delivery parameters) will be presented in the subsections that follow.

Table 1. Core Assurace Model

```
1   Person(firstName("Technician"), lastName("N/A"),
    ↪   email("tech@lightsourcelabs.com"), project("Response & Mitigation"),
    ↪   organisation("LIGHTSOURCE LAB LTD"),activeTo(2025-11-19
    ↪   13:55),description("Technician of the
    ↪   organisation"),roles(technician)),
2   SoftwareAsset (vendor("MariaDB"), version("10.3.18"), name("MariaDB"),
    ↪   kind(Service), type(SAL), project("Response &
    ↪   Mitigation"),organisation("LIGHTSOURCE LAB
    ↪   LTD"),owner("Technician"),description('Open source database solution
    ↪   for modern, mission-critical applications."))
3   SoftwareAsset (vendor("NGINX"), version("1.17.7"), name("NGINX"),
    ↪   kind(Service), type(SAL), project("Response &
    ↪   Mitigation"),organisation("LIGHTSOURCE LAB
    ↪   LTD"),owner("Technician"),description("NGINX accelerates content and
    ↪   application delivery, improves security, facilitates availability
    ↪   and scalability for the busiest web sites on the Internet"))
```

5.1   Core Assurance Model

Table 1 shows a subset of the Response & Mitigation Core Assurance model, specified using the CTTP Specification Language [5]. The model specifies three different assets, two software assets and one person.

5.2   Emulation Sub-model

Table 2 shows a subset of the Response & Mitigation Emulation sub-model converted in an XML format. The XML is then converted (by the Emulation Tool) to a HEAT template and is being deployed in OpenStack [2]. More specifically, this sub-model specifies the creation of a Virtual Machine and its network configuration.

Table 2. Emulation sub-model

```xml
<?xml version="1.0" encoding="Unicode" standalone="yes"?>
<Scenario name="UC1-LSE">
    <CustomVM name="broker_UC1" os="linux">
        <connectionmode port="22" connectiontype="ssh"/>
        <ram val="4096"/>
        <vcpus val="2"/>
        <disk val="40"/>
        <image name="LSE-broker" val="UC1-broker-v7" username="debian"/>
        <Network idref="home_network" fixedip="192.168.33.20"/>
    </CustomVM>
    <Networks>
        <Network id="home_network">
            <gateway name="gateway-home_network" val="192.168.33.1"/>
            <cidr name="cidr-home_network" val="192.168.33.0/24"/>
            <is_external val="false"/>
        </Network>
    </Networks>
</Scenario>
```

5.3   Simulation Sub-model

Table 3 shows a subset of the Response & Mitigation Simulation sub-model in a JSON format. This subset includes two simulation components. The Smart Home root component (see root = true) and the SmartPlug child component (see root = false). The latter includes an attribute that checks if the initial value of the smart plug is set to "WORKING" and specifies that this value can change throughout the simulation phase.

Table 3. Simulation sub-model

```
. . . ,
"SimulationComponents": [
{
    "name": "SmartHome",
    "simulatedComponent": "SmartHome",
    "type": "jasima.core.Simulation.SimComponentContainerBase",
    "root": true,
    "componentContainers": [
    {
        "simpleComponents": [
            {
                "name": "SmartPlug",
                "internalID": "SmartPlug",
                "type": "smarthome.SmartPlug",
                "root": false,
                "attributes": [
                    {
                        "name": "plugState",
                        "initialValue": "WORKING",
                        "type": "smarthome.SmartPlugStateEnum",
                        "canChange": true
                    },
                    . . .
                ]
            },
        ]
    },
    . . .
]
```

5.4 Gamification Sub-model

Table 4 shows the Gamification sub model, specified using the CTTP Specification Language and converted in a JSON format. More specifically, this sub-model includes the PROTECT game with difficulty level of 2, total game time of 12 min and the SmartHome card deck.

5.5 Training Model Generation and Delivery Parameters

Lastly, as mentioned in Sect. 3, the Training Model Generation and Delivery parameters are parsed by the Training Tool in order to instantiate the Training Programme. Table 5 shows a subset of the Response & Mitigation Training Model Generation and Delivery parameters in a JSON format. This subset presents the Training Programme goal, the maximum score the trainee can achieve, the base score he/she needs in order to succeed, its difficulty and the educational materials (see *Bibliography* field) that will be made available to the trainee.

Table 4. Gamification sub-model

```
"games": [
    {
        "gameType": {
            "gameTypeID": 1,
            "game": "Protect"
        },
        "protects": [
            {
                "difficultyLevel": 2,
                "gameTime": 12,
                "cardDeckID": "cd_smarthome",
                "specialPractice": false
            }
        ]
    },
    ...
]
```

Table 5. Training Model Generation and Delivery parameters

```
[
    {
        ...,
        "scenarioGoal": {
            "description": "This scenario trains an end user with no
            ↪   security knowledge on how to response to an abnormal
            ↪   behaviour and take immediate actions in order to
            ↪   mitigate the risk. The scenario is implemented in an
            ↪   Emulation, Simulation and Gamification tool.",
            "maxScore": 10,
            "successScore": 5
        },
        "difficulty": 7,
        "bibliographies": [
            {
                "name": "Incident Response & Abnormal behaviour",
                "text": "Lightsource's incident response guideline"
            },
            ...
        ],
    ...
]
```

6   Conclusions and Future Work

This paper presented the THREAT-ARREST's Cyber Threat and Training Preparation (CTTP) Models and the process followed for the specification of the associated Training Programmes, which are at the core of the platform's model-driven cyber range training approach. While this model-driven approach requires some effort and introduces a level of complexity to create and parse the CTTP Models, it also enables the use of an evidence-based approach to cyber range training, and the provision of programmes that are mapped to the actual cyber system and the results of its security assessment, thus targetting the most pertinent threats in the context of the training. Moreover, the creation of CTTP models facilitates deployment of several variations of the Training Programmes (e.g., to cater for trainees with different levels of expertise) and a thorough evaluation of both the trainee and the programme itself.

As a next step, efforts will focus on specifying all the Training Programmes defined within [6], as well as on identifying new ones, based on the analyses results of the actual pilot cyber systems, provided by the Security Assurance Tool integrated within the THREAT-ARREST platform. This tool will also be used as part of the adaptation of the CTTP Models and Programmes in the piloting environments based on updates to the threat landscape. In this context, an analysis will be carried out on the impact that changes in part of the CTTP Programme can have, while also checking the completeness and consistency of the entire specification of CTTP Models and Programmes in the context of these changes.

Acknowledgements. This work has received funding from the European Union's Horizon 2020 research and innovation programme under grant agreement No. 786890 (THREAT-ARREST).

References

1. Alarming Cyber Security Facts and Stats (2019). https://www.cybintsolutions. com/cyber-security-facts-stats/
2. Braghin, C., Cimato, S., Damiani, E., Frati, F., Mauri, L., Riccobene, E.: A model driven approach for cyber security scenarios deployment. In: Fournaris, A.P., et al. (eds.) IOSEC/MSTEC/FINSEC -2019. LNCS, vol. 11981, pp. 107–122. Springer, Cham (2020). https://doi.org/10.1007/978-3-030-42051-2_8
3. Common Platform Enumeration (CPE) (2020). https://csrc.nist.gov/projects/ security-content-automation-protocol/specifications/cpe/
4. D1.3: THREAT-ARREST platform's initial reference architecture (2020). https:// www.threat-arrest.eu/html/PublicDeliverables/D1.3
5. D3.1: CTTP Models and Programmes Specification Language (2020). https:// www.threat-arrest.eu/html/PublicDeliverables/D3.1
6. D3.3: Reference CTTP Models and Programmes Specifications (2020). https:// www.threat-arrest.eu/html/PublicDeliverables/D3.3
7. D4.2: THREAT-ARREST serious games v1 (2020). https://www.threat-arrest.eu/ html/PublicDeliverables/D4.2

8. D4.3: Training and Visualisation tools IO mechanisms v1 (2020). https://www.threat-arrest.eu/html/PublicDeliverables/D4.3
9. D5.1: Real event logs statistical profiling module and synthetic event log generator v1 (2020). https://www.threat-arrest.eu/html/PublicDeliverables/D5.1
10. Erdogan, G., et al.: An Approach to Train and Evaluate the Cybersecurity Skills of Participants in Cyber Ranges based on Cyber-Risk Models, June 2020
11. Gartner Forecasts Worldwide Information Security Spending to Exceed $124 Billion in 2019 (2020). https://www.gartner.com/en/newsroom/press-releases/2018-08-15-gartner-forecasts-worldwide-information-security-spending-to-exceed-124-billion-in-2019
12. Goeke, L., Quintanar, A., Beckers, K., Pape, S.: PROTECT – an easy configurable serious game to train employees against social engineering attacks. In: Fournaris, A.P., et al. (eds.) IOSEC/MSTEC/FINSEC -2019. LNCS, vol. 11981, pp. 156–171. Springer, Cham (2020). https://doi.org/10.1007/978-3-030-42051-2_11
13. Kubernetes (2020). https://kubernetes.io/
14. NS-3 Network Simulator (2020). https://www.nsnam.org/
15. OpenStack (2020). https://www.openstack.org/
16. PwC's global economic crime and fraud survey 2018(2020). https://www.pwc.com/gx/en/forensics/gecs-2020/pdf/global-economic-crime-and-fraud-survey-2020.pdf
17. Rantos, K., Fysarakis, K., Mani-favas, C.: How effective is your security awareness program? An evaluation methodology. Inf. Secur. J. Glob. Perspect. **21**(6), 328–345 (2012)
18. Russo, E., Costa, G., Armando, A.: Scenario design and validation for next generation cyber ranges. In: 2018 IEEE 17th International Symposium on Network Computing and Applications (NCA), pp. 1–4. IEEE (2018)
19. Schaab, P., Beckers, K., Pape, S.: Social engineering defence mechanisms and counteracting training strategies. Inf. Comput. Secur. **25**, 206–222 (2017)
20. Somarakis, I., Smyrlis, M., Fysarakis, K., Spanoudakis, G.: Model-driven cyber range training: a cyber security assurance perspective. In: Fournaris, A.P., et al. (eds.) IOSEC/MSTEC/FINSEC -2019. LNCS, vol. 11981, pp. 172–184. Springer, Cham (2020). https://doi.org/10.1007/978-3-030-42051-2_12
21. Soultatos, O., et al.: The THREAT-ARREST cyber-security training platform. IOSEC/MSTEC/FINSEC -2019. LNCS, vol. 11981, pp. 199–214. Springer, Cham (2020). https://doi.org/10.1007/978-3-030-42051-2_14
22. THREAT-ARREST (2019). https://www.threat-arrest.eu/
23. Yamin, M.M., Katt, B., Gkioulos, V.: Cyber ranges and security testbeds: scenarios, functions, tools and architecture. Comput. Secur. **88**, 101636 (2020)

Serious Games

A Pond Full of Phishing
Games - Analysis of Learning Games
for Anti-Phishing Education

Rene Roepke[1($\boxtimes$)], Klemens Koehler[2($\boxtimes$)], Vincent Drury[3($\boxtimes$)], Ulrik Schroeder[1],
Martin R. Wolf[2], and Ulrike Meyer[3]

[1] RWTH Aachen University, Ahornstr. 55, 52074 Aachen, Germany
`{roepke,schroeder}@cs.rwth-aachen.de`
[2] University of Applied Sciences Aachen, Eupener Str. 70, 52066 Aachen, Germany
`{k.koehler,m.wolf}@fh-aachen.de`
[3] RWTH Aachen University, Mies-v.-d.-Rohe-Str. 15, 52074 Aachen, Germany
`{drury,meyer}@itsec.rwth-aachen.de`

Abstract. Game-based learning is a promising approach to anti-phishing education, as it fosters motivation and can help reduce the perceived difficulty of the educational material. Over the years, several prototypes for game-based applications have been proposed, that follow different approaches in content selection, presentation, and game mechanics. In this paper, a literature and product review of existing learning games is presented. Based on research papers and accessible applications, an in-depth analysis was conducted, encompassing target groups, educational contexts, learning goals based on Bloom's Revised Taxonomy, and learning content. As a result of this review, we created the publications on games (POG) data set for the domain of anti-phishing education. While there are games that can convey factual and conceptual knowledge, we find that most games are either unavailable, fail to convey procedural knowledge or lack technical depth. Thus, we identify potential areas of improvement for games suitable for end-users in informal learning contexts.

Keywords: Game-based learning · Learning game · Learning content · Review · Analysis

1 Introduction

Recent incidents and reports confirm that phishing is still a relevant threat to end-users' online security [1,2]. Consistently high numbers of new phishing websites and quickly evolving attack schemes try to exploit security's weakest link, the end-user [2]. Although technical solutions to thwart phishing exist, they exhibit various shortcomings and fail to stop the threat completely [3]. Thus,

---

R. Roepke, K. Koehler and V. Drury—Contributed equally.

G. Hatzivasilis and S. Ioannidis (Eds.): MSTEC 2020, LNCS 12512, pp. 41–60, 2020.
https://doi.org/10.1007/978-3-030-62433-0_3

anti-phishing education can be implemented as a complementary approach to support end-users in mitigating phishing attacks.

Since end-users need to be able to detect and avoid phishing attacks, anti-phishing education has the goal to teach the necessary knowledge and skills. Due to a lack of prior knowledge and the domain's complexity, the subject of security may be perceived to have a steep learning curve. Additionally, security is only a secondary task and users' motivation to learn anything about it must be considered to be low.

To overcome these issues educators have turned to game-based learning over a decade ago. These games promise the ability to increase motivation and engage users in learning about phishing. Over the years, several learning games have been proposed and developed (e.g., [4–6]), yet there seems to be little to no comprehensive and comparative analysis as to which content is conveyed within these games, how the content is presented and what game design elements they use.

This paper closes this gap in an interdisciplinary manner by taking on three different perspectives on game-based anti-phishing education. Based on a systematic literature and product review, we present the results of an in-depth analysis of the games, encompassing target groups, educational contexts, learning goals based on Bloom's Revised Taxonomy (BRT) [7], and learning content. The BRT was selected because it connects teaching goals with activities. Games require active participation and usually train the player to improve in the necessary skills. Educational games can leverage this by training skills that can be transferred to real-world situations. By categorizing activities the BRT provides a framework to analyze the resulting skills.

We find that most applications are only presented in literature but not publicly accessible. The BRT-based learning goal analysis suggests, that some games do not convey procedural knowledge on real-life application, but rather convey procedures to pass the game. For available applications, the analysis of learning content revealed a lack of technical detail and conveyed knowledge which makes them less educative and potentially misleading. We, therefore, identify the problem of availability and suitability, as many learning games are either not publicly available or fail to teach adequate knowledge. These results indicate the necessity of additional development and research of new learning games with more sustainable content and publishing choices, including availability as open educational resources.

The remainder of this paper is structured as follows. The next section presents related work, followed by the definition of research objectives and hypotheses in Sect. 3, as well as the methodology of the literature and product search in Sect. 4. Sections 5, 6, and 7 present the methodology and results of our multidimensional analysis, examining target groups and educational contexts, learning goals and taxonomy levels, and learning content, respectively. Finally, we discuss our findings in Sect. 8 and conclude the paper in Sect. 9.

2   Related Work

This paper presents a systematic literature review of anti-phishing learning games from several different perspectives. Though we did not find any similar peer-reviewed publications in the research area of anti-phishing education, there are various articles that take a look at game-based learning for IT security education in general [8–13]. These existing reviews emphasize the potential benefits but also challenges and problems of the application of game-based learning in its various forms. However, as they also look at games on other topics in the IT security domain, the reviews are rather broad and less insightful on the specific topic of phishing.

In 2009, Alotaibi et al. [8] identified the use of gaming technology for IT security education as relatively new and in need of more extensive research. Pastor et al. [14] emphasized the potential of practical training and the use of simulations in game-based learning for IT security education. In later work, the review of Compte et al. [9] presented different serious games and stated observations and suggestions regarding their design. They collected and reviewed academic publications as well as commercial products but did not elaborate on their methodology. Compte et al. [9] concluded that reviewed serious games try to deliver an immersive experience through simulations and interactivity. They also identified that most games are tied to formal learning contexts and available via traditional distribution channels of video games (i.e., they can only be found on the website of the research group which developed them).

More recently, Tioh et al. [13] argued for the potential of game-based learning to combine characteristics of both traditional and hands-on training methods. However, their review of related studies showed that the effectiveness of game-based learning for IT security education was not yet empirically proven. Similarly, Hendrix et al. [11] noted positive effects but criticize small sample sizes and non-discussed effect sizes in several studies.

The authors of [15] and [16] reviewed existing learning games for IT security education. They classified existing applications by target groups, educational contexts, and checked availability. Similar to [11], many games were no longer available due to the discontinuation of the corresponding research projects. In [16], keyword analysis was used to inspect the games' learning goals within Bloom's Revised Taxonomy. Their findings indicate that analyzed learning games do not include learning goals targeting the categories "analyze" and "evaluate", nor do they convey meta-cognitive knowledge, e.g., through self-reflection.

Since we did not find any publications on systematic literature reviews on game-based learning for anti-phishing education, we identify the need for an overview and in-depth analysis of existing publications and available games in this area. This analysis enables us to focus on the specific characteristics of phishing, which stands out among IT security attacks in that it actively depends on user interaction and deception. Thus, this contribution takes a closer look at the research and development in the field of game-based anti-phishing education.

3   Research Objectives and Hypotheses

In order to find out how effective available anti-phishing games are at preparing end-users to resist phishing attacks, this research study takes a three-step approach, guided by the following research objective statements:

- (RO 1) A literature review was conducted to create a comprehensive data set and answer which anti-phishing games are available and what is their intended educational context and target group.
- (RO 2) A further analysis of the literature, using Bloom's Revised Taxonomy for categorization, was then done to establish whether the skills conveyed through the game mechanics are suitable and sufficient to prepare end-users.
- (RO 3) By playing the accessible games, extracting their content, and comparing those to contemporary phenomena in phishing attacks, the correctness and completeness of the conveyed knowledge was assessed.

We refer to end-users as users that have little or no prior formal education in Computer Science and IT security and having no access to organizational resources, such as training programs or immediate IT support. Consequently, learning games that address end-users as target group have to be effective in informal, auto-didactic contexts and provide a safe environment to experiment.

However, to enable end-users to avoid phishing attempts, anti-phishing education has to provide the right content with the right methods. In games, teaching methods are translated through game mechanics [17]. Past research has shown that publications on game-based learning applications often give insight into the content of the games, but not the methods and game mechanics [16]. Additionally, it was suggested that this is more pronounced in single-issue games and digital games. Both characteristics are relevant for anti-phishing learning games: As digital games offer access and require no formal or social context, they are well-suited for end-users. Games that concentrate on the single topic of anti-phishing education are relevant because they address an important weakness of end-users' IT security.

Finally, since games offer an alternative to other learning formats that can be more motivating, they might offer more detailed conceptual knowledge that end-users would otherwise be unwilling to learn. On the other hand, games are costly to implement and update compared to other formats.

Considering these assumptions, the research objectives can be transformed into the following hypotheses:

- (H1) The majority of games are designed for end-users without prior knowledge in IT security.
- (H2) The majority of games are designed for informal learning contexts.
- (H3) The game mechanics aim at specific, shared learning goals, and:
    - (H3a) There is no difference in learning goals between the mechanics of digital and non-digital games.

- • (H3b) There is no difference in learning goals between the mechanics of games that exclusively cover phishing and games that cover additional forms of IT attacks and defense.
- – (H4) The games require learners to utilize procedural knowledge.
- – (H5) The games convey detailed conceptual knowledge.
- – (H6) The games do not contain knowledge on advanced contemporary attacks.

4   Methodology of Literature and Product Search

This section presents our methodology for the literature and product search conducted for this paper, resulting in a set of publications and references of existing anti-phishing learning games. Similar to the approach of [16] and [15], this contribution utilizes the method of systematic literature review. While the focus of [16] and [15] was game-based learning for IT security education in general, for this work, we focused on the collection and analysis of existing research in the field of game-based learning for anti-phishing education.

We followed the prior methodology and queried various digital libraries (ACM Digital Library[1], Google Scholar[2] and IEEE Xplore[3]). All search queries were constructed by a combination of the keyword *phishing* and one keyword k from the following keyword set using the logical conjunction operator ($\wedge$ or AND):

$$k \in \{ \text{ educational game, serious game, learning game,} \atop \text{game based learning, competence developing game }\} \tag{1}$$

We limited our collection of search results to publications written in English. The initial result set contained 497 publications and after omitting all duplicates, it was reduced to 282 results. Next, we analyzed title and abstract for relevance to our research domain, i.e., learning games for anti-phishing education. The result set was reduced to 61 publications. In the reduced result set, we found 7 reviews on learning games. We checked each review for publications on learning games for anti-phishing education but our result already contained all mentioned publications. We, therefore, excluded the review publications to further process only detailed publications on particular games.

Our final *Publications on Games* data set (POG) contains 54 results, describing 40 unique games. For games described in more than one publication, we referenced only one publication in the Appendix Table 6. In the following sections, we present an in-depth analysis focusing on (1) target groups and educational contexts and (2) learning goals based on Bloom's Revised Taxonomy and (3) learning content.

---

[1] https://dl.acm.org/, last accessed on 2020-07-13.

[2] https://scholar.google.de/, last accessed on 2020-07-13.

[3] https://ieeexplore.ieee.org/, last accessed on 2020-07-13.

5 Analysis of Target Groups and Educational Contexts

Methodology. As learning games are usually bound to specific learning goals and learning content, they are often developed for a particular target group and may be used in a specific educational context. While we do not expect these details to be revealed in the games directly, e.g., by stating it at the start of a game, we can look at available publications.

Similar to the approach in [15], we distinguish between the following target groups: (1) *Computer Science (CS) students*, (2) *non-CS students*, (3) *employees*, (4) *IT employees*, and (5) *end-users*. If no target group is mentioned we classify it as (6) *unspecified*. We explicitly differentiate between CS students and non-CS students, since prior knowledge may vary between these two target groups. Similarly, we distinguish between employees and IT employees. We assume that tailoring a game towards a target group with prior knowledge in Computer Science and IT security means building upon this prior knowledge. Thus, it might not be suitable for target groups without prior knowledge.

For the educational context, we consider different levels of education, i.e., (a) *primary school*, (b) *middle school*, (c) *high school* and (d) *college/university*. We also distinguish between (e) *corporate* and (f) *informal* learning contexts. Unknown educational contexts are classified as (g) *unspecified*. The above-mentioned school contexts as well as college/university and corporate can be summarized as formal learning contexts.

Results. The results for the analysis of target groups and educational contexts are summarized in Table 1. Among the 40 games described in publications, we were able to identify 34 games (85%) with an explicit target group and educational context. As a game could be designed for multiple target groups and educational contexts, we allowed the assignment of multiple classes for each game (see Appendix Table 6 for the complete analyses results of identified categories for each game).

Table 1. Analysis results for target groups and educational contexts

Target group	# games	Educational context	# games
CS students	4	Primary school	3
Non-CS students	9	Middle school	5
Employees	6	High school	1
IT employees	3	College/University	7
End-users	13	Corporate	9
Unspecified	6	Informal	14
		Unspecified	6

For the remaining 6 games (15%), no target groups and educational contexts were specified in any of the publications describing them. Thus, we made an educated guess based on the details presented in the publications, e.g., game description, screenshots, participants of user studies. We argue that all 6 games are suitable for end-users and can be used in informal learning contexts.

The results of our analysis show that only a few games are designed for CS students and IT employees. Most games are either for end-users (13), non-CS students (9), or employees (6). During our review, we did not observe explicit notions of required prior knowledge for those games. This supports our first hypothesis (H1). In addition, 14 games are suitable for informal learning contexts, supporting our second hypothesis (H2).

6   Analysis of Learning Goals and Taxonomy Levels

Methodology. This part of the analysis aims at learning goals that are built into game mechanics. Game-based learning has a comparative advantage to other forms of learning because it provides a safe environment to practice and experiment [18]. Furthermore, if activities and content within the game resemble real-world activities and content more closely, knowledge transfer from game to real-world behavior becomes easier [19].

Therefore, game mechanics should enforce actions and behavior that are helpful in real-world situations. By playing, a player will acquire skills necessary to advance in a game, regardless of its content. If these differ from the skills needed in the face of a real IT attack, the game is inefficient at best and can be ineffective. To classify the type of skills developed through playing the game, we use Bloom's Revised Taxonomy (BRT) [7].

The Taxonomy defines activities as learning goals along a cognitive process dimension and a knowledge dimension. We depict it as a discrete Cartesian coordinate system, where each combination of a cognitive process on one axis and a knowledge type on the other constitutes a category. The cognitive processes are *remember, understand, apply, analyze, evaluate,* and *create.* The knowledge dimension defines *factual, conceptual, procedural,* and *meta-cognitive* knowledge. Both dimensions are progressing, i.e., without competency at a lower level (e.g., remembering facts) one cannot achieve a higher one (e.g., understanding facts, or remembering concepts). More detailed information on the concept and use of the BRT can be found in the original publication of the model [7].

Our analysis was conducted on the academic publications in the *POG* data set, assuming that publications on games provide reasoning and reflection on game design choices. Thus, 40 unique games could be analyzed. In each case, the sources contained information on game mechanics.

For data collection, we used an approach modified from [16] by analyzing how authors describe game mechanics, instead of how they define the learning goals of their games. The original semantic analysis extracted learning goals of game-based learning applications by searching academic publications for indicator phrases and verifying that they were used to describe learning goals. This approach has two drawbacks: It relies on authors using the same or similar vocabulary to describe their goals, and it relies on the authors understanding of how to translate the learning goals into their games. For example, many learning games in our analysis take a multiple-choice approach. While these games often include educational texts that convey factual, conceptual, and procedural knowledge, the game mechanics themselves do not require using it. Facts like what constitutes phishing (fact) and how phishing URLs can be distinguished from legitimate URLs (concepts) are represented and must be remembered and understood (cognitive processes) to solve the quiz and advance in the game. A question might be: Where do you find the top-level-domain in the URL. Remembering, and understanding conceptual knowledge is necessary to answer this question type. However, this does not constitute the application of procedural knowledge. Players are told what to do with phishing emails (procedural knowledge), but the actual activity in the game, clicking on the good or bad URL, does not represent the application of that knowledge in reality. Also, the player does not actively apply, analyze, evaluate, or create knowledge in the sense of the BRT.

By refining the method to analyze the descriptions of game mechanics, the actual activities required of the players can be understood. If these in-game activities match activities defined in the BRT, specific categories of the knowledge dimension and the cognitive process dimension can be assigned. Multiple categories can be assigned to each game.

As a result, each game had its own matrix of the BRT, where each category contained either a 1- (representing yes) or 0-value (representing no). For detailed examination according to the hypotheses H3a and H3b, two additional characteristics of each game were included: whether they are (a) *digital* or (b) *non-digital*, and whether (1) *yes*, they are exclusively about phishing, or (2) *no*, they cover additional IT attacks.

Results. The general overview of our results (see Table 2 for a summary and Appendix Table 6 for a detailed analysis of all 40 games) reveals most games to cover factual remembering and understanding, as well as conceptual remembering and understanding. All other categories contain 15 games or less (37.5 %). The abundance of each cognitive learning goal tends to decline going toward more complex cognitive processes and more abstract knowledge.

Table 2. Number of games covering BRT categories ($n = 40$)

	Remember	Understand	Apply	Analyze	Evaluate	Create
Factual knowledge	34	27	14	10	5	2
Conceptual knowledge	35	23	10	4	4	1
Procedural knowledge	15	11	13	5	6	3
Meta-cognitive knowledge	6	3	5	2	2	1

The 15 games with content focused on anti-phishing education concentrate even more on remembering and understanding facts and concepts (see Table 3). No game requires players to evaluate or create knowledge, and only one game conveys meta-cognitive knowledge.

Table 3. Number of anti-phishing learning games in each BRT category ($n = 15$)

	Remember	Understand	Apply	Analyze	Evaluate	Create
Factual knowledge	15	9	4	2	0	0
Conceptual knowledge	15	8	2	1	0	0
Procedural knowledge	6	3	5	0	0	0
Meta-cognitive knowledge	1	0	0	0	0	0

Looking only at the 31 digital games, there is again a complete lack of games requiring players to create knowledge, and a severe lack of meta-cognitive activities (see Table 4).

Table 4. Number of digital games covering BRT categories ($n = 31$)

	Remember	Understand	Apply	Analyze	Evaluate	Create
Factual knowledge	29	22	9	5	2	0
Conceptual knowledge	30	19	5	2	2	0
Procedural knowledge	12	6	11	1	1	0
Meta-cognitive knowledge	2	1	0	0	0	0

Another finding is that some games "skip categories". The theory behind the BRT suggests that this is not possible. On closer examination these games usually are meant to complement other educational formats, which provide the left-out activities.

In summary, the results support the acceptance of H3, while H3a, H3b, and H4 have to be rejected. H3 is true since the vast majority of all games require remembering facts and concepts. A majority also requires understanding facts and concepts. Generally, as one advances along both axes of the BRT toward more complex learning goals, the number of games that convey them declines.

H3a and H3b - the hypotheses that digital games and games exclusively about phishing attacks have similar learning goals as the complete sample - have to be rejected. Although the pattern mentioned above can be found no matter which sub-sample is considered, no digital game asks the player to create, and no game exclusively about phishing asks the player to create or evaluate. Additionally, digital and pure anti-phishing games do not cover most activities that require meta-cognitive knowledge.

Finally, H4 has to be rejected, as remembering procedural knowledge is only required in 15 games, and other cognitive processes in combination with procedural knowledge are necessary in even fewer games.

7   Analysis of Learning Content

Methodology. The results of the previous section show that many games require factual and conceptual remembering and understanding for in-game advancement. In this section, we add an additional dimension to this analysis by examining the specific topics the games present and teach during a typical playing session. This reveals which subjects are popular or missing in current anti-phishing games, the level of detail with which they are presented and whether specific topics are missing even if a broader subject is included in the game. To this end, this section takes a closer look at the content of available digital learning games and presents an analysis of their content based on a number of subjects and topics. We analyze the 9 available games in the *POG* data set (cf. Table 6), and also extend our collection by 4 reference games without academic publications that were found using the Google search engine ($9 + 4 = 13$ games, see Table 5). These reference games represent games about phishing emails, URLs, and websites as offered by several companies.

We begin our analysis by defining several subjects that are concerned with phishing and that we encountered in the games. We find the most common subjects of the analyzed games to be *URLs and Websites* (main subject of 4 games), *Emails* (main subject of 4 games), *Other/Various* (5 games). The games in the *Other/Various* category do not focus on phishing, and instead include learning content about phishing as well as several other topics of online security.

In the next step, we define more specific topics for each subject, again based on the actual content of the games, while also including topics derived from research on common and advanced phishing attack techniques. We argue that the more specific topics a game covers, the more complete the presented knowledge of a subject and the less likely that users are to fall victim to a class of phishing attacks.

For URLs, we define topics based on (1) the structure of URLs, (2) types of deceptive content, and (3) advanced topics. Regarding (1), it has been shown that attackers can make use of different parts of the URL to insert deceptive keywords [20]. The types of deceptive content (2) include common transformations in phishing URLs as well as advanced techniques like abusing Internationalized Domain Names (IDNs) [21]. Lastly, for (3), we look at a selection of URL types that users are likely to encounter in their daily browsing or in specific phishing attacks, like redirection, link-shortening, or services that host user-generated content (e.g., Dropbox[4]).

---

[4] https://www.dropbox.com/, last accessed on 2020-04-27.

For emails, we look at (a) specific traits, (b) sender spoofing, (c) email structure, and (d) email attachments. Specific traits (a) are a common topic in games, even though they can sometimes be easily avoided by attackers. There are also several types of sender spoofing (b), with differences in the display-name and sender address [22]. Finally, knowledge about the email structure (c), e.g., email headers, can often be used to detect anomalies in emails [23]. Games that focus on emails often also include some examples or lessons on domain names, as they commonly appear in email headers and are also presented in the user interface of popular email clients.

Lastly, we look at various auxiliary topics, including different message media (e.g., SMS, social media), advanced protection strategies (e.g., multi-factor authentication (MFA)), and common traits of the body of phishing websites.

The games are processed as follows: We first download and set up all available digital games. In this step, we only look at games that are generally available online, requiring no payment, membership, or request for access. We then analyze the games from a player's perspective while keeping note of the subjects and specific topics appearing in the game. We rate each specific topic according to four classes: 0 - *does not appear*, 1 - *does appear in game elements or examples*, 2 - *mentioned but not fully explained*, 3 - *fully explained*. These distinctions are based on the assumption that detailed explanations (class 3) are more likely to convey an understanding of the actual detection or protection strategy, while shallow descriptions (class 2) can be confusing and might lead to misunderstandings (e.g., [5]).

Still, we argue that these aforementioned instances of classes (2) or (3) are more likely to be actively considered by players than seemingly accidental information that may be hidden in examples or game elements (class 1).

Note that we always focus on phishing when presented with a choice during our analysis of the games. We do not claim to have encountered all examples or exhausted all possible selections, successes, and failures, though we did try to cover all content that is related to phishing, or, if the focus of the game is phishing, complete one gaming session.

Results. We determined the availability for all digital games in the *POG* data set by searching the corresponding research paper, querying a search engine, as well as searching popular code repository GitHub[5] for references to the game. In all; we were able to obtain 13 games, which includes the 4 reference games that were found using a search engine and 9 games from the *POG* data set (cf. Table 6).

After downloading and setting up the games as required, we analyzed them for the topics described in the previous section (see Table 5 for a summary of the results). Our main finding is, that few games include detailed explanations of conceptual knowledge. There are only two games (NoPhish and Anti-Phishing Phil) which focus on URLs, and explain how to determine the registrable domain

---

[5] https://github.com/, last accessed 2020-04-07.

Table 5. Analysis of game content ($n = 13$)

	Anti-Phishing Phil [5]	ATMSG/CSAG [24]	Birds Life [25]	codecanyon[d]	cyberaware [26]	CyberCraft [27]	GHOST [28]	NoPhish [29]	OpenDNS[e]	Sophos[f]	whatdothack [30]	whatthehack [31]	WithGoogle[g]
Registrable domain	3	1	0	1	0	0	0	3	2	0	1	0	2
Deception	2	1	0	1	0	0	0	3	1	0	1	0	2
Other URL features	2	1	0	1	0	0	0	3	2	0	1	0	2
Email traits	0	1	2	0	0	1	0	0	0	1	2	0	2
Sender spoofing	0	1	2	0	0	0	0	0	0	1	1	0	1
Advanced attacks	2[a]	2[b]	0	0	0	0	0	0	1[c]	0	2[c]	0	0

[a]Hex IP-addresses, [b]Pop-ups, [c]Hosting service abuse
[d]https://codecanyon.net/item/anti-phishing-awareness-game/20935555, last accessed on 2020-04-16
[e]https://www.opendns.com/phishing-quiz/, last accessed on 2020-04-16
[f]https://www.sophos.com/en-us/lp/games/play-spot-the-phish.aspx? cmp=35375, last accessed on 2020-04-16
[g]https://phishingquiz.withgoogle.com/, last accessed on 2020-04-16

(RD) of a URL (as defined by the WHATWG URL standard[6]). NoPhish goes beyond this and takes apart the structure of URLs in detail, making it the game with the most detailed explanations. It is, however, only available in German. Anti-Phishing Phil also includes detailed explanations on how to locate the RD, however, it misses some details compared to NoPhish, including information on subdomains and the separation of different domain labels.

For games in the *Other/Various* category, it is interesting to note, that they tend to have a more developed story (ATMSG, Cybercraft, and GHOST), while other games have no or only few story elements, with a focus on education and exercises. Apart from that, games in this category typically do not offer detailed explanations about phishing or anti-phishing protection strategies.

The remaining games typically cover a specific subject (e.g., URLs), and present an example for classification followed by revealing the correct answer and an explanation on how to detect the malicious parts. Note, that none of these games ask the user for the reasons for their classification decisions. As such, users that guess or use a sub-optimal detection strategy might still be rewarded with positive results, which might lead to misconceptions or confusion.

In general, we did not find any games that offer detailed conceptual knowledge about emails; none of the games explain email headers or how to verify email authenticity. Though sender spoofing is a common theme, the only way to really

---

[6] https://url.spec.whatwg.org/, last accessed 2020-04-07.

verify an email's authenticity as presented by the analyzed games is to contact the help desk or IT support, which is usually not a viable option for private end-users. The lack of detailed explanations might be due to the game creators' perception of the email structure being more complicated, email sender `From:` spoofing being uncommon, or email headers being less reliable in identifying phishing emails than other indicators. As for attachments, seven games include information on malware in attachments or links in emails. Two games also address other message types beyond email (e.g., instant messaging). This leads us to reject H5, as it seems that most games are either used to motivate different types of educational material or to test knowledge that was acquired differently.

An additional finding is the lack of advanced phishing techniques in available games, supporting H6. None of the games include information on IDN or percent-encoding in URLs, and only a few include hosting platform abuse. This might be due to the low expected occurrence of this type of attacks in phishing, or due to the fact that the emergence of advanced techniques are comparatively recent developments. Note that users, depending on their locality, might be confronted with techniques such as IDN in their benign surfing activities as well.

On the other hand, six games include examples of benign websites with uncommon characteristics. Examples here include the use of "www3" as subdomain instead of "www" or information on unexpected domain names (e.g., "dropbox-mail.com" instead of "dropbox.com"). We argue that including these examples can potentially demonstrate to users, that benign websites might also exhibit uncommon behavior, thus reducing false positives in their decisions. Many games also include hints on additional protection strategies, like using a search engine to determine the authenticity of a website (3 games) or hovering over a link to display the actual destination (3 games). Using MFA was recommended less often, only one game included it as a method to protect against phishing.

Note, that we only analyze the content of the games and do not claim that including or omitting these topics has an effect on learners. However, the relevance of the selected topics is still valid due to the body of knowledge on phishing.

8   Discussion

The analysis in previous sections revealed that many games are suitable for end-users in informal learning contexts, thus supporting our hypotheses (H1 & H2 accepted). It also showed that most of the games require specific categories of player action, namely remembering and understanding conceptual and factual knowledge (H3 accepted), regardless of their scope or digital nature. The majority of games do not require procedural or meta-cognitive knowledge (H4 rejected), however. Furthermore, considering only digital and mono-thematic anti-phishing games, those require an even smaller range of activities (H3a & H3b rejected). Finally, the effect of game-based learning on motivation is not used to introduce more complex content (H5 rejected) and lacks information on advanced contemporary phishing techniques (H6 accepted).

The main problem concerning all findings is that few games are actually available and accessible. This severely hinders attempts to extract general findings, which in turn hurts attempts to replicate research and improve on the development of game-based learning applications. Nevertheless, the hypotheses were tested and warrant some discussion and interpretation.

The content of the accessible games is comparably easy to discuss, as it concerns verifiable technical information. In general, few games offered detailed explanations that would allow users to gain a fundamental understanding of key concepts. As a consequence, most games would need additional, accompanying educational material. The most detailed explanations we encountered focus on URL classification, in particular locating the registrable domain, but leave out more advanced techniques, although some games offer examples. Additionally, though emails were a topic of several games, none of them offered detailed knowledge on phishing emails, making this common attack vector severely underrepresented. Evaluating the severity of these gaps in user education poses the question, how much detail and depth would be enough. This question is hard to answer, as attack and defense knowledge co-evolve, changing the necessary knowledge over time. Also, it is hard to discern which contents are most efficient and effective at improving security, necessitating further research.

In Sect. 6 we found that the learning goals and game mechanics of analyzed games are suitable to convey conceptual knowledge, as players at least need to remember and understand some concepts. Even so, as argued above, only a few games use the mechanisms to convey conceptual or procedural knowledge in depth. Acquiring only punctual and isolated knowledge might impede the creation of accurate mental models that help users develop secure online behavior.

While some publications refer to the *conceptual-procedural principle*, it is often not leveraged. Basically, the idea is to present knowledge (conceptual) and then use it to solve in-game problems (procedural). However, the procedures needed to advance in the game are generally not applicable to deal with real-world attacks, i.e. pointing at a phishing URL would not solve the problem in a real phishing attack. Consequently, the games are suitable as an assessment tool to identify factual and conceptual knowledge gained elsewhere, not as a stand-alone learning tool.

This is especially true for digital games and games that focus exclusively on phishing, as these characteristics are good predictors to find some form of a gamified multiple-choice test. We found that no digital game needs creative activities for players to advance. We also found that no game exclusively about phishing made the players create or evaluate knowledge. In reality, end-users without institutional help need to create, apply, and evaluate their own security procedures against IT attacks. This poses the question, whether it is possible to design games that create these skills. The alternative is to surround available games by additional teaching material, briefings, and debriefings, while at the same time conserving their motivation advantage.

While our methods were not suited to identify *why* non-digital games generally covered a wider range of activities, we can offer some educated guesses for future research. Most non-digital games require a facilitator to play, who would often be a subject matter expert on the contents, a source of knowledge digital games lack. Facilitators are also humans and potentially capable of empathy: They sense if participants are curious, or lack curiosity about more intricate details. It is a challenge to integrate this kind of player-interaction into digital games. In contrast, facilitated games can be updated, potentially before each use, which requires domain-specific knowledge on phishing attacks.

Digital games, especially those that originated in now finished research projects, are often not up to date with newer advanced attacks, a problem that could be solved by periodic updates. Finally, non-digital games often create a scenario with a role for each player. The players need to evaluate their resources and find strategies to leverage them. This again creates the problem of human facilitation, as non-professional end-users might find it difficult to communicate creative ideas to a computer program. Future research might reveal possibilities to develop scalable digital games with human facilitation, mitigating each approach's weaknesses.

To summarize, available anti-phishing learning games do not contain detailed information on the threats and do not train adequate behavior when faced with it. On the other hand, most games are designed for an informal learning context (see Sect. 5), where users can not be expected to have additional material or advice available. We argue that a lack of detailed information might thus lead to confusion when presented with unknown or unexpected situations (e.g., an advanced attack using IDN or a link using an IP-address on a benign website), while inadequate understanding of secure behavior can lead to fatigue (e.g., if users check the URL after every click) or harm (e.g., when failing to check for indicators of malicious websites after being redirected).

9   Conclusion

Our research suggests that it is possible to design games that enable end-users in informal contexts to successfully deal with phishing attempts. However, most games do not seem to accomplish that. We found that many games address end-users and are meant to be used in informal, even self-teaching contexts. At the same time, some of the more extensive games provide a learning experience that can even be used in formal contexts. A closer examination of the game mechanics and activities necessary to advance in the games showed that most of them do not teach procedural knowledge that is easily transferable to the real world. While users learn how to operate the game, they do not learn how to integrate anti-phishing techniques into their everyday behavior. Even the conceptual knowledge that most games are designed to convey is often inadequate. This is only partly the result of fast-paced developments in IT attacks.

The variance of the games in each analysis suggests the possibility to design suitable anti-phishing learning games. That is games that teach end-users in informal contexts to independently cope with phishing threats. However, to integrate adequate conceptual and procedural knowledge with methods to convey that knowledge by enabling active, experimental learning by users, requires further work.

Acknowledgements. This research was supported by the research training group "Human Centered Systems Security" sponsored by the state of North Rhine-Westphalia.

Appendix

Table 6. Summarized analysis results of POG data set (x = identified category; g = guessed category; y = yes; n = no; − = n/a)

Reference	Target Gr.					Edu. Context									factual						Conceptual						Procedural						Meta-cognitive					
	End-users	Non-CS students	CS Students	Employees	IT employees	Primary School	Middle school	High school	College/university	Corporate	Informal	Available?	Focus: phishing?	Digital?	Remember	Understand	Apply	Analyze	Evaluate	Create	Remember	Understand	Apply	Analyze	Evaluate	Create	Remember	Understand	Apply	Analyze	Evaluate	Create	Remember	Understand	Apply	Analyze	Evaluate	Create
[5]	x										x	y	y	y	x						x	x					x		x									
[6]	x										x	n	y	y	x	x	x				x	x	x				x	x	x									
[24]		x									x	y	y	y	x	x					x	x																
[25]			x								x	y	y	y	x	x					x																	
[26]		x				x	x					y	n	y	x	x	x	x	x	x	x	x	x	x	x	x	x	x										
[27]			x								x	y	n	y	x	x	x	x	x	x	x	x	x	x	x	x	x	x	x	x	x	x						
[28]			x							x		y	n	y	x	x					x	x	x							x								
[29]	x										x	y	y	y	x	x					x	x					x											
[30]	x										x	y	y	y	x	x					x	x																
[31]	x										x	y	n	y	x	x					x	x					x		x									
[32]	x										x	n	n	y	x	x					x	x																
[33]	g										g	n	y	y	x						x																	
[34]	g										g	n	y	y	x						x																	
[35]	x										x	−	y	n	x	x	x				x	x	x				x	x	x									
[36]	x					x	x					n	n	y	x	x					x	x																
[37]			x								x	−	n	n	x						x	x	x				x	x	x	x	x	x	x	x	x	x	x	x
[38]		x									x	−	n	n	x	x	x				x	x	x				x	x										
[39]	x										x	n	n	y	x	x					x	x																
[40]	x										x	n	n	y	x												x		x									
[41]		x									x	n	y	y	x	x					x	x					x		x									
[42]		x									x	n	y	y	x	x					x								x	x								
[43]		x									x	n	n	y	x						x																	
[44]		x									x	−	n	n			x	x	x					x	x					x	x	x	x			x	x	x	
[45]	x										x	−	n	n	x	x	x	x			x		x				x		x	x					x			
[46]				x							x	n	y	y		x					x						x											
[47]	g										g	n	n	y							x									x								
[48]	g										g	n	n	y	x	x					x	x																
[49]	x					x						n	y	y	x	x	x	x																				
[50]	x					x	x					n	n	y	x	x	x				x	x	x				x	x	x				x	x				
[51]	x										x	n	y	y	x	x					x	x																
[52]			x								x	n	n	y	x						x						x		x									
[53]	x								x			n	n	y	x	x	x	x			x						x		x									
[54]	g										g	n	n	y	x	x	x				x	x																
[55]			x								x	−	n	n			x	x	x					x									x	x	x	x	x	x
[56]	x										x	−	y	n	x						x	x	x															
[57]	g										g	n	n	y	x	x					x	x																
[58]	x	x					x				x	−	n	n	x						x																	
[59]	x										x	n	n	y	x	x					x	x																
[60]	x										x	n	y	y	x						x																x	
[61]		x									x	−	n	n	x	x	x	x			x						x	x					x	x	x			

References

1. Shi, F.: Threat Spotlight: Coronavirus-Related Phishing (2020). https://blog.barracuda.com/2020/03/26/threat-spotlight-coronavirus-related-phishing/
2. Anti-Phishing Working Group: Phishing Attack Trends Report, 4th Quarter 2019. Report, Anti-Phishing Working Group (2020). https://docs.apwg.org/reports/apwg_trends_report_q4_2019.pdf
3. Gupta, B.B., Tewari, A., Jain, A.K., Agrawal, D.P.: Fighting against phishing attacks: state of the art and future challenges. Neural Comput. Appl. **28**(12), 3629–3654 (2016). https://doi.org/10.1007/s00521-016-2275-y
4. Canova, G., Volkamer, M., Bergmann, C., Borza, R.: NoPhish: an anti-phishing education app. In: Mauw, S., Jensen, C.D. (eds.) STM 2014. LNCS, vol. 8743, pp. 188–192. Springer, Cham (2014). https://doi.org/10.1007/978-3-319-11851-2_14
5. Sheng, S., et al.: Anti-phishing phil: the design and evaluation of a game that teaches people not to fall for phish. In: Symposium on Usable Privacy and Security, SOUPS 2007, pp. 88–99. ACM, New York (2007)
6. Hale, M.L., Gamble, R.F., Gamble, P.: CyberPhishing: a game-based platform for phishing awareness testing. In: Hawaii International Conference on System Sciences, Kauai, vol. 48, pp. 5260–5269. IEEE (2015)
7. Krathwohl, D.R.: A revision of bloom's taxonomy: an overview. Theory Pract. **41**(4), 212–218 (2002)
8. Alotaibi, F., Furnell, S., Stengel, I., Papadaki, M.: A review of using gaming technology for cyber-security awareness. Inf. Secur. Res. **6**(2), 660–666 (2016)
9. Compte, A.L., Elizondo, D., Watson, T.: A renewed approach to serious games for cyber security. In: International Conference on Cyber Conflict: Architectures in Cyberspace, Tallinn, pp. 203–216. IEEE (2015)
10. Dewey, C.M., Shaffer, C.: Advances in information SEcurity EDucation. In: International Conference on Electro Information Technology, Grand Forks, pp. 133–138. IEEE (2016)
11. Hendrix, M., Al-Sherbaz, A., Bloom, V.: Game based cyber security training: are serious games suitable for cyber security training? Serious Games **3**(1), 53–61 (2016)
12. Monk, T., Van Niekerk, J., Von Solms, R.: Concealing the medicine: information security education through game play. In: Information Security for South Africa, Pretoria, pp. 467–478. ISSA (2009)
13. Tioh, J.N., Mina, M., Jacobson, D.W.: Cyber security training a survey of serious games in cyber security. In: 2017 IEEE Frontiers in Education Conference (FIE), Indianapolis, pp. 1–5. IEEE (2017)
14. Pastor, V., Díaz, G., Castro, M.: State-of-the-art simulation systems for information security education, training and awareness. In: EDUCON, Madrid, pp. 1907–1916. IEEE (2010)
15. Roepke, R., Schroeder, U.: The problem with teaching defence against the dark arts: a review of game-based learning applications and serious games for cyber security education. In: International Conference on Computer Supported Education, Heraklion, vol. 2, pp. 58–66. SciTePress (2019)
16. Köhler, K., Röpke, R., Wolf, M.R.: Through a mirror darkly - on the obscurity of teaching goals in game-based learning in IT security. In: Simulation & Gaming Through Times and Across Disciplines, pp. 324–335. Akademia Leona Kozminskiego, Warsaw (2019)

17. Arnab, S., et al.: Mapping learning and game mechanics for serious games analysis. Educ. Technol. **46**(2), 391–411 (2015)
18. König, J.A., Wolf, M.R.: A new definition of competence developing games. In: ACHI 2016, pp. 95–97. IARIA, Venice (2016)
19. Wolf, M.R., Wiese, U.: A comparative transformation model for process changes using serious games. In: International Conference on Serious Games and Applications for Health, Vilamoura. IEEE (2013)
20. McGrath, D.K., Gupta, M.: Behind phishing: an examination of phisher modi operandi. In: USENIX Workshop on Large-Scale Exploits and Emergent Threats, LEET 2008, San Francisco (2008)
21. Elsayed, Y., Shosha, A.: Large scale detection of IDN domain name masquerading. In: 2018 APWG Symposium on Electronic Crime Research (eCrime). IEEE (2018)
22. Resnick, P.: Rfc 5322: Internet message format (2008)
23. Hu, H., Wang, G.: End-to-end measurements of email spoofing attacks. In: USENIX Security Symposium (USENIX Security 18), pp. 1095–1112. USENIX Association (2018)
24. Huynh, D., Luong, P., Iida, H., Beuran, R.: Design and evaluation of a cybersecurity awareness training game. In: Munekata, N., Kunita, I., Hoshino, J. (eds.) ICEC 2017. LNCS, vol. 10507, pp. 183–188. Springer, Cham (2017). https://doi.org/10.1007/978-3-319-66715-7_19
25. Weanquoi, P., Johnson, J., Zhang, J.: Using a game to improve phishing awareness. Cybersecur. Educ. Res. Pract. **2018**(2), 2 (2018)
26. Giannakas, F., Kambourakis, G., Gritzalis, S.: CyberAware: a mobile game-based app for cybersecurity education and awareness. In: International Conference on Interactive Mobile Communication Technologies and Learning (IMCL), Thessaloniki, pp. 54–58. IEEE (2015)
27. Lu, Y.: CyberCraft, a security serious game. Master's thesis, Politecnico di Torino, Torino (2018)
28. König, J.A., Wolf, M.R.: GHOST: an evaluated competence developing game for cybersecurity awareness training. Adv. Secur. **11**(3 & 4), 274–287 (2018)
29. Bergmann, C., Canova, G.: Design, implementation and evaluation of an anti-phishing education app. Master's thesis, Technische Universität Darmstadt, Darmstadt (2014)
30. Wen, Z.A., Lin, Z., Chen, R., Andersen, E.: What. Hack: engaging anti-phishing training through a role-playing phishing simulation game. In: CHI Conference on Human Factors in Computing Systems, CHI 2019. ACM, New York (2019)
31. Geywitz, J.: "What the Hack?" - Konzeption und Implementierung eines erweiterbaren und adaptiven Serious Game zur Verbesserung von Information Security Awareness. Master's thesis, University of Applied Sciences, Düsseldorf (2019)
32. Aladawy, D., Beckers, K., Pape, S.: PERSUADED: fighting social engineering attacks with a serious game. In: Furnell, S., Mouratidis, H., Pernul, G. (eds.) TrustBus 2018. LNCS, vol. 11033, pp. 103–118. Springer, Cham (2018). https://doi.org/10.1007/978-3-319-98385-1_8
33. Arachchilage, N.A.G., Love, S., Maple, C.: Can a mobile game teach computer users to thwart phishing attacks? Infonomics **6**(3/4), 720–730 (2015)
34. Baral, G., Arachchilage, N.A.G.: Building confidence not to be phished through a gamified approach: conceptualising user's self-efficacy in phishing threat avoidance behaviour. In: Cybersecurity and Cyberforensics Conference (CCC), Melbourne, pp. 102–110. IEEE (2019)

35. Baslyman, M., Chiasson, S.: "Smells Phishy?": an educational game about online phishing scams. In: 2016 APWG Symposium on Electronic Crime Research (eCrime), Toronto, Ontario, Canada, pp. 1–11. IEEE (2016)
36. Bauer, G., Martinek, D., Kriglstein, S., Wallner, G., Wölfle, R.: Digital game-based learning with "Internet Hero": a game about the internet for children aged 9–12 years. In: Mitgutsch, K., Huber, S., Wagner, M., Wimmer, J., Rosenstingl, H. (eds.) Context Matters!, pp. 148–161. New Academic Press, Wien (2017)
37. Beckers, K., Pape, S.: A serious game for eliciting social engineering security requirements. In: International Requirements Engineering Conference (RE), Beijing, pp. 16–25. IEEE (2016)
38. Beckers, K., Pape, S., Fries, V.: HATCH: hack and trick capricious humans - a serious game on social engineering. In: International BCS Human Computer Interaction Conference: Companion Volume, HCI 2016, pp. 1–3. BCS Learning & Development Ltd., Swindon (2016)
39. Bhardwaj, J.: Design of a game for cybersecurity awareness. Master's thesis, North Dakota State University, Fargo (2019)
40. Chiasson, S., Modi, M., Biddle, R.: Auction Hero: the design of a game to learn and teach about computer security. In: Ho, C., Lin, M.F.G. (eds.) E-Learn: World Conference on E-Learning in Corporate, Government, Healthcare, and Higher Education 2011, pp. 2201–2206. AACE, Honolulu (2011)
41. Gokul, C.J., Pandit, S., Vaddepalli, S., Tupsamudre, H., Banahatti, V., Lodha, S.: PHISHY - a serious game to train enterprise users on phishing awareness. In: Annual Symposium on Computer-Human Interaction in Play Companion Extended Abstracts, CHI PLAY 2018 Extended Abstracts, pp. 169–181. ACM, New York (2018)
42. Cone, B.D., Irvine, C.E., Thompson, M.F., Nguyen, T.D.: A video game for cyber security training and awareness. Comput. Secur. 26(1), 63–72 (2007)
43. Filipczuk, D., Mason, C., Snow, S.: Using a game to explore notions of responsibility for cyber security in organisations. In: Extended Abstracts of the 2019 CHI Conference on Human Factors in Computing Systems, CHI EA 2019. ACM, New York (2019)
44. Frey, S., Rashid, A., Anthonysamy, P., Pinto-Albuquerque, M., Naqvi, S.A.: The good, the bad and the ugly: a study of security decisions in a cyber-physical systems game. IEEE Trans. Softw. Eng. 45(5), 521–536 (2019)
45. Gondree, M., Peterson, Z.N.J.: Valuing security by getting [d0x3d!]: experiences with a network security board game. In: Workshop on Cyber Security Experimentation and Test (CSET). USENIX Association, Washington, D.C. (2013)
46. Hebert, A.J., Reynolds, C.O., Stack, K.J., Lindsay, R.C.: Lock_out: a cybersecurity MQP and game. Final Report, Worcester Polytechnic Institute, Worcester (2017)
47. Katsadouros, E., Kogias, D., Toumanidis, L., Chatzigeorgiou, C., Patrikakis, C.Z.: Teaching network security through a scavenger hunt game. In: IEEE Global Engineering Education Conference (EDUCON), Athens, pp. 1802–1805. IEEE (2017)
48. Kulkarni, V.K.: Basic cybersecurity awareness through gaming. Master's thesis, North Dakota State University, Fargo (2019)
49. Lopes, I., Morenets, Y., Inácio, P.R.M., Silva, F.: Cyber-detective: a game for cyber crime prevention. In: Play2Learn, Lisbon, Portugal, pp. 175–191 (2018)
50. Mikka-Muntuumo, J., Peters, A., Jazri, H.: CyberBullet - Share Your Story: an interactive game for stimulating awareness on the harm and negative effects of the internet. In: African Conference for Human Computer Interaction: Thriving Communities, pp. 287–290. ACM, New York (2018)

51. Misra, G., Arachchilage, N.A.G., Berkovsky, S.: Phish phinder: a game design approach to enhance user confidence in mitigating phishing attacks. In: Furnell, S., Clarke, N.L. (eds.) International Symposium on Human Aspects of Information Security & Assurance (HAISA 2017), Adelaide, pp. 41–51 (2017)

52. Monk, T., van Niekerk, J., von Solms, R.: Sweetening the medicine: educating users about information security by means of game play. In: Annual Research Conference of the South African Institute of Computer Scientists and Information Technologists, SAICSIT 2010, pp. 193–200. ACM, New York (2010)

53. Olano, M., et al.: SecurityEmpire: development and evaluation of a digital game to promote cybersecurity education. In: USENIX Summit on Gaming, Games, and Gamification in Security Education, San Diego (2014)

54. Olanrewaju, A.S.T., Zakaria, N.H.: Social engineering awareness game (SEAG): an empirical evaluation of using game towards improving information security awareness. In: International Conference on Computing and Informatics, Istanbul, pp. 187–193 (2015)

55. Rieb, A., Lechner, U.: Operation digital chameleon: towards an open cybersecurity method. In: International Symposium on Open Collaboration, OpenSym 2016, pp. 1–10. ACM, New York (2016)

56. Stockhardt, S., Reinheimer, B., Volkamer, M.: Über die Wirksamkeit von Anti-Phishing-Training. In: Mensch und Computer 2015 - Workshopband, pp. 647–656. Oldenbourg Wissenschaftsverlag, Stuttgart (2015)

57. Tseng, S., Chen, K., Lee, T., Weng, J.: Automatic content generation for anti-phishing education game. In: International Conference on Electrical and Control Engineering, Yichang, pp. 6390–6394. IEEE (2011)

58. Tseng, S.S., Yang, T.Y., Weng, J.F., Wang, Y.J.: Building a game-based internet security learning system by ontology crystallization approach. In: International Conference on e-Learning, e-Business, Enterprise Information Systems, and e-Government (EEE), p. 6. CSREA Press, Las Vegas (2015)

59. Vuksani, E.: Device dash: designing, implementing, and evaluating an educational computer security game. Thesis, Wellesley College & MITLincoln Laboratory, Wellesley (2012)

60. Yang, C., Tseng, S., Lee, T., Weng, J., Chen, K.: Building an anti-phishing game to enhance network security literacy learning. In: International Conference on Advanced Learning Technologies, Rome, vol. 12, pp. 121–123. IEEE (2012)

61. Yasin, A., Liu, L., Li, T., Wang, J., Zowghi, D.: Design and preliminary evaluation of a cyber Security Requirements Education Game (SREG). Inf. Softw. Technol. **95**, 179–200 (2018)

Conceptualization of a CyberSecurity Awareness Quiz

Sebastian Pape[1,2](✉) ⓘD, Ludger Goeke[1], Alejandro Quintanar[1],
and Kristian Beckers[1]

[1] Social Engineering Academy (SEA) GmbH,
Eschersheimer Landstrasse 42, 60322 Frankfurt am Main, Germany
Sebastian.Pape@m-chair.de
[2] Faculty of Economics and Business Administration, Goethe University Frankfurt,
Theodor-W.-Adorno-Platz 4, 60323 Frankfurt am Main, Germany

Abstract. Recent approaches to raise security awareness have improved a lot in terms of user-friendliness and user engagement. However, since social engineering attacks on employees are evolving fast, new variants arise very rapidly. To deal with recent changes, our serious game *Cyber-Security Awareness Quiz* provides a quiz on recent variants to make employees aware of new attacks or attack variants in an entertaining way. While the gameplay of a quiz is more or less generic, the core of our contribution is a concept to create questions and answers based on current affairs and attacks observed in the wild.

Keywords: Serious game · CyberSecurity Awareness · Human factor

1 Introduction

Social engineering attacks represent a continuing threat to employees of organizations. With a wide availability of different tools and information sources [5], it is a challenging task to keep up to date of recent attacks on employees since new attacks are being developed and modifications of known attack scenarios are emerging. The latest Data Breach Investigations Report [2] reports another increase of financially motivated social engineering, where the attacker directly ask for some money, i. e. by impersonating CEOs or other high-level executives. However, during the writing of the report, scammers have already varied their approach and also ask for purchase and transfer of online gift cards[1] in order to scam employees. Additionally, scammers also base attacks on the current news situation, such as COVID-19 Ransomware [15]. While a couple of defense methods and counteracting training methods [16,17] exist, at present, most of them can not be adapted fast enough to cope with this amount and speed of new variations.

---

[1] https://twitter.com/sjmurdoch/status/1217449265112535040.

© Springer Nature Switzerland AG 2020
G. Hatzivasilis and S. Ioannidis (Eds.): MSTEC 2020, LNCS 12512, pp. 61–76, 2020.
https://doi.org/10.1007/978-3-030-62433-0_4

The *CyberSecurity Awareness Quiz* is a serious game in form of an online quiz to raise the security awareness of employees, in particular against social engineering attacks. The game follows the approach that quiz questions are based on real-world social engineering attacks. Additionally, the pool of questions will constantly be extended by new questions in relation to current social engineering attacks. For this purpose, a specific process for the procurement of appropriate information is developed, which is described in detail in Sect. 3.2. Our contribution within this paper is the conceptualization of the *CyberSecurity Awareness Quiz* with a focus on the concept how to generate questions for the quiz game based on current affairs and attacks observed in the wild.

The remainder of the paper is structured as follows: Sect. 2 lists some related games, explains the relationship of the *CyberSecurity Awareness Quiz* with previously developed games and how it integrates into a more general training platform. Its concept is explained in Sect. 3 along with the planned components in Sect. 4. We conclude in Sect. 5.

2   Background and Related Work

There is a large number of tabletop games for security training or awareness raising [3,4,6,8,14] targeting different domains, asset and areas in the academia.

However, the ones which are closer to *CyberSecurity Awareness Quiz* are mostly commercial without a detailed description. Nevertheless, we give a brief overview of them in the following. The "Emergynt Risk Deck" highlights IT-security risks to business leadership [7]. "OWASP Snakes and Ladders" is an educational game to raise security awareness about application security controls and risks [13]. Within the game "Quer durch die Sicherheit" players move towards the target by answering questions correctly [10]. "Stadt Land HACK!" is a quiz about data privacy and security [11].

Since the above mentioned games are all tabletop or card games, they can not be adapted to recent security incidents easily. While there is only a limited variation of different variants of a quiz-style game, our main contribution of this conceptual paper is the process for the creation of questions along with the idea to mostly use the *CyberSecurity Awareness Quiz* to keep users informed about recent attacks in an entertaining way.

2.1   Relation to Existing Games

Naturally, the aim and scope of a game can not be too broad. Similar to security awareness campaigns [1], serious games also benefit from an adaption to the user and his/her specific needs. Therefore, *CyberSecurity Awareness Quiz* is part of a series of games dovetailed to a chain aiming at raising security awareness (cf. Fig. 1). For security requirements engineering, employees are playing HATCH [3], in order to identify relevant attacks and develop countermeasures. All identified threats which can not be technically addressed need to be integrated into the organisation's security policy. Once the security policy is developed or updated, employees can train to apply it and get an understanding how it addresses certain attacks by playing PROTECT [9]. However, naturally different attacks or variations of attacks will sprout faster than the security policies can be adapted. Thus, *CyberSecurity Awareness Quiz* is used to raise awareness about the latest attacks and their variations, based on the player's general understanding developed in the game sessions of HATCH and PROTECT.

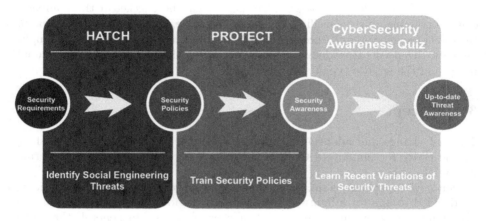

Fig. 1. The relation of HATCH [3], PROTECT [9] and *CyberSecurity Awareness Quiz*

2.2 Embedding into a CyberSecurity Training Platform

Besides the use and interplay of *CyberSecurity Awareness Quiz* with other serious games, it is also important to integrate them into a more general training platform, such as the THREAT-ARREST [12] advanced training platform (cf. Fig. 2).

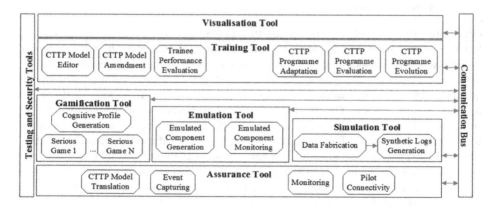

Fig. 2. The THREAT-ARREST advanced training platform [12]

This way it is not only possible to train employees during their use of the serious games, but also to embed and manage their efforts in a broader way.

The result of *CyberSecurity Awareness Quiz* sessions contribute to THREAT-ARREST's continuous evaluation of the individual trainees' performance and the effectiveness of the training programs. Within the platform for each trainee results of the serious games, the emulation, the simulation and the training tool are brought together to spot possible gaps in the employee's knowledge or awareness. If knowledge gaps are identified, it can be checked if there already exists a training on the specific topic as serious game, simulation or emulation of the cyber range system. If no appropriate training can be identified, this might indicate the need of producing a new training, tailored to the organizational needs and the trainee types.

3   Concept

The fast change and adaption of attacks as sketched in the introduction show the necessity for employees to keep their knowledge about social engineering up-to-date.

Since we expect only a reasonable amount of new attacks or attack variations, we decided to aim for a lightweight game with the idea that it could be played occasionally (e.g. when traveling in trams or subways). In general, the game should be playable alone since this avoids any necessity to find or wait for other players, but in particular for long term motivation, comparisons with or games against other players should be possible. In summary, we identified the following requirements:

- Questions refer to recent real-world threats
- Lightweight
- Playable on mobile devices
- Single and multi-player modes

3.1   Game Concept

One game type which fulfills the requirements is a quiz game, where players have to answer a set of questions. In *CyberSecurity Awareness Quiz[,]* a question describes a certain social engineering attack scenario which is based on a recent attack observed in the real world in an abstract and general way. For every question, the possible answers contain one or more correct answers and one or more incorrect answers. Correct answers will represent consequences which result from the attack that is described in the question. Accordingly, incorrect answers will represent effects which can not result from the attack. A mockup of the planned GUI which also shows a sample question is illustrated in Fig. 3.

CyberSecurity Awareness Quiz will provide different modes in which a quiz can be played. Either by a single player or in competition between two players. These modes are described in the following:

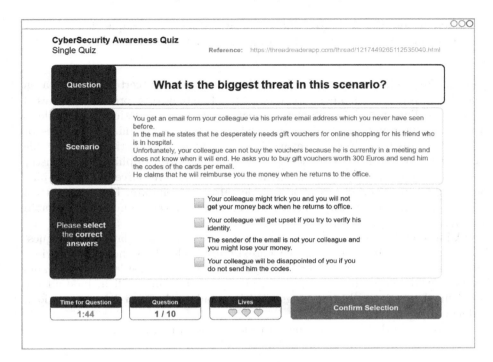

Fig. 3. Mockup of the user interface along with a sample question

Single Quiz: A player will answer the questions of a quiz alone.

Context Quiz: Single-player quiz with specific questions depending on the preferences of a player. Examples for specific questions are scenarios concerning a certain location, industry sector or role/position in the company. Furthermore, it is possible to play only recent added questions, e.g. questions added in the last 3 months.

Versus Quiz: Two players will compete in a quiz against each other. A question will be asked simultaneously to both players. The player who will answer a question correctly gets a point. If both players are correct, the faster player wins. The player who will answer more questions correctly, wins the quiz round.

Pick Quiz: In this mode, two players will answer questions one after the other. Here, the player who has answered his/her last question correctly chooses the next question for the opponent out of different options until the opponent answers a question correctly. If this is the case, the right for choosing questions changes and so on. Only the first question will be asked to both players simultaneously. The player who answers this question correctly first will have the right to choose the next question for the opponent.

Draw Quiz: This mode will have the same rules as the *Pick Quiz* mode with the following modification: Instead of choosing the next question out of different options, the player who has answered his/her last question correctly will choose the industry/sector to which the next question for the opponent relates.

For the modes context quiz, pick quiz and draw quiz, certain metadata on the scenarios is needed. Therefore, question will be tagged by predefined types of metadata. This metadata will enable a categorization of questions which allows it to combine questions to different quizzes for certain training objectives or specific groups of players. For example, a specific set of questions will be able to reference a certain type of attacks (e.g. different forms of phishing), industry sector (e.g. energy suppliers), department (e.g. human resources), a geographic area (e.g. Europe) or all new attacks added after a given date. The possibility of adapting a quiz to the players needs aims to enable players to map the mediated learning content directly to their work routine.

Additionally, the metadata will enable an on the fly compilation of the questions for a quiz round played in the Context Quiz mode. Here, the player provides information which refers to certain aspects of social engineering he/she wants to be considered in the next quiz round. This quiz round will include all the predefined questions which are tagged with metadata that matches the provided information.

We describe the different types of metadata used in Sect. 3.2.

3.2   Process for Information Procurement and Question Generation

A key feature of *CyberSecurity Awareness Quiz* will be the fact that its questions are based on real-life attacks whereby the amount of questions will be permanently expended to cover new social engineering attacks. To fulfill this requirement, an appropriate process for gathering content regarding attacks and the creation of corresponding questions and answers is needed. This process is sketched in Fig. 4.

The first step of the process includes the procurement of information with respect to current social engineering attacks. While the number of relevant attacks might be feasible, there is a huge amount of reports of attacks, privacy breaches, data losses, etc. Due to the high frequency in which they occur as well as the multitude of information sources, the information procurement presents an enormous challenge. To meet this challenge, the information procurement will include automated tasks which are discussed later in this section.

The second step of the process for the creation of questions and answers includes the formulation of questions for a quiz. Usually, questions will be created based on content about social engineering attacks which has been collected in Step 1. If this is the case, the game content designer will check for a new relevant web feed first if a corresponding question already exists. For this check he/she will filter the existing questions by the types of metadata which are relevant for the new web feed.

In the third step, a created question will be tagged with metadata. This metadata will represent characteristics of an attack like the category of an attack

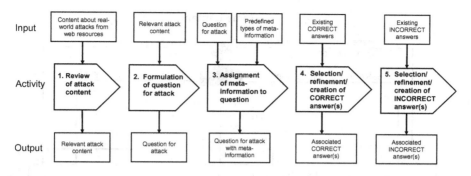

Fig. 4. Process for the creation of questions and answers for social engineering attacks

(e.g. phishing). *CyberSecurity Awareness Quiz* will provide predefined types of metadata, which are specified in Table 1. This table includes the name of a metadata type and its description. The metadata of questions is important for the reuse of questions during the creation of certain predefined quizzes and the compilation of on the fly quizzes within the Context Quiz mode (see Sect. 3.1). As discussed in the previous section, metadata allows to filter questions by special categories when creating a quiz with a certain topic. For example, if a quiz shall refer to attacks which are targeting employees of the human resources department, questions whose metadata parameter of the type *Department* has the value "human resources" should be assessed for consideration. The same concept is applied when a quiz round is played in the Context Quiz mode. Here, the player provides information regarding his/her preferences and the started quiz comprises only such questions whose metadata corresponds to the provided information. For example, if a player is interested in all types of new phishing attacks from a certain point in time, he/she can selects the value "phishing" for the metadata type *Attack category* and the value "from 01.06.2020" for the metadata type *Time of attack*.

In the fourth step of the process **correct** answers are assigned to a question. In this context, new correct answers can be created or already existing correct answers can be reused.

The last step of the process includes the assignment of **incorrect** answers to a question. As for correct answers, incorrect answers can be newly created or already existing incorrect answers can be reused.

Information Procurement. One objective of the information procurement is to gather content related to social engineering attacks which is published on appropriate web resources like news websites, websites about information security, websites of institutions, blogs or even twitter. In this context, in particular websites which provide information about their new content in a structured manner (e.g. web feeds) will be considered. Figure 5 shows an overview of the steps for the information procurement.

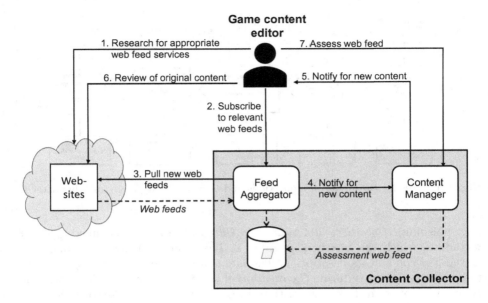

Fig. 5. Tasks for gathering and analysing content about attacks

Web feeds present a form of pull data. This means, that users can request frequently information in relation to new content on subscribed websites by using appropriate tools (e.g. feedreaders). Web feeds are machine-readable files which are provided in standardized formats like RSS[2] or Atom[3]. They include data which addresses among others the title and a short description of the new content, the URL of the original resource, the publishing date and the name of the author.

As Fig. 5 illustrates, some tasks for the information procurement need to be performed manually by the *game content editor*. Other steps will be performed automatically by a component of *CyberSecurity Awareness Quiz* which is named *Content Collector*. The different steps of the process for information procurement are explained in the following.

In the initial step of the process, the game content editor will search for websites which publish content about social engineering attacks and implement a web feed service. This step will be repeated periodically to check if new appropriate web resources are available. In the second step, the game content editor will subscribe to the found web feed services by using the *Feed Aggregator* which is a subcomponent of the Content Collector. The Feed Aggregator will query automatically and periodically the subscribed websites for new web feeds (step 3). If new web feeds have been found, it will notify the *Content Manager*

---

[2] depending on the version RSS means: RDF Site Summary or Really Simple Syndication.

[3] Atom Syndication Format is an XML language used for web feeds.

(step 4) which is another subcomponent of the Content Collector. The Content Manager, which is responsible for the management of gathered web feeds, will inform the game content editor that new content is available (step 5). Then, the game content editor will review the original content of the corresponding web feed (step 6). Afterwards he/she will assess in the Content Manager if the content to the web feed is relevant or not (step 7).

Web feeds which will be marked as relevant can be used for the formulation of new quiz questions (see Fig. 4, step 2).

Types of Metadata. As already discussed, questions need to be tagged by metadata in order to allow the categorization of questions during the creation of predefined quizzes and within on the fly compilation of quizzes with respect to the Context Quiz mode (see Sect. 3.1). The different types of metadata are specified in Table 1. Additionally, (correct and incorrect) answers will be also tagged with metadata (cf. Table 2). The *Multiplicity* will specify the number of data items which have to be assigned at least and can be assigned at most.

Table 1. Types of metadata for tagging of questions

Type of metadata	Description	Multiplicity
Title	Title of an attack	1
Type of attack execution	Specification if an attack is executed (i) directly on site by an attacker (e.g. an attacker tries to get access to a secured server room by pretending to be a service technician), (ii) indirectly by using a technical medium (e.g. phishing via email) or (iii) different combinations of direct and/or indirect executions	1
Attack category	Categories which typify an attack (e.g. vishing). In this connection, an attack can be assigned to exactly one category or to several categories. For example, an attack which uses dumpster diving can only be associated to the category *dumpster diving*. An attack in which emails with malicious links are sent to CEOs can be assigned to the categories *email fraud*, *phishing*, *email phishing* and *whaling*	1..*
Type of attacker	Typing of the attacker who executes an attack (e.g. cyber criminal, fraudster, intelligence service, hacker)	1..*
Feigned identity	Defines the identity of the entity/person which/who is feigned by the attacker during an attack. Regarding enterprises or institutions, a feigned identity could refer to internal persons like colleagues, C-level personnel and employees from other branches or external persons like customers, technicians and cleaning stuff. In the private context, an attacker could pretend to be a relative, friend or a person who seeks for help. When feigning an entity, an attacker could pretend to be an employee of a state authority (e.g. tax authority) or a private institute (e.g. banks)	1..*
Context of victims	Specifies the context(s) of the victims who are targeted by an attack. For this parameter the values *individual* and *organisation* are predefined	1..2
Characteristics of private victim	Specifies the characteristic(s) for a group of victims in person of *individual* who are threatened by an attack. For individuals this could be demographic characteristics (e.g. age, gender, interests, internet usage)	0..*

(*continued*)

Table 1. (*continued*)

Type of metadata	Description	Multiplicity
Sector	Specifies the sector/industry of organisations which are threatened by an attack (e.g. energy suppliers, financial institutes, state institutions)	0..*
Department	Defines certain departments of an organisation (e.g. human resources, finance, IT) which are affected by an attack	0..*
Role	Indicates certain roles of employees of an organisation (e.g. CEO, administrator, financial accountant) which are threatened by an attack	0..*
Motivation for attack	Specifies the motivation for the execution of an attack (e.g. espionage, criminal intend, interest in hacking)	1..*
Objective description	Defines the objective of an attack (e.g. illegal financial transactions, gaining of sensitive information, data, identity theft)	1..*
Exploited psychological pattern	Psychological pattern which is tried to be exploited by an attack (e.g. authority, good faith, laziness)	1..*
Used technology	Technology which has been used during the attack (e.g. email for phishing or telephone for vishing)	0..*
Geographical spreading	The geographical area where the attack has been conducted (e.g. worldwide, Europe, United States, California, Milan)	1..*
Time of attack	Period(s) of time in which the attack has been conducted	1..*
Sources	Sources of the content on which the attack bases	1..*

CONDITION: This parameter is only used when the parameter *Context of victims* has the value *individual*
CONDITION: This parameter is only used when the parameter *Context of victims* has the value *organisation*

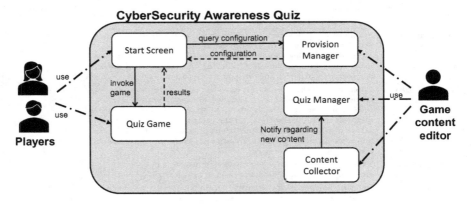

Fig. 6. Components of *CyberSecurity Awareness Quiz*

Table 2. Types of metadata for tagging of answers

Type of metadata	Description	Multiplicity
Attack category	Specifies the attack category or rather different attack categories of questions to which an answer could be assigned	1..*
Answer type	Indicates if an answer is correct or incorrect in the context of its attack categories	1

4 Architecture and Components

This section discusses the different components of *CyberSecurity Awareness Quiz* which will implement the concepts described in Sect. 3. Figure 6 provides an overview of these components and the rudimentary communication between them. Additional, it shows the different roles which will use certain components. For the sake of clarity, a representation of the database and the corresponding communication between the database and components has been omitted.

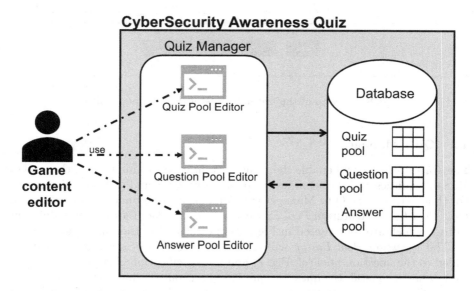

Fig. 7. Editors provided by the quiz manager

4.1 Content Collector

We have already introduced the *Content Collector* in Sect. 3.2, thus the following description is limited to the essentials.

The Content Collector will provide functionality for the collection of new content about social engineering attacks in the form web feeds. To this, it will check the subscribed web feed services frequently for new content.

A further functionality of the Content Collector will enable the management of collected web feeds. It will inform the game content designer when new content has been collected and will allow to assign his/her assessments regarding its relevance to the related web feeds. If a web feed will be considered as relevant by the game content editor, the Content Collector will notify another component in form of the *Quiz Manager* (see Sect. 4.2) that new relevant content is available.

The content collector will be exclusively used by the game content editor.

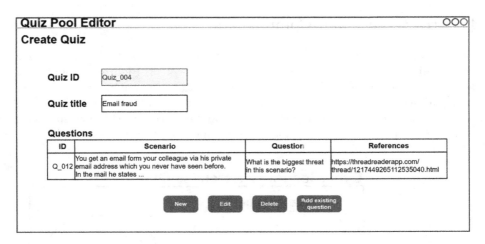

Fig. 8. Mockup of the user interface of the quiz pool editor

4.2   Quiz Manager

The *Quiz Manager* will enable the game content editor to manage (i) the pool of available quizzes and the separate (ii) pool of questions and (iii) pool of answers. For that purpose, the Quiz Manager will implement corresponding editors named *Quiz Pool Editor*, *Question Pool Editor* and *Answer Pool Editor*. These different editors, which are represented in Fig. 7, are discussed in the following.

The *Question Pool Editor* will enable the creation of questions which are added to the question pool (cf. Fig. 7) and the specification of the corresponding metadata. In general, the questions are based on content that has been collected by the *Content Collector* (see Sect. 4.1). Additionally, the Question Pool Editor will allow the editing of questions in the pool and their deletion.

In the context of creating or editing a question, the Question Pool Editor will also implement the assignment of correct and incorrect answers to a question. For that purpose, it will supply a dialogue for the creation of new answers and the related metadata. When the input is finalized, a created answer will be added to the answer pool (cf. Fig. 7).

The Question Pool Editor will also display a list of existing answers from the answer pool which could be relevant for the current question because of their assigned attack categories. Besides adding new answers, it will be possible to assign any existing answer to the edited question.

With respect to the management of the answer pool (cf. Fig. 7), the *Answer Pool Editor* will implement the creation of new answers and the related metadata as well as the editing and deletion of answers.

The functionality of creating new quizzes and adding them to the pool of available quizzes (cf. Fig. 7) will be implemented by the *Quiz Pool Editor* (cf. Fig. 8). In the mockup of the user interface of the Quiz Pool Editor it is shown that every quiz has a title and is identified by an unique identifier.

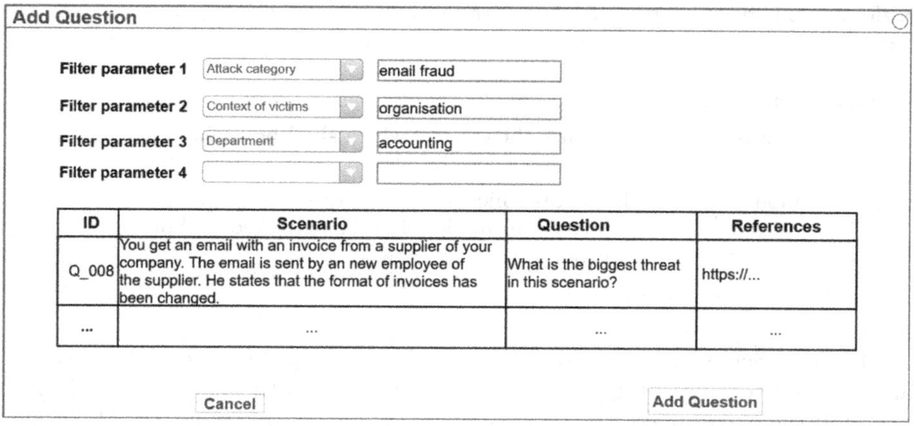

Fig. 9. Mockup of the user interface of the add question dialogue of the quiz pool manager

It will be possible to reuse predefined questions from the question pool for a new quiz. For that purpose, the Quiz Pool Editor will display a list of predefined questions from the question pool which can be filtered by the metadata of the questions. This way, the game content designer will be able to restrict the number of displayed questions.

During the creation of a quiz, the Quiz Pool Editor will also allow the creation of new questions and the related answers. A newly created question will be added additionally to the question pool, when it is finalized. If newly created answers will be assigned to a created question, these answers will be also added to the answer pool. Figure 9 shows the dialogue for adding existing questions to a quiz. Here, the set of displayed questions corresponds to the selected filter parameters.

Functionalities for the editing and deletion of quizzes will also be supplied by the Quiz Pool Editor.

4.3 Provision Manager

The *Provision Manager* facilitates configurations with respect to provisions of *CyberSecurity Awareness Quiz* These configurations will be managed by the game content editor. The different configuration parameters are represented in Table 3.

4.4 Start Screen

When a player will start the *CyberSecurity Awareness Quiz* client, the *Start Screen* will appear. Depending on the configuration provided by the *Provison Manager*, the Start Screen will show which gaming modes are activated and which quizzes can be played.

Table 3. Configuration parameters for the provisioning of *CyberSecurity Awareness Quiz*

Configuration parameter	Description
Available quizzes	Specifies the quizzes which shall be available for the player to be played
Activated modes	Indicates which single-player modes and/or multi-player modes shall be activated within a provision

The Start Screen acts as a frontend of *CyberSecurity Awareness Quiz* to start games in the component *Quiz Game* (see Sect. 4.5) with one of the activated quizzes. If the player plays a game in the *Context Quiz* mode (see Sect. 3), he/she will be able to provide the information which determines how the content of the quiz to be played will be compiled.

If any multi-player mode is activated, the Start Screen will display other players which are currently online. Accordingly, a player will be able to arrange a game in one of the multi-player modes with an available competitor.

4.5 Quiz Game

The component *Quiz Game* will implement the actual quiz game. A certain quiz game can be invoked by the *Start Screen* (see Sect. 4.4). For that purpose, the Start Screen will pass the required parameters for a quiz to the Quiz Game. These parameters will include among other information, the set of questions and the mode in which the quiz will be played.

The graphical user interface (GUI) of the Quiz Game will differ depending on the gaming mode in which the quiz is played. A mockup was already presented in Fig. 3 in Sect. 3.1.

5 Conclusion

We presented a conceptualization of *CyberSecurity Awareness Quiz* based on the requirements defined in Sect. 3. From a conceptual perspective, all requirements are fulfilled. In particular, one of our contributions is a detailed description of the process for information procurement and deduction of questions based on recent social engineering attacks. The game offers different quiz modes to maintain the players' long-term motivation and interest to gather knowledge on new attacks. Besides the obvious implementation of *CyberSecurity Awareness Quiz*[,] in future work we intend to investigate by user studies if the implementation is also perceived as lightweight by the players and if players perceive the game suitable for occasional playing.

Acknowledgements. This work was supported by European Union's Horizon 2020 research and innovation program from the project THREAT-ARREST (grant agreement number: 786890) and CyberSec4Europe (grant agreement number: 830929).

References

All URLs haven been last accessed on July 22nd, 2020.

1. Bada, M., Sasse, A.M., Nurse, J.R.C.: Cyber security awareness campaigns: why do they fail to change behaviour? CoRR abs/1901.02672 (2019). http://arxiv.org/abs/1901.02672
2. Bassett, G., Hylender, C.D., Langlois, P., Pinto, A., Widup, S.: Data breach investigations report (2020). https://enterprise.verizon.com/resources/reports/2020-data-breach-investigations-report.pdf
3. Beckers, K., Pape, S.: A serious game for eliciting social engineering security requirements. In: Proceedings of the 24th IEEE International Conference on Requirements Engineering, RE 2016. IEEE Computer Society (2016). https://doi.org/10.1109/RE.2016.39
4. Beckers, K., Pape, S., Fries, V.: HATCH: hack and trick capricious humans - a serious game on social engineering. In: Proceedings of the 2016 British HCI Conference, Bournemouth, United Kingdom, 11–15 July 2016 (2016). https://ewic.bcs.org/content/ConWebDoc/56973
5. Beckers, K., Schosser, D., Pape, S., Schaab, P.: A structured comparison of social engineering intelligence gathering tools. In: Lopez, J., Fischer-Hübner, S., Lambrinoudakis, C. (eds.) TrustBus 2017. LNCS, vol. 10442, pp. 232–246. Springer, Cham (2017). https://doi.org/10.1007/978-3-319-64483-7_15
6. Denning, T., Lerner, A., Shostack, A., Kohno, T.: Control-alt-hack: the design and evaluation of a card game for computer security awareness and education. In: Proceedings of the 2013 ACM SIGSAC Conference on Computer & Communications Security, pp. 915–928 (2013)
7. Emergent Network Defense: Emergynt risk homepage. https://emergynt.com/risk-deck/
8. Frey, S., Rashid, A., Anthonysamy, P., Pinto-Albuquerque, M., Naqvi, S.A.: The good, the bad and the ugly: a study of security decisions in a cyber-physical systems game. IEEE Trans. Software Eng. 45(5), 521–536 (2017)
9. Goeke, L., Quintanar, A., Beckers, K., Pape, S.: PROTECT – an easy configurable serious game to train employees against social engineering attacks. In: Fournaris, A.P., et al. (eds.) IOSEC/MSTEC/FINSEC -2019. LNCS, vol. 11981, pp. 156–171. Springer, Cham (2020). https://doi.org/10.1007/978-3-030-42051-2_11
10. Known Sense: Quer durch die Sicherheit game reference. http://www.known-sense.de/quer_durch_die_sicherheit_folder.pdf
11. Known Sense: Stadt Land HACK! homepage. http://www.known-sense.de/stadt_land_hack.pdf
12. Koshutanski, H., et al.: Threat-arrest platform's initial reference architecture. Technical report, Threat-Arrest, Deliverable 1.3 (2019)
13. OWASP: Owasp snakes and ladders homepage (2013). https://owasp.org/www-project-snakes-and-ladders/
14. Rieb, A., Lechner, U.: Operation digital chameleon: towards an open cybersecurity method. In: Proceedings of the 12th International Symposium on Open Collaboration, pp. 1–10 (2016)

15. Saleh, T.: Covidlock update: deeper analysis of coronavirus android ransomware (2020). https://www.domaintools.com/resources/blog/covidlock-update-coronavirus-ransomware
16. Schaab, P., Beckers, K., Pape, S.: A systematic gap analysis of social engineering defence mechanisms considering social psychology. In: 10th International Symposium on Human Aspects of Information Security & Assurance, HAISA 2016, Frankfurt, Germany, 19–21 July 2016, Proceedings (2016). https://www.cscan.org/openaccess/?paperid=301
17. Schaab, P., Beckers, K., Pape, S.: Social engineering defence mechanisms and counteracting training strategies. Inf. Comput. Secur. **25**(2), 206–222 (2017). https://doi.org/10.1108/ICS-04-2017-0022

Emulation and Simulation Studies

Towards the Monitoring and Evaluation of Trainees' Activities in Cyber Ranges

Chiara Braghin[1]([✉]) [ID], Stelvio Cimato[1] [ID], Ernesto Damiani[1,2] [ID],
Fulvio Frati[1] [ID], Elvinia Riccobene[1] [ID], and Sadegh Astaneh[1]

[1] Computer Science Department, Università degli Studi di Milano, Milan, Italy
{chiara.braghin,stelvio.cimato,ernesto.damiani,fulvio.frati,
elvinia.riccobene,sadegh.astaneh}@unimi.it
[2] Research Centre on Cyber-Physical Systems (C2PS), Khalifa University,
Abu Dhabi, UAE

Abstract. Cyber ranges are virtual environments used in several contexts to enhance the awareness and preparedness of users to cybersecurity threats. Effectiveness of cyber ranges strongly depends on how much realistic are the training scenarios provided to trainees and on an efficient mechanism to monitor and evaluate trainees' activities.

In the context of the emulation environment of the THREAT-ARREST cyber range platform, in this paper we present a preliminary design of our work in progress towards the definition of a model-driven approach to monitor and evaluate the trainee performance. We enhance the platform emulation environment with an agent-based system that checks trainees' behavior in order to collect all the trainee's actions performed while executing a training exercise. Furthermore, we propose a modular taxonomy of the actions that can be exploited for the description of the trainee's expected behavior in terms of the expected trace, i.e., the sequence of actions that is required for the correct execution of an exercise. We model the expected and actual trainee activities in terms of finite state machines, then we apply an existing algorithm for graph matching to score the trainee performance in terms of graph distance.

Keywords: Cyber ranges · Emulation frameworks · Monitoring frameworks

1 Introduction

Cyber ranges are virtual environments used in several contexts to enhance the resistance of users to the huge amount of cybersecurity threats coming from individual attackers or criminal organizations. They are a virtual playground where both customers and employees can be trained and instructed in mitigating and reacting to several typologies of attacks. Cyber ranges are being used by military agencies as well as commercial companies as a mean to train their personnel and protect their strategic assets. Academic courses have being relying

© Springer Nature Switzerland AG 2020
G. Hatzivasilis and S. Ioannidis (Eds.): MSTEC 2020, LNCS 12512, pp. 79–91, 2020.
https://doi.org/10.1007/978-3-030-62433-0_5

on cyber ranges too, giving students the opportunity to improve their security skills, through an hands-on experience in alternative to traditional methods such as lectures and seminars.

Indeed, since many sectors in business and society are critically depending on the underlying digital infrastructure, there is an increasing need to maintain and control its trustworthiness and security, preventing and forecasting new threats and attacks that derive from new technologies and their novel combinations.

Cybersecurity experts need to continuously increase their skills and adapt their competences to continuously evolving scenarios where sophisticated cyber attacks are mounted exploiting the wide surface of ICT systems and services. Cyber ranges allow cybersecurity professionals to be involved in a constant learning process that is in strict relation with the fast rate of evolution of threats, attacks and vulnerabilities.

Interest in this innovative way of preparing security experts, is testified by a number of national and sovranational funding programs (in UE and US for example), with the common goal to implement cyber range frameworks and also to extend their capabilities in order to address specific domains, such as IoT or Industrial Control Systems such as SCADA. The THREAT-ARREST project aims to provide an advanced training platform including emulation, simulation, serious gaming and visualization capabilities to adequately prepare users at different levels of expertise to face known and new cyber attacks [6].

However, building cyber ranges and realistic training scenarios is a difficult task. In general, the adaptation of a virtualized environment to represent realistic scenarios to fit the testing objectives is a time consuming operation, that requires expertise and is often done manually. At the same time, the environment should provide tools and configuration management services available for the generation of benign and malicious events supporting the execution of cyber threats and adequate countermeasures.

The THREAT-ARREST platform adopts a model driven approach, where Cyber Threat and Training Preparation (CTTP) models are used either to specify the potential attacks, the security controls, and the tools that can be used, providing the opportunity to plan and drive the training process integrated with security assurance mechanisms to ensure the relevance of training [2,5,6].

In this paper we focus on the last aspect, that is the monitoring of the activities needed to control that the training process is correctly executed, and the trainees are evaluated according to their performance. This task is not so easy, since standard log systems could not be sufficient for different reasons. In some cases, the events that should be traced are not included in standard logs. In some other cases, they generate a large amount of raw data including events that are difficult to interpret and need to be filtered in order to retrieve the sequence of actions executed by the trainee.

What we propose is a model-driven approach that drives the generation of an agent-based system to monitor trainees' behavior integrated with the cyber range environment. For this reason, we propose a modular taxonomy of trainee's actions that can be deployed for the description of the expected behavior of the trainee in terms of *expected trace* (the event sequence that is required for the correct execution of the exercise). The expected trace is specified by the trainer and is included in the CTTP model of the training scenario. In the deploying phase, the CTTP model is used to configure the cyber range environment and at the same time it instantiates a set of monitoring agents selected on the basis of the actions that are included in the expected trace. In this way, trainees' behavior can be monitored and evaluated by matching the collected actions with the ones included in the expected trace, and a score attributed on the basis of the coverage of the required actions that have been performed by the trainee.

This paper reports some preliminary results of our work in progress. It is organized as follows: Sect. 2 presents the related work in cyber security training frameworks with a run-time monitoring system, whilst Sect. 3 briefly presents the model-driven approach used by the THREAT-ARREST platform to generate training scenarios that we use as a starting point for the solution we propose. Section 4 details the platform architecture and the underlying modules in charge of collecting and analyse the trainee's actions performed during a training session. Finally, Sect. 5 concludes this work.

2 Related Work

Interest in cyber ranges is increasing and a number of research projects and papers have been published recently.

Most common cyber ranges evaluate the trainee in terms of goal fulfilment (e.g., in CTF challenges), rather than evaluating her behavior during the whole training session. For example, the KYPO [8] cyber range, funded by the Ministry of the Interior of the Czech Republic since 2013, provides a virtualised environment for performing complex cyber attacks against simulated cyber environments. Although the environment is controlled and monitored at run-time, in [7] the authors discuss the data they collected during a cyber ranges exercise and describe how they use all the data they collect, at the moment only for ex post evaluation. Indeed, their actual scoring system is based either on goals fulfilment or on service availability, since they organize Capture The Flag challenges with red-blue teams [9]. The dataset including network traffic traces and event logs collected during a cyber defense exercise has been made available by the authors.

An approach for the evaluation of the performance of the trainees involved in cyber ranges has been proposed in [1]. The authors define a distributed monitoring architecture enabling the collection of data about trainees activity and an algorithm for modeling their behavior relying on directed graph matching. A scoring algorithm is also proposed to evaluate the performance of a trainee by considering also different aspects, such as speed and precision. Our approach relies on the same notion of event graphs, somehow derived by the notion of attack trees, that were introduced by Bruce Schneier to model threats against computer systems [4]. In addition, we propose a taxonomy-based modelling of trainee's actions for the description of trainee's expected behavior allowing us to exploit the model driven approach to automatically derive a tailored monitoring system.

3   Background: The THREAT-ARREST Platform

The platform under development within the THREAT-ARREST project [6] follows a model-driven approach to deploy advanced training scenarios incorporating emulation, simulation and serious gaming (see Fig. 1 for a simplified sketch of the overall THREAT-ARREST architecture).

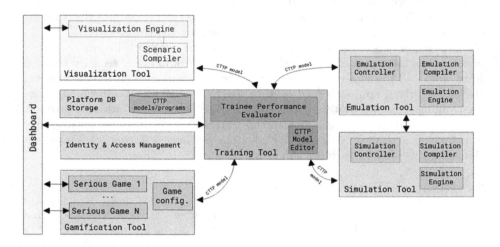

Fig. 1. THREAT-ARREST platform architecture

A *Cyber-Threat Training and Preparation (CTTP)* model defines the training programme in terms of (*i*) the scenario components and their relations (i.e., hosts and network topology), (*ii*) application and services available, together with configuration information and predefined accounts, (*iii*) the type (simulated, emulated or both) and number of planned training sessions. Furthermore, it specifies (*iv*) the goal of the cyber training programme and the actions trainees are expected to take to complete it (called *Expected Trace*).

The model is used within the platform by each specific tool to automatically instantiate a specific training session: the Dashboard sends the sub-model to the required tool, whereas the tool internal *compilers* translate the respective part of the CTTP model into an internal representation (an OpenStack template in case of an emulated session, a Jasima[1] template in case of a simulated session) used to create the requested instance of the training session. The platform offers both a repository of predefined CTTP models and a CTTP *model editor* to be used by the trainer to create a training programme from scratch, tailored on her specific needs.

Both the trainer and the trainee may use the *Dashboard* to access the platform. After an authentication phase, it is responsible to provide content according to the user role and to show the status of a training session. When a trainee

---

[1] https://www.simplan.de/en/software-2/jasima/.

enters a training program, she can choose what to do. Depending on what she chooses, the emulation, simulation, or game scenario is created in an automatic way by extracting the relevant information from the respective CTTP submodel.

4   An Enhanced Platform with Trainee Activity Monitoring and Evaluation

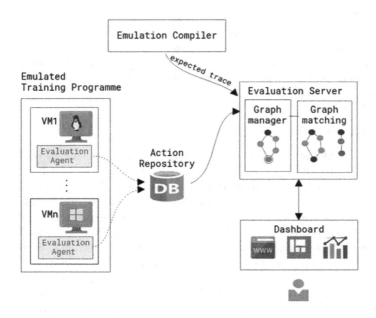

Fig. 2. Emulation environment during the execution of a training programme

As depicted in Fig. 2, we extended the THREAT-ARREST platform with the ability to monitor and evaluate trainee's activities. By following a common client-server architecture, we added an *evaluation agent* in each virtual machines of the emulated training programme, which is responsible to observe the actions performed by the trainee during the play, and to record them into the *action repository*. The main task of the *Evaluation Server* is to evaluate the trainee's performance with the data collected by the agents.

The new feature has been designed with the objective to follow the underlying model-driven approach adopted by the project. To this aim, the *expected trace* contained in the CTTP model, i.e., a finite sequence of events that represents (or in some case approximates) the set of actions or activities expected to be performed by the trainee during a training session, is used for two purposes:

– on the one hand, before instantiating the emulated training programme, to establish which activities to monitor and where to embed the evaluation agent;

– on the other hand, to allow the server to evaluate the trainee's performance not only in terms of time spent on the training session, or on training goals fulfilment, but also by comparing the expected trace with the actual *trainee trace*, i.e., the (possibly partial) sequence of activities performed so far by the trainee and built from the actions collected by the agents. For this purpose, both traces are represented as graphs.

In the rest of the section, we discuss the model-driven approach in detail. In particular, in Sect. 4.1 we describe how we defined a taxonomy of actions to be able to specify what to collect, and to formalise the language used to specify the expected trace. In Sect. 4.2, we describe how the evaluation server internally represents both the expected and the trainee trace as a graph and the matching algorithm. Finally, in Sect. 4.3, we describe how we exploit an object-oriented language, in particular class hierarchy and method overriding, to efficiently implement evaluation agents.

4.1 Actions Taxonomy

The purpose of the evaluation system is to monitor the activities performed by the trainee during the training session in order to assess her work. An activity is a sequence of actions performed by the trainee and caught by the evaluation system. The actions performed by the trainee may vary depending on the parameters of the training programme, such as the expertise level, the ultimate goal, or the components of the virtual environment. Possible activities range from command execution, application activities, log-in attempts, Web browsing and network activities, to OS kernel changes or GUI interactions.

Instead of using a flat list of raw events, we defined a hierarchy of categories and sub-categories of actions (see Fig. 3). In this way, we have more granular control over which information is logged by the agents, and we are able to work at different levels of abstraction. For example, we can reason in terms of actions and their side effect on the system, rather than in terms of the execution of a specific command, or the usage of a tool. Action categories towards the root of the tree hierarchy are more abstract and group similar type of actions, whereas action categories in the leaves may map to a specific command. The big advantage of using subcategories is the ability to limit the number of actions that result from the related category, thus reducing (though not eliminating) unnecessary noise.

In the current version of our prototype, we identified three major categories:

1. *Application Action*: this category contains actions that are related to applications.
2. *Operative System Action*: this category contains actions such as system changes, software installation, access to file system, registry, or kernel object.
3. *Network Action*: this category contains actions that are related to network traffic and management.

We plan to finalise the subcategories during the implementation of the monitoring agents with respect to the types and goals of the training actions included in the framework. Anyway, nothing prevents the taxonomy from being extended in any moment with new categories or subcategories to express new attacks or new defence mechanisms.

Fig. 3. Actions taxonomy

The actions taxonomy allows us to express also expected traces at different level of granularity. In particular, the expected trace in the CTTP model has the following syntax:

$VM_1 : action_1[args].VM_2 : action_2[args].VM_n : action_n[args]$, where:

- VM_i specifies the VM where the action has been performed;
- $action_i$ is a string indicating the name of the action, belonging to the action taxonomy;
- $args$ is an optional string that may represent the argument of the command executed by a trainee, the name of a file that the trainee is supposed to modify, or a value edited/changed in a file.

4.2   Evaluation Server

The evaluation server component is responsible for evaluating the trainee activity. Before explaining the way how it is evaluated, we present a model of the trainee program and the trainee's activity while executing the program. The trainee performance is evaluated on the base of such models.

Trainee Program Modeling. Given a CTTP program, upon that the Emulation tool of the platform compiles the respective CTTP submodel, a *trainee program* P, i.e., the training exercise proposed to the trainee, is provided together with its expected desired execution (*expected trace*) T.

The execution of P is informally described as a sequence of desired system configuration states; each state is obtained from the previous one by performing a (set of) actions. A possible taxonomy of such actions has been proposed in Sect. 4.1. Here, we assume that a change of system configuration is caused by a trainee's action and we consider such action as performed in 0-time. Therefore, an action can be viewed as a (call) *event* labelling a state transition[2].

Formally, we can model the operational semantics of P in terms of a Finite State Machine (FSM) $M = (S, I, \delta)$, where S is the set of possible system configuration states – an initial state s_o and an end state s_f model the beginning of the trainee actions and the conclusion of the exercise, respectively –, I is the set of (input) actions and $\delta : S \times I \rightarrow S$ is the transition function which yields a target configuration state from a source state and a given input action. The FSM M can be graphically represented as a graph whose nodes correspond to the states and the edges represent the transition function. An edge from a source state s_i to a target state s_j is labelled by the (input) action that cause the transition from s_i to s_j (we use the notation (s_i, e, s_j) to indicate the labeled transition). An *execution* of P is a possible run of M.

The graphical representation of M corresponds to the concept of *reference graph* in [1]; such a graph is meant as the model of the ideal behavior of a trainee during the exercise. In the sequel, we also make use of this terminology.

The **Graph manager** sub-component of the **Evaluation Server** is responsible of building the FSM from the program P and the expected trace T. In a naive way, if s_o and s_f are, respectively, the start and end states of the FSM modeling P, the reference graph is a linear graph from state s_o to state s_f and the edge from s_i to s_{i+1} is labelled by the i-th action (or command) occurring in the expected trace T.

As an example, let us suppose to have a CTTP training program for system administrators or security experts, where they need to practically secure their server, by discovering open ports accessible from outside and closing unnecessary ports and services. In this case, the server in the emulated virtual environment is running on a Linux machine (VM1) and is deliberately vulnerable, with the Telnet service active on port 23. The actions the trainee has to perform in order to fulfill the task are: (i) do a scanning for open ports on $VM1$, (ii) edit file */etc/xinetd.d/telnet* and disable the Telnet service (by changing the line *disable = no* into *disable = yes*), and (iii) restart the *xinetd* service. By using the Actions taxonomy depicted in Fig. 3, the expected trace in the CTTP program for this training session is:

$VM1 : PortScan[127.0.0.1].VM1:Editing[/etc/xinetd.d/telnet, disable = yes].$
$VM1 : ServiceRestart[/etc/rc.d/init.d/xinetd]$

Figure 4 shows the reference graph of the trainee program according to the expected trace above.

Trainee Activity Modeling. The execution of the training program by the trainee succeeds if the trainee performs as expected, but during training activity the trainee performance may differ from what expected. We therefore need to keep track of the trainee performance in order to compare it to the desired behavior.

---

[2] This restriction on the use of atomic actions as transition labels does not limit our approach since, on the base of model granularity, a state transition can be labelled by *completion events* associated to complex activities.

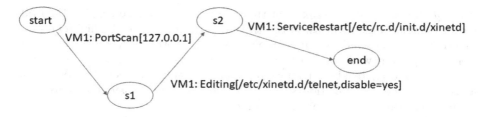

Fig. 4. An example of a reference graph

To this aim, we take advantage of the approach described in [1] and adapt it to our purposes.

At the end of the trainee activity, the `Graph manager` and the `Graph matching` sub-components build the *trainee graph*, which keeps track of the trainee actions. They use the reference graph and the trainee traces collected by the evaluation agents (see Sect. 4.3). The construction of the trainee graph works similarly to the algorithm in [1]; it relies on a set of distributed agents and plugins that collect data (then saved on the event repository) directly on the deployed Virtual Machines (VMs) where the trainees' activity is executed. Such architecture is briefly explained in the following section. From the action repository, an *action timeline* is built for a specific trainee program and a trainee activity. From the action timeline and a reference graph, the trainee graph is built as follows.

The trainee graph starts with the same starting state s_0 of the reference graph. The actions in the action timeline are considered in linear order, namely in the same time order in which the trainee executed them. Let e be the current considered event (i.e., action) of the timeline.

If the Graph matching reveals a labelled transition (s_i, e, s_j) occurring in the reference graph and the state s_i already exists in the trainee graph, the Graph Manager updates the trainee graph by adding the state s_j – if it does not exist –, and the transition (s_i, s_j) with label e. If any transition (s_i, e, s_j) occurs in the reference graph, it means that the trainee is not following the correct solution or she has followed some steps of the exercise but she is having some difficulties. We need to keep track of these situations.

Let s_i be the last correct current state in the trainee graph and s_j the next expected state, i.e, the transition (s_i, e', s_j) is in the reference graph, for some $e' \neq e$ (checking is performed by the Graph matching); in the worst case, s_j can be the start state s_0 if the trainee has not yet performed any correct step of the expected solution, or it can be one of the intermediate states. The trainee graph is updated by the Graph Manager by adding the labeled transition (s_i, e, s_{j-err}).

In our first implementation of the `Graph manager`, the trainee graph construction is offline (at the end of an exercise). It may also be computed at run-time, during the exercise execution to track live trainee progress. By the trainee graph construction, the Graph matching may contribute to reveal correct solution paths that have not been considered by the instructor.

Scoring Algorithm. On the base of the reference and trainee graphs, the evaluation server is able to measure the trainee performance. In [1], different score functions are presented. As an example, we here report a very basic score function from [1], but we leave a better evaluation to future work.

Let G_r and G_t be the reference and trainee graphs, respectively. We define a *score* function as a function $s : G_r \times G_t \rightarrow [0, 1]$ that measures how well the trainee performs w.r.t. the expected solution.

If l_r is the length of the reference linear graph G_r and l_t the length of the shortest path from the start to the end states in the trainee graph G_t, a *basic score function* that is able to measure how fast correctly a trainee performs is the following:

$$s(G_r, G_t) = \begin{cases} l_r/l_t & \text{if a path from start state to end state exists in } G_t \\ 0 & \text{otherwise} \end{cases}$$

(1)

This measure does not work in case a trainee finds an unexpected but correct solution path. The definition of more accurate measures will be investigated in the future.

4.3   A Distributed and Agent-Based Plugin Architecture

The deploying activities of the training programme are managed by the THREAT-ARREST internal tool called *Emulation Tool (ET)*, that takes in input the CTTP Emulation sub-model, compiles it in a YAML template readable by HEAT, and invokes the OpenStack CLI interface[3]. The input compiled template is deployed to create and configure a new stack of virtual instances. In detail, the YAML template contains all the information needed by Open-Stack for the generation and configuration of the Virtual Machines, including the Network Topology needed to put in place the required emulated environment. Furthermore, the template include also a set of ad-hoc scripts to configure at deploy-time each individual VM. Those scripts will be run during the booting of the operating system exploiting the applications cloudinit[4], for Linux, and cloudbase-init[5] for Windows systems.

As described in Sect. 4.2, the proposed framework is composed of a centralized *Evaluation Server*, that takes care of the analysis and of the scoring of the activities reported, and of an agent-based *Plugin Manager*, deployed in each VM and responsible for the collection of the events data generated by trainee's actions.

---

[3] https://docs.openstack.org/python-openstackclient/latest/.
[4] https://cloud-init.io/.
[5] https://cloudbase.it/cloudbase-init/.

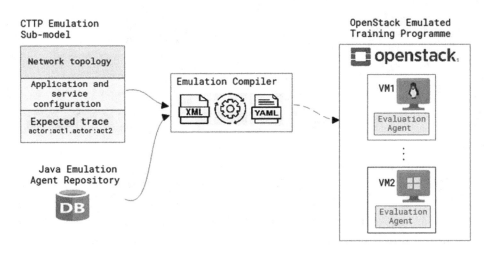

Fig. 5. The trainee evaluation framework deployment process

The system relies on the Emulation Tool compiler of the THREAT-ARREST platform to trigger the distributed agent and configure it at VM boot-time, in order to capture specific actions of the trainee from the emulated instances. The model-driven approach adopted by THREAT-ARREST will allow the system to be configured to intercept only the actions that are of interest of the training programme. The specific plugins to be loaded and the details needed to configure the listeners are specified in the expected trace that is included in the CTTP emulation sub-model (see Fig. 5).

Under the developing point of view, the agent has been designed exploiting the *Factory Method design pattern* [3], a design pattern that uses factory methods (i.e. plugins) to deal with the problem of creating objects without having to specify the exact class of the object that will be created. Figure 6 depicts the structure of the plugin-based system that characterizes the Plugin Manager.

The software classes involved in the architecture of the Plugin Manager are the following:

- *EmulPluginManager*, a class that loads the plugin classes indicated at deploying time in the YAML, collects data from the running plugins, and sends the data to the Action repository;
- *iEmulPlugin*, a common interface implemented by the plugins, it defines the common methods invoked by the manager, like for instance *run*, *sendData*, and *monitor*;
- *Plugin1, Plugin2, ..., PluginN*: the specific plugins, implementing the common interface *iEmulPlugin*, that listens and collects specific data. The Java classes are stored in a common repository at the level of the Evaluation Server and loaded, in the form of JAR archives, at boot time.

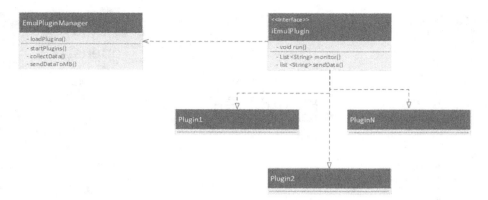

Fig. 6. Architecture of the plugin manager

The architecture will rely on the open source Java Plugin Framework[6] (PF4J).

As an example, the plugin *Editing*, triggered in the expected trace shown in Sect. 4.2 by the second action, will periodically check if the file indicated as parameter (*/etc/xinetd.d/telnet*) has been modified. As soon as it detects that the file has been modified, the plugin will return a Boolean value to the Plugin Manager, that in turn notifies the Evaluation Server. In this way, only the subset of actions that the expected trace has indicated, will be monitored and reported to the server. The model-driven approach has been guaranteed with this approach given that only the required plugins will be downloaded and executed inside the specific VM.

5   Conclusion and Future Works

In this position paper, we present the structure and the design of a framework for the evaluation of trainees' performance in cyber range based training sessions. Our work will be part of the THREAT ARREST platform, enhancing the capabilities of the current version of the Emulation Tool.

In particular, our system will exploit and enforce the model-driven approach that is at the basis of the THREAT-ARREST platform, enabling the monitoring of a specific subset of trainee's actions relying on the description provided in the project-specific CTTP models. Data collected from trainees' VMs will be further analysed by our Evaluation Server, in order to provide the THREAT-ARREST framework with a complete and holistic evaluation of the trainee, or, in case of team exercises, of the whole team performance.

In the next future, we plan to implement the evaluation server with the graph construction and matching mechanisms. We also plan to evaluate the

---

[6] https://pf4j.org/.

effectiveness of our approach on some pilot case studies taken from the THREAT-ARREST project, and to extend our approach and framework in order to support also the red team/blue team exercises.

Acknowledgements. This work has been partly funded by the European Commission within the H2020 project THREAT-ARREST (contract n. 786890).

References

1. Andreolini, M., Colacino, V.G., Colajanni, M., Marchetti, M.: A framework for the evaluation of trainee performance in cyber range exercises. Mob. Netw. Appl. **25**(1), 236–247 (2020). https://doi.org/10.1007/s11036-019-01442-0. https://link.springer.com/article/10.1007/s11036-019-01442-0
2. Braghin, C., Cimato, S., Damiani, E., Frati, F., Mauri, L., Riccobene, E.: A model driven approach for cyber security scenarios deployment. In: Fournaris, A.P., et al. (eds.) IOSEC/MSTEC/FINSEC -2019. LNCS, vol. 11981, pp. 107–122. Springer, Cham (2020). https://doi.org/10.1007/978-3-030-42051-2_8
3. Gamma, E., Helm, R., Johnson, R., Vlissides, J.M.: Design Patterns: Elements of Reusable Object-Oriented Software, 1st edn. Addison-Wesley Professional (1994)
4. Schneier, B.: Attack trees. Dr. Dobb's J. **24**(12), 21–29 (1999)
5. Somarakis, I., Smyrlis, M., Fysarakis, K., Spanoudakis, G.: Model-driven cyber range training: a cyber security assurance perspective. In: Fournaris, A.P., et al. (eds.) IOSEC/MSTEC/FINSEC -2019. LNCS, vol. 11981, pp. 172–184. Springer, Cham (2020). https://doi.org/10.1007/978-3-030-42051-2_12
6. Soultatos, O., et al.: The THREAT-ARREST cyber-security training platform. In: Fournaris, A.P., et al. (eds.) IOSEC/MSTEC/FINSEC -2019. LNCS, vol. 11981, pp. 199–214. Springer, Cham (2020). https://doi.org/10.1007/978-3-030-42051-2_14
7. Tovarňák, D., Špaček, S., Vykopal, J.: Traffic and log data captured during a cyber defense exercise. Data Brief **31**, 105784 (2020). https://doi.org/10.1016/j.dib.2020.105784
8. Vykopal, J., Ošlejšek, R., Čeleda, P., Vizváry, M., Tovarňák, D.: KYPO cyber range: design and use cases. In: ICSOFT 2017 - Proceedings of the 12th International Conference on Software Technologies, pp. 310–321. SciTePress (2017). https://doi.org/10.5220/0006428203100321
9. Vykopal, J., Vizvary, M., Oslejsek, R., Celeda, P., Tovarnak, D.: Lessons learned from complex hands-on defence exercises in a cyber range. In: Proceedings - Frontiers in Education Conference, FIE, October 2017, pp. 1–8. Institute of Electrical and Electronics Engineers Inc., December 2017. https://doi.org/10.1109/FIE.2017.8190713

Automatically Protecting Network Communities by Malware Epidemiology

Xiao-Si Wang[1(✉)], Jessica Welding[1,2], and Tek Kan Chung[1,3]

[1] Applied Research, British Telecommunications plc., Adastral Park, Ipswich, UK
selina.wang@bt.com
[2] Lancaster University, Lancashire, UK
[3] Cambridge University, Cambridge, UK

Abstract. Malware epidemiology, specifically the modelling and simulation of malware propagation, has been theorised to improve malware outbreak preparedness and drive decision making during real time epidemics. However, practical methods to make use of malware epidemiology are significantly lacking at every level, whether within organisations or at country and global levels. To fill this gap, we present a novel and automatic method to protect networks with a community structure using the malware epidemic final size, one of the most important metrics of a malware outbreak. We treat the final size probabilities abstracted from the simulations as a "signal". We process the "signal" so that the final sizes can be correlated with communities identified within the network to gain practically usable insights. Finally, we define thresholds and rules built on such insights to deploy automatic protection on the network of concern. To our knowledge, this is the first attempt to make use of malware propagation simulation results as a signal. We show that not only theoretically, but practically malware epidemiology can be used in an automatic manner to protect networks. This study should act as the foundation and inspiration for industrial deployments of malware epidemiology.

Keywords: Malware epidemiology · Malware propagation · Model · Simulation · Epidemic final size · Outbreak severity · Signal processing · Signal smoothing · Rule · Threshold · Network · Community · Cluster · Stochastic model · Agent-based model

1 Introduction and Motivation

Computer systems are being embedded into day-to-day activities of modern society at an unprecedented speed. As such, securing computing systems and infrastructure has become more critical than ever. The huge losses and damages from cybercrimes, e.g., WannaCry [2], NotPetya, and Equifax Data Loss, just highlight the importance of robust and agile cyber security.

Protecting the networks and computing systems has been predominately achieved through malware and intrusion detection mechanisms which are reactive in nature. Any detection means that adversarial events such as malware

© Springer Nature Switzerland AG 2020
G. Hatzivasilis and S. Ioannidis (Eds.): MSTEC 2020, LNCS 12512, pp. 92–107, 2020.
https://doi.org/10.1007/978-3-030-62433-0_6

infection or propagation have already taken place or are taking place in real time. Therefore it is imperative to introduce predictive measures to the anti-malware arena. Malware epidemiology, especially the modelling and simulation of malware propagation, has long been theorised to provide predictive insights and drive decision making, with the first malware epidemiology study published in 1991 [3]. However, agent-based malware propagation models, including network-based models, are significantly lacking, as also noticed by a recent review on mathematical modelling of malware propagation [6], and practical methods to make real world use of malware epidemiology have not been seen.

When producing simulation results from an agent-based network malware propagation model, or more generally any stochastic spatial spreading model, due to such models' probabilistic nature and the innate spatial heterogeneity, different runs of a model would result in different simulation results. A common approach when simulating outbreaks in malware propagation models, or even in infectious disease spreading models, is to seed the infection source(s)/starting point(s) from different part(s) of the spatial structure and run simulations multiple times to produce the predicted infection numbers. The predicted infection numbers from multiple simulation runs, either randomly selected or selected using some criteria, are subsequently presented as multiple curves in a plot as they are or are averaged to show an average curve of predicted infected numbers over time, e.g. covid-19 modelling of non-pharmaceutical interventions [1].

The authors consider two major problems about this approach. Firstly this approach is very limited to an academic setting in that a plot of several simulations can be presented in an academic paper but cannot simply be used in an industrial setting. An industrial setting places the emphasis on automation and on making simulation results usable in a systematic way, and more importantly can be built into a user-friendly tool. Simply producing a curve plot does not meet such needs. Secondly, because of the complexity introduced through the stochastic and spatial nature of the model, the simulation results can be fundamentally different from one another and averaging simulation results from multiple runs will hide certain infection patterns, in particular it can hide spatial patterns which are meaningful and usable. Therefore the authors seek a systematic way of quantifying model simulation results seeding from all the possible infection starting points, i.e. all the network nodes, so that statistically meaningful infection patterns can emerge. The authors then carry out a sequence of systematic analytical procedures to analyse these patterns to produce real-world usable results, e.g. statistical analysis of recognised and grouped patterns, on which industrial operational thresholds can be used to set.

Typical predictive metrics of any spreading agent, whether infectious disease or malware, include: predicted epidemic final size, predicted infection onset time, predicted infection peak size and peaking time, and predicted epidemic size for a fixed period. We have chosen the epidemic final size as our metric, i.e. How big is an outbreak likely to be. This is because first and foremost it is a very important predictive metric. In the real world of fighting malware, it represents how severe the damage would be if an organisation let the malware run its natural course without any additional measures. With limited resources and the possibility of hundreds and even thousands of attacks to deal with on a daily basis, for many organisations it is unrealistic to expect that all malware attacks are dealt with using extra measures and efforts, in addition to the intrusion detection and anti-malware defences in place. Secondly, some of the time dependent metrics bring in extra complexity through time, e.g. infection peaking time in some simulation runs will result in one peak but in other runs will result in multiple peaks. Such complexities will distract the focus of this paper, which is a first attempt to lead the way to a more systematic procedure to analyse and use simulation results from malware epidemiology.

We will use a simple SIR model as the malware epidemiology model to produce the simulation results. The SIR model assumes nodes can have one of three states: susceptible, infectious, or removed. The nodes move through the states from S $\rightarrow$ I $\rightarrow$ R over time and once removed, a node cannot be reinfected. The choice of infection spreading model is less relevant for this study and as such will not be the focus of this paper. In summary, whether we choose a SIR model or a SIS model (no removed state, nodes can be reinfected) or a SEIR model (additional exposure period before a node becomes infectious), all of which are referred to as SIR families or SIR variants, it matters little in our case as all these models will produce the metric we are interested in, which is the epidemic final size.

We will further use a social network obtained from a public data set as the spatial structure to overlay our SIR model on. According to regular recent statistics published by Center for Internet Security, the top 10 malware types compose around 50% of total malware activities in the contemporary malware world; within the top 10, Trojan malware types consistently occupy several positions[1]. Many of them, such as Emotet, use social and business networks among businesses and societies to spread[2]. These Trojans, often equipped with detection evasion components, make traditional anti-malware detection difficult. Stealthy and widely spread Trojan malware, different from WannaCry and Not-Petya which are catastrophic but happen on rare occasions, are one of the most challenging problems to be dealt with on a day-to-day basis by many organisations across the globe. Therefore using a social network to demonstrate our methods has its own value for tackling Trojan attacks in the real world.

In the following sections, the authors present a novel method to quantify and analyse the simulation results from stochastic network malware propagation models. The method processes the simulation results as a signal and summarises the results in a way to directly aid automatic network protections. To our knowledge, this is the first practical and quantitative method to make use of malware propagation simulation results in network protection. As the method developed is complex in nature, we do not use the traditional scientific publishing format of methods and results to present it; rather, we discuss the method and an

---

[1] https://www.cisecurity.org/blog/top-10-malware-may-2020.

[2] https://www.kryptoslogic.com/blog/2018/10/emotet-awakens-with-new-campaign-of-mass-email-exfiltration.

experiment to demonstrate its use in a combined way. We begin in Sect. 2 by using community detection methods to identify the communities within the network we are interested in. This is useful for understanding the behaviour of outbreaks which begin in different social clusters. Next, in Sect. 3 we simulate outbreaks on the network using a malware propagation model. In Sect. 4 we smooth the simulation results and in Sect. 5 we group the smoothed results to help identify patterns of behaviour. In Sect. 6 we analyse the results to investigate patterns and identify the relationship between the final size and the community in which the outbreak began. Finally in Sect. 7 we use the results to produce an automatic method of protecting network communities and reducing the severity of the malware spread before discussing our results in Sect. 8.

2   Identify the Network Communities

2.1   The Network Structure

We first explain several graph terms and how we define nodes, edges and network structures in this paper:

1. Node/vertex
   In graph theory, the terms of node and vertex are used equivalently. We will primarily use the term node, unless stated otherwise.
   (a) A node represents a computing device or system.
   (b) The node changes infection status, e.g. susceptible to infected, infected to removed.
   (c) Each node can also carry attribute information, e.g. node ID, business affiliation, IP subnet.
2. Edge
   (a) An edge connects two vertices, representing that these two vertices have direct interactions between each other which can result in malware infection.
   (b) Each edge can also carry attribute information, e.g. edge ID, which edge connects which nodes, frequency of interactions per edge.

The data set we will be primarily working with is a network of anonymised Facebook friends. This is a network consisting of 4039 nodes with 88234 edges connecting those who are friends. The network data set used was obtained from the Stanford Large Network Dataset Collection [4] and the detailed description of this data set can be found in Leskovec et al. [5]. We consider the Facebook network as a typical social network. As reported on the data repository where the data set is reported and stored, the average clustering coefficient, which measures the average degree the nodes within a network group to, of the Facebook data set is 0.6055. This is very similar to a much larger Twitter network consisting of 81306 nodes and 1768149 edges reported in the same repository with an average clustering coefficient of 0.5653.

To prepare for further analysis, we need to group all the nodes and edges into different communities either by network graph features or by other definitions.

Such communities in the real world reflect lines of businesses, the collaborating teams and the IP subnets the devices are connected into, depending on community definitions. For the social network data, we use graph features to group the nodes into communities as community for this data set is not pre-defined and network community detection algorithms can be applied widely to other networks.

2.2   Detect and Group Nodes into Communities

After experimenting with several community detection methods, we chose the asynchronous fluid method due to its relatively fast computational speed. As previously, for this paper the specific community detection algorithm to use is less relevant as our focus is to showcase an example in which nodes belong to different communities. The grouped communities of the Facebook data set are shown in Fig. 1, where the different communities are clearly marked in different colours. It is noticeable that some bridging nodes connect the different communities and these bridging nodes will play a vital role in either delaying or stopping the spreading of malware, or helping malware spread into other communities. In summary, we used a publicly available social network data set to demonstrate our method, however the application to a social network should not be seen as exclusive. Our method applies to any spatial structure in which malware can propagate and communities can be identified.

To investigate the relationship between different communities and different epidemic final sizes, we need to simulate the epidemic final sizes starting from different nodes within the communities.

3   Simulate Epidemic Final Sizes Using Malware Propagation Models

We performed 20 malware propagation simulations beginning at each node, i.e. patient zero, within this network, with a moderate average node to node infection transmission rate of $\beta_t = 0.05$ and an average removal rate of $\gamma_t = 0.2$ for time unit t. In total this resulted in approximately $80,000$ simulation runs. Our simulations were run until all the infected nodes had become removed nodes and we recorded the epidemic final sizes for all of the runs. The final sizes are plotted against the epidemic starting node in Fig. 2.

Visibly there is a distinctive pattern that certain starting nodes will result in very different final sizes, e.g. epidemics starting from certain nodes between ID 500 and ID 1000 are quite likely to result in small epidemics with around 250 infected nodes. This is hardly seen in epidemics starting from other nodes. It is also worth noting that a significant number of simulations are required to see this pattern, otherwise randomness dominates. With the complexity of the network being studied increasing, the number of simulations should increase accordingly.

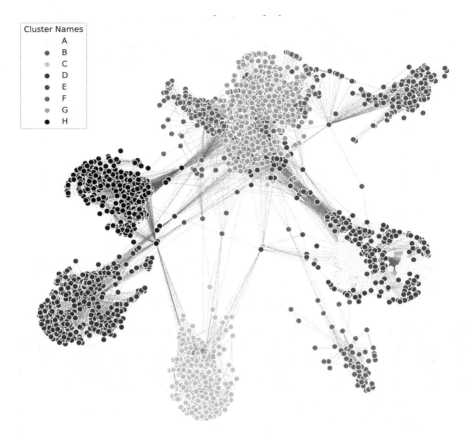

Fig. 1. A visualisation of the communities detected by the asynchronous fluid method in the Facebook data set.

4   Smooth the Final Size Probabilities as a Signal

4.1   Calculate the Probability of Each Final Size

The aim is to group the final size into subsets of high density. For example, if we were to do this visually using Fig. 2, we might decide to split the final sizes into the following ranges: [1], [2, 100], [100, 250], [250, 3300], [3300, 3600], [3600, 3750], [3750, 4039], each of which exhibits different behaviour.

We first calculate the estimated probability of observing each final size in all simulations. This is a frequency probability calculated by adding up the number of times we observed this final size within the simulations, divided by the total number of simulations. An example of which is shown as Fig. 3.

As stated in earlier sections, the idea is to find the high-density final size ranges that can aid malware infection preparedness. Therefore we are interested in the boundaries of the value ranges. The results shown in Fig. 3 clearly have

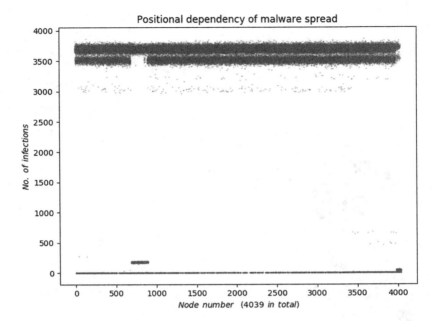

Fig. 2. Positional dependency of malware epidemic final size to the epidemic starting node from approximately 80,000 epidemic simulations. The Y axis shows the final sizes and the X axis is the starting node ID. Note: The node IDs also correlate with the communities they belong, i.e. the node IDs are sequential when the nodes belong to the same community, which makes the patterns more visible when plotted in this way.

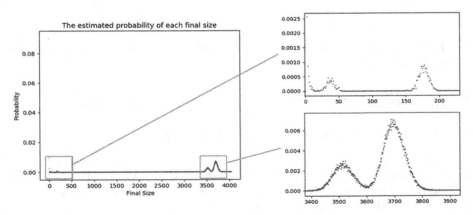

Fig. 3. The probability density dot plot of each final size in the Facebook example. The Y axis is the probability of getting a specific epidemic size and the X axis is the epidemic size. On the right hand side we include zoomed in high-density probability areas.

some kind of noise, particularly around the local minima and maxima. Should we apply algorithms to find the local minima and maxima to the raw data, the ranges found are likely to be affected by this noise. Hence we need to apply smoothing functions to remove such noise.

4.2   Apply a Smoothing Function

There exist many different algorithms to smooth data, a large portion of which come from the field of signal processing. Although our requirement is different, we can note that we expect the probability of a final size of "X" to be related to the probability of a final size of "X+1". As such we can apply these methods to smooth our data.

The aim is to pick out the key features of the final sizes, to be successful in this we need to remove the noise to ensure we do not just pick out random fluctuations. As such we choose to use one-dimensional Gaussian filter to smooth the data. In the experiments, we used $scipy.ndimage.filters.gaussian\_filter1d$ within the scipy module in Python as it produces a good, smooth fit to the data. Additionally, within the methods we have developed we allow for two additional smoothing choices: triangle moving average and a kernel smoother. Together with the Gaussian filter these three functions have been selected as they ensure the curve is smooth and thus we can use methods already developed to find the key features. Throughout we choose to use the Gaussian filter; however, during the process of experimenting different smoothing algorithms, we note that the kernel smoother results in almost identical smoothed data. The Gaussian smoothing function requires the parameter σ to be selected, with larger σ indicating that we require more smoothing. We expect this to be related to the number of simulations we have run. Additionally we expect that we may always require some smoothing as the true underlying distribution will not necessarily be smooth due to the network structure. Therefore to automate this we choose to set σ as a function of the standard deviation of the data, with a minimum value (σ_{min}) placed so that we always perform some smoothing. Therefore

$$\sigma = max\left(\sigma_{min}, \sqrt{\frac{var(data)}{M}}\right) \tag{1}$$

i.e. the smoothing parameter is the standard deviation of the simulated data divided by the square root of the number of simulations. We take $\sigma_{min} = 5$ for the experiments as this seems appropriate. This choice of σ makes intuitive sense as with greater number of simulations the standard error decreases and therefore we require less smoothing of the data. We plot the smoothed data with the original data in Fig. 4. We can see that the high-density areas and the local minima that separate these areas are still present.

5   Group the Final Sizes into Ranges

5.1   Find All the Boundary Values Marked by Local Minima in the Smoothed Probability

To find the subset of high-density and low-density areas, we need to identify the boundaries that separate these ranges. Again, we treat the problem as a signal processing problem but also as an optimisation problem. We use a signal processing method to find all the local minima among the smoothed probability "signal" curve by comparing the neighbouring values surrounding each value. In the experiment, we reverse the curve along the Y axis and use a peak finding method (*signal.find.peaks* within the scipy module in Python) to find the maxima and the corresponding x axis values which are the boundaries we are interested in. The boundaries identified are presented in Fig. 5.

5.2   Merge the Original Ranges Using Thresholds/Rules

Using the above approach alone, the ranges identified can be very short, as seen in Fig. 5. This is as, although we smoothed the curve, there is still noise. Short ranges are not suitable for further analysis and network protection because we are not interested in a final size range with a low probability to reach, therefore we must merge the ranges. In other words, we need to avoid having ranges in which the probability of reaching such a final size range is very small. We achieve this by automatically and sequentially going through the ranges following some thresholds or rules, e.g. maximum 10 groups, range probability values.

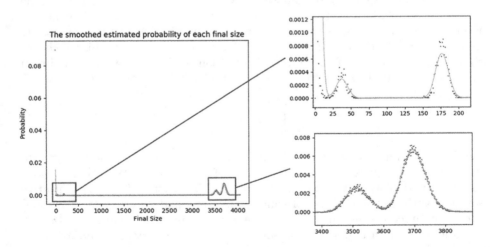

Fig. 4. The smoothing probability curve overlaying the probability density dot of each final size in the Facebook example. The Y axis is the probability of getting a specific epidemic size. The X axis is the epidemic size. On the right hand side we include zoomed in the high-density probability areas and the smoothing curve of those areas.

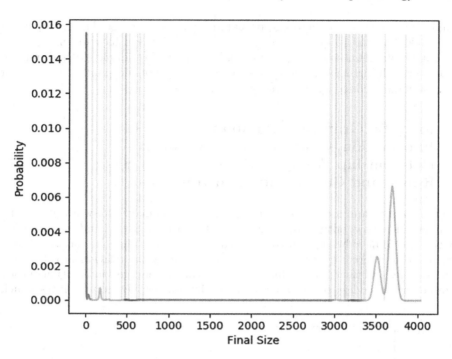

Fig. 5. The high-density and low-density ranges of the smoothed probability "curve" as separated by the boundaries. The boundary values are marked by the vertical lines.

In the experiment, we first add up the probability of reaching each value within one range as shown in Fig. 5, e.g. if the range before merging is [250, 251, 252], its range probability is P(final size 250) + P(final size 251) + P(final size 252). Doing this for all ranges, it forms a series of range probability values. We then go through the range probability values; and if the range probability is less than merging parameter M, we then check to see if its neighbour's probability is also less than M, if so then join the two ranges. We choose to set M so that it satisfies $M = min(0.01, M_q)$ and $M = max(0.001, M)$ where M_q is the qth percentile of the range probabilities, usually we use M_{10}. This ensures that if we have small peaks these are still given the chance to be picked out.

Additionally we set a max number of ranges as $r_{max} = 15$. Then if we have too many ranges we increase M by 0.1 and perform the collapsing from scratch with the new M, this is repeated until we have at most r_{max} intervals. This is to ensure the final output is readable and usable.

After merging the ranges using this method, the final ranges for the experiment are shown in Fig. 6. We can see that there are eight ranges left after merging. These ranges will be analysed together and the community information detected from the network in the next step. How many final ranges for network protection depends on practical needs and what makes sense. We could simply use quantiles of the range probability values to merge. For example, we could calculate the 10-quantiles of the range probability values and merge with the cut points defined by 10-quantiles, additionally this simple method may be improved with further rules to insure the ranges are not too small when some of the cut points defined by quantiles are very small values.

6 Identify Granular Community Information/Characteristics Through Relationship Analysis Between Final Size Range and Community Contributions

We next aim to find a concise but meaningful way to make real-world use of the findings. Until now, both the communities introduced in Sect. 2 and the final sizes (Sects. 3 to 5) have been grouped automatically. We can therefore now carry out a number of different types of analysis which quantify the relationships between communities and the epidemic final sizes, e.g. the percentage contribution of each community of nodes to the different final size ranges, the communities which

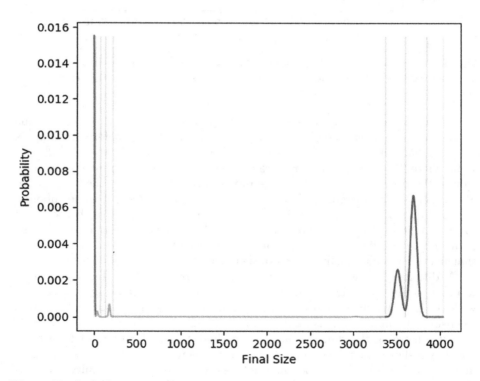

Fig. 6. The high-density and low-density areas of the smoothed probability "curve" as separated by the new boundaries after merging. The boundary values are marked by the vertical lines.

resulted in the most infection cases. We use the experiment to demonstrate how to analyse such data and draw useful knowledge which can inform on thresholds and rules to be used for network protections.

6.1 Epidemic Starting Community and Final Size

The number of nodes within each community from the Facebook data set is presented in Table 1. There are eight communities detected within the network, each containing hundreds of nodes.

Table 1. The number of nodes within each community.

Community name	A	B	C	D	E	F	G	H
Number of nodes	553	209	348	545	267	525	840	752

For each distinct final size range and for each epidemic simulation starting community, we calculate the frequency relative to approximately 80,000 malware propagation simulation runs, i.e. the relative frequencies, which are shown as percentages in Table 2. Such analytics provide a way to quantify the damage of malware infection in terms of the total number of infected systems, should there be no additional measures to stop the malware from infecting the machines but only the routine removal rate. Certain quantitative community epidemic knowledge can be drawn from the contribution probabilities to the epidemic final sizes presented in the table below:

- All of the communities have at least a 50% chance of producing an outbreak of greater than 3600 individuals.
- Communities A, G and H have the largest chance of producing a severe (> 3600) outbreak. In other words, these communities are prone to large scale spread within the community and therefore are considered more vulnerable to malware attacks.
- Communities B and F contribute to different rare final size ranges which means they are isolated communities which are more resilient to malware attacks. Malware attacks are less likely to spread out from them if started there or are less likely to spread into them if not started there.

To summarise, Table 2 informs us about the relationship between the epidemic final size and community in which the outbreak begins.

Table 2. The probability of observing a particular final size, given the outbreak begins in each community represented in percentage.

	A	B	C	D	E	F	G	H
Final size range	%							
[0, 19]	3.4	17.4	23.2	14.6	16.6	14.3	6.1	4.8
[20, 75]	0.0	0.0	0.0	0.0	0.0	4.5	0.0	0.0
[76, 129]	0.0	0.0	0.0	0.0	0.0	0.0	0.0	0.0
[130, 217]	0.0	29.0	0.0	0.0	0.0	0.0	0.0	0.0
[218, 3374]	0.5	0.0	0.3	0.2	0.2	0.3	0.3	0.3
[3375, 3599]	27.4	0.4	20.5	24.1	24.0	22.2	27.2	27.2
[3600, 3852]	68.8	53.2	56.0	61.0	59.1	58.7	66.4	67.8
[3853, 4039]	0.0	0.0	0.0	0.0	0.0	0.0	0.0	0.0

7 Protect Network Communities Automatically

7.1 Set up Rules and Thresholds

The ultimate goal is to protect the network communities automatically using the insights gained from the algorithms presented in the preceding sections. As described above, modelling and simulation results have to be summarised into probabilistic findings which can be used to inform the appropriate protection of the network communities. In particular, any values can be used to set up rules or thresholds so that once rule conditions are met, protective measures including prevention and intervention measures are deployed automatically, e.g. re-routing, alerting choking nodes, increasing traffic scans on choking nodes. Such protective measures can include but are not limited to: an anti-malware facility; a malware filter; a malware detector; a block, preclusion or cessation of interaction; and a reconfiguration of one or more computer systems.

Here is one example on how to use the experiment results above to set up rules:

- If
  (a final size >= a threshold value, e.g. >= 3600 infected cases
  AND
  a probability of reaching such a final size given a starting community >= a certain percentage, e.g. probability of reaching >= 3600 infected cases >= 60%)
- Prepare for malware attacks and deploy protective measures to those communities should a malware be detected, e.g. raising alerts/increasing traffic scans to the users or user communities to be most likely affected.

It is worth noting that we presented a fixed value for the threshold to be set in the above example and a more systematic approach would be to look at the cost function and balance out the cost of a large outbreak against the cost of potential disruptions by any network protection measure, e.g. air-gapping will protect systems but will also stop systems and network to function normally and incur cost.

7.2   Real World Use

In the real world of cyber security operations, an end to end automation or human-in-the-loop automation is important. As described above, a number of the steps require parameter values to be set, algorithms to be chosen and rules to be set to make the method work well, e.g. the choices of community detection algorithms, infection spreading parameters, smoothing algorithms, range merging thresholds and different methods. These parameter choices can be built into the backend of the modelling and simulation tool and the user can choose algorithms or define parameter values at the front end of the tool, which is very likely to be a software tool; or an optimal algorithm can be pre-selected by technical experts for the users so that certain parameters cannot be modified by the user. We have also experimented with a higher infection transmission rate $\beta_t = 0.1$ and a lower infection transmission rate $\beta_t = 0.025$, the proposed method of analysing the simulation results systematically discovered the expected patterns the same way it did with the infection transmission rate $\beta_t = 0.05$. To avoid presenting too many simulation results and distracting the audience from the main method, we do not present the results here.

8   Discussion

In this paper, we describe a quantitative and automatic method of making use of simulation results from stochastic network malware propagation models. We show that although the simulation results are complex and difficult to quantify, significant progress can be made by analysing the simulation results as a signal and in a systematic way. There are many steps in the method presented in this paper; each step also includes a number of sub-algorithms. We summarise the major steps as follows:

1. Identify the network communities
2. Simulate epidemic final sizes using malware propagation models
3. Smooth the final size probabilities as a signal
4. Group the final sizes into ranges
5. Identify community epidemic information/characteristics
6. Protect network communities automatically with rules and thresholds

There have been many theoretical and academic studies to address malware epidemiology, however the majority only focus on demonstrating the possibility of modelling. For studies which focused on stochastic models, the results presented were usually simulation examples which cannot be directly used in real world protections [7]. Hardly any research looks into analysing all the possible simulation results in a collective way. In an ideal and simple world, the problems can be modelled using mathematical methods with analytical solutions. However, usually this is not possible as malware propagation on a large network consisting of many nodes and edges cannot be modelled analytically. We seek to use stochastic models and simulation results to gain insights to this complex problem.

We use epidemic final size as an example to demonstrate how to analyse modelling and simulation results quantitatively and subsequently use such results to serve protection purposes. The general method of treating the simulation results as a probabilistic signal are generalisable to using simulation results on other key measures of malware epidemics or even other spreading agents, e.g. infectious disease spreading. We acknowledge that network information is not always easy to obtain, but with data becoming increasingly accessible and advancements in data sharing technologies [8], we expect to see more information on large and complex networks become available for modelling and simulation. We also acknowledge quantifying simulation results focusing on different measures of epidemics will require different considerations, but we argue that treating simulation results as a signal is a good way to identify patterns and to develop methods for the automatic deployment of network protections. We also acknowledge that this method is usable only on any network or spatial structure in which communities or clusters can be identified, which largely means "small-world" types of networks which are probably mostly social or business networks in the malware propagation scenario and the population mobility networks in the human infection spreading setting.

To our knowledge, this is the first attempt to make use of malware propagation simulation results as a signal to aid network protection. We show that not only theoretically, but practically too, malware epidemiology can be used in an automatic manner to protect networks. This study should therefore act as the foundation and inspiration for industrial deployments of malware epidemiology.

Acknowledgments. We thank all the anonymous reviewers for their feedback. The views expressed in this paper are solely those of the authors and do not necessarily represent the views of their employers.

References

1. Ferguson, N., et al.: Report 9: impact of non-pharmaceutical interventions (NPIs) to reduce COVID19 mortality and healthcare demand (2020)
2. Ghafur, S., Kristensen, S., Honeyford, K., Martin, G., Darzi, A., Aylin, P.: A retrospective impact analysis of the WannaCry cyberattack on the NHS. NPJ Digit. Med. **2**(1), 1–7 (2019)
3. Kephart, J.O., White, S.R.: Directed-graph epidemiological models of computer viruses. In: Proceedings of the 1991 IEEE Computer Society Symposium on Research in Security and Privacy, pp. 343–359 (1991)
4. Leskovec, J., Krevl, A.: SNAP Datasets: Stanford large network dataset collection, June 2014. http://snap.stanford.edu/data

5. Leskovec, J., Mcauley, J.J.: Learning to discover social circles in ego networks. In: Advances in Neural Information Processing Systems, pp. 539–547 (2012)
6. del Rey, A.M.: Mathematical modeling of the propagation of malware: a review. Secur. Commun. Netw. **8**(15), 2561–2579 (2015)
7. Wang, P., González, M.C., Hidalgo, C.A., Barabási, A.L.: Understanding the spreading patterns of mobile phone viruses. Science **324**(5930), 1071–1076 (2009)
8. Wang, X.S., Herwono, I., Di Cerbo, F., Kearney, P., Shackleton, M.: Enabling cyber security data sharing for large-scale enterprises using managed security services. In: 2018 IEEE Conference on Communications and Network Security (CNS), pp. 1–7. IEEE (2018)

Attacks

Chasing Botnets: A Real Security Incident Investigation

George Hatzivasilis[1,2(✉)] ⓘ and Martin Kunc[3]

[1] Foundation for Research and Technology, Heraklion, Greece
hatzivas@ics.forth.gr
[2] Department of Electrical and Computer Engineering,
Hellenic Mediterranean University (HMU), Heraklion, Greece
hatzivas@hmu.gr .
[3] CZ.NIC, ZSPO, Prague, Czech Republic
martin.kunc@nic.cz

Abstract. Botnets form a special type of malware that nowadays constitute one of the biggest threats in cyber-security. Ordinarily, the hacker exploits existing vulnerabilities to infiltrate the system and install a command-and-control (C&C) infrastructure. Thereupon, the system is "botnized" and performs the bot-master's commands. In most cases, the attacker does not intend to destroy the compromised assets but to utilize them in order to perform other type of attacks, such as crypto-mining or Denial of Service (DoS) campaigns to targeted websites. Nevertheless, ransomware or other disruptive attacks can also be launched at some point and harm the owner of the infected equipment. This paper starts with an overview of botnet cases, attacker's tactics, and relevant defense mechanisms. Then, we present a real step-by-step digital forensics investigation on a customer's bare-metal server in the cloud. The attack was performed in 2020. We describe the storyline from the server's installation, the infection, the investigation, the proper mitigation actions, as well as, the economic implication. Finally, we sum-up which were the main mistakes that enable the attack and propose a silver bulletin for server setup in the cloud.

Keywords: Botnet · Malware · Forensics · Digital investigation · Attack tactics · Miner · DoS · Cloud · OpenStack · Economic crime

1 Introduction

For more than a decade now, the battle against botnets has gone more intensive. Microsoft estimates that around 1% of the recorded computers that execute automatic updates are infected with malicious software [1]. In a twelve-months period, the majority of the affected machines are unique, revealing that around 10% of users will face an infection within the next year.

Defense mechanisms are surveyed in [2–4], engaging industry and governmental organizations, Internet Service Providers (ISPs), and end-users. The infection rate is

© Springer Nature Switzerland AG 2020
G. Hatzivasilis and S. Ioannidis (Eds.): MSTEC 2020, LNCS 12512, pp. 111–124, 2020.
https://doi.org/10.1007/978-3-030-62433-0_7

reduced since the beginning of this war, and it seems to be relatively stabilized [5] since 2009.

On the other hand, the financial losses and costs on the global economy are still significant [6]. Malwares were evolved from highly visible and disruptive at early 2000s (ILOVEYOU, CODE RED, etc.), to stealthy code laying undetectable in the infected equipment and acting as part of a larger criminal infrastructure (GAMEOVER ZEUS). Today, cybercrime is structured as a Service Oriented Architecture (SoA) with malware authors and botnet herders trading their assets in a market of attack-tools and integrated malicious strategies [7, 8]. The malicious operations include, among others, crypto-mining, user credentials harvesting, Distributed Denial-of-Service (DDoS) attacks, financial fraud, ransomware, hosting of phishing sites, click fraud on advertising networks, spamming, and so on [9].

Ordinarily, the end-users do not bear the whole cost of the botnet scourge, as ISPs undertaking main mitigation actions with the support of national initiatives (e.g. the London Action Plan (LAP) [10] which promotes anti-spam and anti-botnet strategies). Nevertheless, ISPs are not motivated by the market to moderate bot-net operations and several ISPs try to evade the addable costs [11].

Nonetheless, end-users still play a core role in the overall Internet security [12]. This fact is becoming more-and-more essential with the evolution of the Internet of Things (IoT) where mobile and personal devices in high numbers have to be safeguarded against "botinization" [13–16]. Marai constitutes an indicative botnet case that exploited IoT devices [17]. In just six months, the malware infiltrated in almost 600,000 smart devices (e.g. CCTV cameras with default credentials). On October 2016, the botnet launched massive DDoS attacks, overwhelming several high-profile victims and getting unreachable much of the Internet on the US east coast [18]. While the creators of the Mirai bot were arrested, its techniques and source code inspired many other actors to build sophisticated IoT botnets, like Tori-bot. Thereupon, the users' active involvement is considered as a next step towards the safer Internet and the further decrement of the abovementioned infection ratio [5]. WARDOG functionality [12] as well as the active participation of users is crucial. Security certification and cyber insurance are also instruments to establish trust and reduce risk in the provision of a wide spectrum of industries and services [19–21]. Insurance and certification can also enhance the trustworthiness of potential customers.

This paper presents a real step-by-step digital forensics investigation on a set of compromised virtual machines in a cloud setting with OpenStack administrating them. Cloud environments form a popular target for attackers as a successful assault would be feasible to several machines with the same setting as well. Also, cloud applications usually provide a specific set of known services and have sufficient computational/communicational capabilities.

The rest paper is structured as follows: Sect. 2 overviews the overall concept of the emerging botnet threats and countermeasures. Section 3 outlines the storyline of the examined security incident. Section 4 details digital investigation on the compromised server. Section 5 discusses the economic implication for the victim and the excess usage charges for the cloud services. Section 6 summarizes a proposed silver bulletin for cloud server set-up. Finally, Sect. 7 concludes the results of this work.

2 Related Works

Nowadays, security experts have managed to neutralize a few botnets and analyze their underlying features [22, 23]. The generic botnet architecture was initially revealed through the investigation of Torbig [22], with other remarkable studies including the analysis of Botters [8] and Conficker [23]. Surveys for botnet attacks, malicious tools, and countermeasures are documented in [2, 4, 9, 24], and [25]. Furthermore, several botnets target specific application domains, like social media [26] and the banking sector [27]. Legal aspects of botnet mitigation are examined in [28].

2.1 Botnet Infrastructure

Typically, botnets are defined as networks of compromised end-hosts, known as *bots or zombies*. The whole infrastructure is controlled by one or more persons, called *bot-master/s*. The botnet recruits vulnerable hosts across the Internet via various methods which are exploited by different malware types (e.g. default system configurations, social engineering, software flaws, etc.). The infected bots establish a *Command and Control (C&C)* mechanism between them, to get instructions from the bot-master and coordinate malicious campaigns. The core C&C operations:

1. Support monitoring and recovery by the bot-master
2. Offer robust network connectivity
3. Constrains the exposure of the malicious network which is visible to individual bot
4. Provide individual control traffic dispersion and encryption.

Therefore, the bot-master sends commands to the bot armies through the C&C infrastructure. Usually, the hacker builds intermediate bot layers, known as *handlers*. Handlers forward the bot-master's instructions to other bots which they are controlling directly. The commands will eventually reach the end-bots, which are actually performing the attacks. Henceforth, the bot-master's real identity and location are concealed and he/she evades the law authorities.

The C&C channels can work across various (logical) networks and use several communication techniques. Botnet administration includes a set of tools and systems which ordinarily install malicious software and control the victim through the Internet Relay Chat (IRC). Nevertheless, the attacker can change the communication approach, with many botnets nowadays providing more than one protocol to harden their detection.

2.2 Attacks

Usually, botnets are utilized for DDoS attack campaigns on targeted applications, networks, and/or the Web in general. The current trends include the execution of DDoS operations at the application layer. These are still remaining among the most difficult cases to defend online, especially for web servers.

The typical attack strategy launches *HTTP/S flooding traffic* which is sent from the end-bots to the victim. The campaign presupposes an adequate number of bots which are exhausting the victim's bandwidth, and thus, constraining the access of legitimate users.

As the involved end-bots do not require any response from the victim, they can transmit requests with spoofed (false) IPs. Thus, bots attack the victim with several fake IPs and their true IP addresses are hidden. The deployed defense mechanisms, such as black-listed IPs in firewalls or other network monitoring modules, are overcome as the bots keep altering IPs.

Also, the attacker could further conceal the end-bots through a reflectors' layer and hit the victim indirectly. *Reflectors* constitute non-compromised systems which exclusively send replies to requests. The bots make requests towards the reflectors setting as spoofed IP, the IP address of the victim. Thereafter, the reflectors will answer back to the victim, executing the actual assault.

Apart of flooding, *Slowloris* forms another state-of-the-art type of DDoS. The attacker makes several connections to the target and keeps them open with minimum effort for as long as possible. The assault is effectively launched with less bots than flooding. Furthermore, the bots devote less resources, and thus, enhance the possibility of remaining undetected by the owner of the compromised equipment.

Unquestionably, botnets are utilized for a high variety of malicious operations. The latest cyber threat landscape by ENISA [29] reports actions like spam campaigns and click frauds, crypto-mining or crypto-jacking, as well as, data breaches, extortion, and/or ransomware.

The main variation among botnets and to ordinary malwares is the subsistence of the C&C. Therefore, if we discover the C&C location, the botnet can be traced and removed. This approach exploits the potential weaknesses of the botnet's communication channels. It is relatively more feasible to break down a centralized setting. Thus, as the detection strategies become more effective, hackers start adopting Peer-to-Peer (P2P) and hybrid infrastructures. This comes with a cost of higher delay as the interaction between the bots and the bot-master passes via many peers before reaching the target (i.e. HTTP flooding). On the other hand, it provides higher untraceability from law authorities and botnet's persecutors.

2.3 Countermeasures

The botnet defense mechanisms can be grouped in three categories. The first category blocks the botnet's setup, prevents the infection of secondary victims, and detects/neutralizes the botnet's handlers. The second category responds to ongoing botnet attacks, incorporating countermeasures that detect, prevent, or mitigate the malicious activity at runtime. The third category applies forensics techniques that examine the botnet characteristics, after a performed attack.

The usual methods for safeguarding systems from getting infected involve anti-viruses/anti-malwares, firewalls, and patching. Therefore, malicious code is detected based on digital signatures, behavior and/or heuristic features. Afterwards, it is quarantined for further examination or permanent deletion. Valuable information is also gathered, disclosing the hacker's strategies. The system's vulnerabilities are revealed and the legitimate software/hardware is updated accordingly. These countermeasures form an integral part of the overall defense. Apart from protecting individual machines or networks, such functionality is now extended to the cloud [30, 31].

However, those methods cannot always defend the legitimate assets. For example, anti-viruses only detect malicious patterns which are already known. Thus, an attacker could test the scanning capabilities of the defense mechanism and perform a policy to evade detection (e.g. zero-days).

Thereupon, anomaly detection techniques are suggested. The normal system operation is traced by machine learning modules (e.g. based on fingerprinting, deep learning, synergetic neural networks, or fuzzy estimators). When a new attack type is launched, the abnormal activity is noticed and mitigation strategies are performed. So, DDoS attacks could be tracked by network monitoring components that scan the traffic at runtime [12]. Then, prevention techniques, such as the Moving Target Detection (MTD) [32], can constrain the malicious side-effects. BotFlex is a state-of-the-art community-driven tool for network monitoring. Raw data from the inspected networking functions, which were performed by the examined machines, are transformed in high-level events (e.g. download form site, port scan, or other transactions). A deduction engine processes this information and discovers symptoms of malicious patterns (modelled as logic rules). However, it needs a vast amount of data which have to be processed. Therefore, singular value decomposition from the Big Data domain is applicable here. The high-order data dimensions are decreased, even for encrypted transactions, and the computational overhead is considerably decreased.

On the other hand, stealthy DDoS campaigns with the attacker combining various attack patterns instead of a single and easily traced one, could overcome statistical analysis and anomaly detection. Furthermore, the legitimate entity has to devote sufficient effort to apply and keep up-to-date the defense mechanisms.

Except from these main security controls at the system level, Internet-wide mechanisms are also deployed by ISPs to marshal the networking traffic without the active involvement of the end-users. While ISPs would not take full responsibility and lock down every compromised machine, they will at least ensure that they do not serve traffic containing malicious packets. The main ISP countermeasures include:

1. **IP-spoofing:** ISPs should not forward traffic with spoofed IP addresses and all packets containing any RFC 1918 or reserved IP address in the source or destination must be immediately discarded.
2. **Filtering:** *Ingress filtering* has to be performed for all the incoming packets to the ISP's network. For traffic which is originated from a customer's site, it should be validated that the NET_ID field in the source IP address matches the assigned NET_ID for this specific customer. *Egress filtering* has to be also performed to monitor the outgoing traffic to upstream and peer ISPs.
3. **Broadcast:** Directed IP broadcasts has to be deactivated.
4. **High-profile entities:** Special attention should be paid for high-profile customers and servers.
5. **Dissemination:** Customers should be educated to protect themselves and enhance the security awareness.

In several botnet cases, the compromised machines tend to connect malicious domains or Domain Name System (DNS), which are under the control of the bot-master, to get and respond to instructions. If the relevant communication patterns to the C&C are detected by the ISP (e.g. router-based TCP/UDP monitoring, honeypots, etc.), the communication can be stopped (e.g. blocking malicious domains/IPs, routing and DNS blacklist).

However, relying on identifying bot communications is not considered viable in the long term. The C&C interactions could be extremely polymorphic and flexible, using encryption and other masking methods.

Digital forensics are applied throughout these processes to collect juridical artifacts. These mainly involve honeypots, network and computer forensics. Still, the high amounts of affected users/machines, the global coverage of bots, and thus, the different law authorities from various involved countries, pose significant difficulties in the prosecution of the wily entities.

3   The Storyline of the Security Incident

The digital investigation concerns a successful attack on a bare-metal server for a cloud customer in Europe. The server has a quite powerful machine (20 physical/40 logical CPU cores, 192 GB RAM, 960 GB hard disk, 250 TB Bandwidth) where a training platform would be implemented. In the main machine, it was installed the Open-Stack framework, which would manage several underlying Virtual Machines (VMs). There were VMs that performed i) the core functionality of the developed platform and were deployed once and ii) the training session modules per trainee which would be deployed dynamically at runtime. The OpenStack installation and the permanent VMs were deployed first and were affected by the attack. One of the core VMs had external connection capabilities and acted as a proxy for the rest ones.

Due to lack of time for the delivery of the final product, the platform was exposed to direct Internet access almost from the beginning in order to speed-up the development and testing procedures. This was the main mistake, as: i) server administrators were not assign from the start, ii) the proper security controls (e.g. HTTPS connections) were not in place, iii) installed software modules with pre-defined default credentials (e.g. accounts) and configurations (e.g. ports), and iv) a secure communication channel was not established with some credentials (i.e. pairs of username/password) being initially sent via unencrypted emails.

The server and the development started in January 2020 and the malicious behavior begin almost immediately a few days later. At first, the malware compromised the proxy and then some of the other core VMs behind it. Then, the malware was trying to spread to other servers within the cloud, by trying SSL connections for ordinary accounts (e.g. admin, superuser, etc.) with default or weak passwords. The activity was blocked initially by the cloud provider and then by the customer (e.g. by restricting outgoing SSL connections). The spreading phase stopped and the botnized server started DoS attacks to external websites. This activity requires some time to be detected and was identified via collaborative intrusions detection and early warning systems between the cloud providers, raising an alarm that they were under attacks. The accountable cloud provider blocked the public IP and Internet connection of the server for a while. Thereafter, the disruptive activity was stopped and the infected VMs start exhibiting high CPU and memory usage from crypto-mining.

Finally, it was completed the digital investigation that is detailed in the next section and the malware was detected and removed. The VMs were set properly under a safe environment, the security primitives were activated, and the server went online again.

4 The Investigation – Incident Report

This was a second incident in about six months. During the first incident, couple of machines were compromised and abused for DDoS attacks. That was visible as a significant outgoing traffic which actually resulted in increased cost of the platform. Higher outgoing traffic can be often expected with highly visited web servers (or other service providing platform) – which was not our case in that moment. Another giveaway was that during regular connections i.e. downloading files a reasonable amount of related incoming traffic is expected – which was not our case. Short packet capture on outgoing interface clearly showed a high number of outgoing SYN packets with no reply, as depicted in Fig. 1.

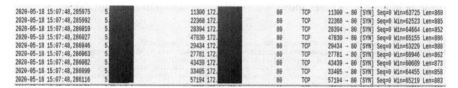

Fig. 1. Snapshot – SYN packets

From there it was just about identifying the compromised machine by the high traffic and the way it communicates with command and control server. The list of active TCP sessions (i.e. *netstat -t*) then clearly showed active IRC connection, which is often used for this. At that time, we decided to go the way of rolling back all the machines to an uncompromised state and securing SSH by denying authentication with username and password and allow only public key authentication as is often referred as best practice.

The second incident was spotted as high CPU load on one of the virtual machines by a process named *mdadmd*. Short search led to conclusion that it might be process coupled with RAID storage. That could have swayed the investigating team into thinking that it's a legitimate application that has something to do with the way the virtual machine is setup. Unfortunately for the process, the list of installed packages (*dpkg -l*) proved that no such package is currently installed. From that point it was clear that the machine was compromised. After checking the other machines, it was clear that a total number of 6 virtual machines were compromised. The location of the original binary (*/root/.mdadmd/mdadmd*) was found via *ls -la/proc/x/exe* (where *x* is *pid* of the running process) which show the path from which the file was executed.

One of the other indicators of compromise was found in syslog (Fig. 2).

```
May 29 19:29:18 x systemd[1]: Started mdadmd daemon monitoring MD devices.
May 29 19:29:18 x mdadmd[8421]: #033[1;32m * #033[0m#033[1;37mABOUT          #033[0m#033[1;36mXMRig/5.11.1-mo1#033[0m#033[1;37m gcc/7.3.1#033[0m#033[0m
May 29 19:29:18 x xmrig[8421]:  * ABOUT        XMRig/5.11.1-mo1 gcc/7.3.1
May 29 19:29:18 x mdadmd[8421]: #033[1;32m * #033[0m#033[1;37mLIBS           libuv/1.8.0 #033[0m#033[0m
May 29 19:29:18 x mdadmd[8421]: #033[1;32m * #033[0m#033[1;37mHUGE PAGES     #033[0m#033[1;32msupported#033[0m#033[0m
May 29 19:29:18 x mdadmd[8421]: #033[1;32m * #033[0m#033[1;37m1GB PAGES      #033[0m#033[1;33munavailable#033[0m#033[0m
May 29 19:29:18 x mdadmd[8421]: #033[1;32m * #033[0m#033[1;37mCPU            Intel Core Processor (Skylake, IBRS) (2)#033[0m #033[1;32mx64 #033[1;32mAES#033[0m#033[0m
```

Fig. 2. Snapshot – Syslog

XMRig is name of a cryptomining application. That was actually a good sign because there was high chance it was "just miner" instead of a destructive malware. Even-though sings of persistence are to a trained eye visible from the syslog. More information was found when issuing the find command find */-name "mdadmd*"*. That resulted in the following output:

/etc./systemd/system/mdadmd.service

/etc./systemd/system/multi-user.target.wants/mdadmd.service

/root/.mdadmd/mdadmd

After clearing the persistence, the only question left to answer was how did the attacker get in. The included syslog output actually refers to a first time the *mdadmd* process was started (the same output was then written several times later). Having the first time help a lot with pinpointing the similar timestamp in *authlog. e* (Fig. 3).

```
May 29 19:29:16 x sudo:      root : TTY=tty1 ; PWD=/root ; USER=root ; COMMAND=/bin/true
May 29 19:29:16 x sudo: pam_unix(sudo:session): session opened for user root by superuser(uid=0)
May 29 19:29:16 x sudo: pam_unix(sudo:session): session closed for user root
May 29 19:29:17 x sudo:      root : TTY=tty1 ; PWD=/root ; USER=root ; COMMAND=/bin/true
May 29 19:29:17 x sudo: pam_unix(sudo:session): session opened for user root by superuser(uid=0)
May 29 19:29:17 x sudo: pam_unix(sudo:session): session closed for user root
May 29 19:29:17 x sudo:      root : TTY=tty1 ; PWD=/root ; USER=root ; COMMAND=/bin/systemctl stop mdadmd.service
```

Fig. 3. Snapshot – Authlog

Log shown that a user *superuser* logged via tty1 just before the mdadmd was first run. What was puzzling here was that the tty that was used to login did not point to SSH. That meant that the attacker used another way to get in. That lead to host machine being pulled into investigation. Since the host machine authlog and wtmp didn't show any discrepancy the next thing to check were open ports and related applications. The list of open ports (netstat -tulnp) shown that there is a number of open ports just above *5900*. On those ports was a process *qemu-system-x86* that was listening. Since the same process was used for running the virtual machines things began to be clear. Port *5901* is a default port for VNC which is one of the protocols used for remote desktop. Upon connection to that port a user obtained a terminal where the user could just provide a username and password a gain access to the machine it belongs to. Using this an attacker could that bypass the public key restriction posed on the SSH server configuration and gain access to actually any machine since all have the maintenance account *superuser* and same password. The attacker did not even have to enumerate or randomly discover the IP address of those machines since all ports were situated one after another (*5901, 5902, …*).

The next steps were then clear. First block access to those ports, and then change the compromised password.

Final step was to check the compromised machines on any changes that could have been made by the attacker. Utility called *debsums* serves exactly this purpose. It gathers hashes of all system files and compares them with their original counterpart that comes with the package during installation (Fig. 4).

```
debsums: changed file /etc/securetty (from login package)
debsums: changed file /etc/sysctl.conf (from procps package) changed
debsums: changed file /etc/sudoers (from sudo package)
debsums: changed file /etc/tomcat8/server.xml (from tomcat8 package)
```

Fig. 4. Snapshot – Debsums

From the output above we can clearly see which files were changed and we can then manually check if any changes were introduced by the attacker. The only change that was made by the attacker was enabling *hugepages* option in the *sysctl.conf* which is expected to increase the performance of the miner.

Luckily the attacker did not display any really malicious behavior and the damage done was easily fixed. There is still speculation on how did the attackers obtained the quite strong password in the first place. One option is that during the first incident the attackers could have guessed easier password get access to the system, obtain the hashes from */etc./shadow* and crack them. Other option is they eavesdropped it from an unencrypted email (the password was at least once transferred in plain text). But that we will never know.

5   The Economic Implications

This section discusses the economic implications that the attack had to the server owner. Figure 5 depicts the bandwidth of the infected server during the period January-May 2020. The server was hired in January 1st and, as it is visualized, the malicious activity began a few days later at January 27th. As the server would be used for development, it was not secured properly from the start and before being exposed directly to Internet access. Also, adequate monitoring and auditing procedures had not been established as well as the involvement of the responsible personnel (e.g. administrators). As the setup of the server and the related services proceeded, the abnormal incoming traffic was noticed, the digital investigation analysis was performed as described in the previous section, and the attack was mitigated completely at May 18th.

However, as mentioned in the beginning, the server was hired by a cloud provider. Therefore, it was subject to volume charges (i.e. when traffic exceeded a specified threshold). The legitimate service was supposed to require a low incoming/outgoing bandwidth, so the contract included the default traffic and usage thresholds. This had the implication that when the malicious traffic exceeded by far these thresholds, the monthly charge was excessively raised. The owner had hired the server for 12 months (January to December) for around 2,800 euros. The additional charges due to the attack for February alone would

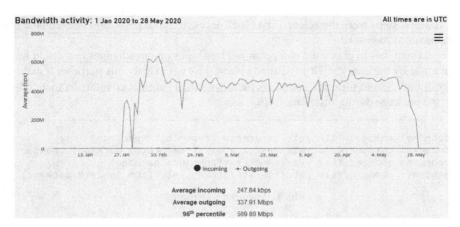

Fig. 5. Bandwidth activity of the infected server during the period January to May 2020.

be around 7,500 euros. Fortunately, the cloud provider noticed the extreme charges and the produced traffic, and inform the owner accordingly. It was agreed to purchase an additional package for around 120 euros per month that would cover the malicious traffic threshold, leaving the owner the opportunity to fix the problem and continue from then on. Thus, the owner paid an additional amount of around 1,450 euros to cover the whole contracting period and avoid the extreme monthly chargers. Furthermore, cyber insurance of digital infrastructure nowadays could cover such security incidents and reduce the risk for the customer [19–21].

6   Silver Bulletin for Setting a Server in the Cloud

As a main comment of this investigation is to "secure first, then go public". It must be strongly avoided to expose a development server directly to the Internet. One must first complete the development phase, deploy the relevant security controls and policies, and then make the service/application public.

Concerning cloud applications, one must also be familiarized and leverage the security controls that are offered by the cloud provider. Most cloud providers support IDS functionality, both for their operation, as well as, a panel for the customers. Also, a customer must enable the provided early-notification functionality and set low-traffic (or other) thresholds.

Other technical best practices for secure server configuration include:

- Apply server-hardening techniques

    - update and upgrade the utilized packages and the operating system
    - remove unnecessary packages
    - verify that no accounts have empty passwords
    - disable USB devices
    - secure any Apache server running in this machine

- examine which services start at boot time in order to verify that there are no malicious services starting with booting and running in the background
- delete all world-writable files
- configure *iptables* to block common attacks, like SYN flooding and spoofing
- secure configuration of SSH
- disable telnet
- secure configuration of *sysctl* to prevent the main flooding attacks and IP spoofing
- lock user accounts after some failed login attempts
- use *netstat* and check for hidden open ports
- set root permissions for the core system files
- install security software and scan for rootkits, viruses, malware, etc.

- Use strong passwords
- Do not send passwords unencrypted

  - Extra point: When sending encrypted passwords (i.e. in zip file) distribute password for the zip file across another channel (i.e. phone)
  - Extra point: Even if password is securely transferred, force the user to change it
  - Extra point: Do not share accounts ("admin", "superuser", etc.)
  - Extra point: Deny root login

- Allow only ssh-key-based login for ssh
- Set all firewalls defaults to deny and only allow ports that are required and justified

  - Never let ports like VNC, SQL, RDP (in case of Windows) be accessible from Internet

    - SSH, HTTP/S are justifiable

  - Set up such default firewall on all machines

- Document all internet accessible ports and monitor version of the software running there for vulnerabilities and patches

  - Have that document updated, private, but easily accessible.
  - Conduct regular port scans to verify

- If compromised, change all passwords that could have been affected

  - i.e. in case of root level compromise, change all user passwords after rollback

  Extra points for:

- Monitoring of authentication logs
- Check traffic – especially outgoing (only updates are expected and they are easy to rule out)

  - Look for IRC connections (highly suspicious, nicely visible)

7 Conclusions

This study presented on overview of current botnization threats and relevant counter-measures, as well as, a step-by-step digital forensics analysis for a real attack case on a customer server in the cloud. The core mistake that lead to the infection was the fact that the server was immediately exposed to direct Internet access, once it was delivered by the cloud provider. It took several days for the administration team to set the full security controls, while in the meantime the server had been compromised. The rapid infection of the server reveals that the cloud infrastructures have become of great importance for attackers, who seem to be aware of the relevant public IP ranges and monitor them. This is also reasonable as cloud applications usually provide a specific set of known services (i.e. OpenStack) and acquire sufficient computational/communicational resources. Moreover, a successful assault would be feasible to several machines with the same setting. The investigated botnet was eventually detected and mitigated. However, as the security monitoring procedures were not in place from the beginning, the attacks were ongoing for several weeks. This has an economic side-effect as well, in contrast to the usual botnet cases on machines which are fully-owned by the legitimate party. As the cloud services are subject to volume charges (e.g. with threshold for bandwidth consumption) a DoS attack from a compromised node would cause excessive charges for the related customer. This is an issue both for the users – who must be aware and put cyber-security as a high priority; and the cloud providers – who must install early notification mechanisms for raising charges to protect their customers. The study ends with a proposed bulletin for setting up a server in cloud environments.

Acknowledgements. This work has received funding from the European Union Horizon's 2020 research and innovation programme under the grant agreements No. 786890 (THREAT-ARREST) and No. 830927 (CONCORDIA).

References

1. Microsoft: Microsoft security intelligence report, Microsoft, vols. 9–17 (2010–2014)
2. Zargar, S.T., Joshi, J., Tipper, D.: A survey of defense mechanisms against Distributed Denial of Service (DDoS) flooding attacks. IEEE Commun. Surv. Tutor. **15**(4), 2046–2069 (2013)
3. Liu, S.: Surviving distributed Denial-of-Service attacks. IT Prof. **11**(5), 51–53 (2009)
4. Specht, S.M., Lee, R.B.: Distributed Denial of Service: taxonomies of attacks, tools and countermeasures. In: 17th International Conference on Parallel and Distributed Computing Systems (ICPADS), San Francisco, CA, USA, 15–17 September 2004, pp. 543–550 (2004)
5. Asghari, H., van Eeten, M.J.G., Bauer, J.M.: Economics of fighting botnets: lessons from a decade of mitigation. IEEE Secur. Priv. **13**(5), 16–23 (2015)
6. Sood, A.K., Zeadally, S., Enbody, R.J.: An empirical study of HTTP-based financial botnets. IEEE Trans. Dependable Secure Comput. **13**(2), 236–251 (2016)
7. Moore, T., Clayton, R., Anderson, R.: The economics of online crime. J. Econ. Perspect. **23**(3), 3–20 (2009)
8. de Santanna, J.J.C., et al.: Booters – an analysis of DDoS-as-a-Service attacks. In: IFIP/IEEE International Symposium on Integrated Network Management (IM). IFIP/IEEE, Ottawa, Canada, 11–15 May 2015, pp. 243–251 (2015)

9. Khattak, S., Ramay, N.R., Khan, K.R., Syed, A.A., Khayam, S.A.: A taxonomy of botnet behavior, detection, and defense. IEEE Commun. Surv. Tutor. **16**(2), 898–924 (2014)
10. Brown, I., Marsden, C.: Co-regulating Internet security: the London action plan. In: Academic Symposium on Global Internet Governance Academic Network (GigaNet), SSRN, Rio de Janeiro, Brazil, 11 November 2007, pp. 1–18 (2007)
11. Garcia, A., Horowitz, B.: The potential for underinvestment in Internet security: implications for regulatory policy. J. Regul. Econ. **31**(1), 37–55 (2007). https://doi.org/10.1007/s11149-006-9011-y
12. Hatzivasilis, G., et al.: WARDOG: awareness detection watchdog for Botnet infection on the host device. IEEE Trans. Sustain. Comput. Spec. Issue Sustain. Inf. Forensic Comput. **4**, 1–15 (2019)
13. Habibi, J., Midi, D., Mudgerikar, A., Bertino, E.: Heimdall: mitigating the Internet of Insecure Things. IEEE Internet Things J. **4**(4), 968–978 (2017)
14. Lu, Z., Wang, W., Wang, C.: On the evolution and impact of mobile botnets in wireless networks. IEEE Trans. Mob. Comput. **15**(9), 2304–2316 (2016)
15. Karim, A., Shah, S.A.A., Salleh, R.B., Arif, M., Noor, R.M., Shamshirband, S.: Mobile botnet attacks – an emerging threat: classification, review and open issues. KSII Trans. Internet Inf. Syst. TIIS **9**(4), 1471–1492 (2015)
16. Traynor, P., et al.: On cellular botnets: measuring the impact of malicious devices on a cellular network core. In: 16th ACM Conference on Computer and Communications Security (CSS), 9–13 November 2009, pp. 223–234. ACM, Chicago (2009)
17. Antonakakis, M., et al.: Understanding the Mirai botnet. In: 26th Usenix Security Symposium (SS), Vancouver, BC, Canada, 16–18 August 2017, pp. 1093–1110 (2017)
18. Fruhlinger, J.: The Mirai botnet explained: how teen scammers and CCTV cameras almost brought down the Internet. CSO Online, article 3258748. https://www.csoonline.com/article/3258748/security/the-mirai-botnet-explained-how-teen-scammers-and-cctv-cameras-almost-brought-down-the-internet.html. Accessed 9 March 2018
19. Pritchett, W.: Insurtech 10: Trends for 2019. The Digital Insurer, KPMG, pp. 1–36, March 2019
20. Hatzivasilis, G., et al.: Cyber insurance of information systems. In: 24th IEEE International Workshop on Computer Aided Modeling and Design of Communication Links and Networks (CAMAD 2019), 11–13 September 2019, pp. 1–7. IEEE, Limassol (2019)
21. Hatzivasilis, G., et al.: Towards the insurance of healthcare systems. In: Fournaris, A.P., et al. (eds.) IOSEC/MSTEC/FINSEC -2019. LNCS, vol. 11981, pp. 185–198. Springer, Cham (2020). https://doi.org/10.1007/978-3-030-42051-2_13
22. Stone-Gross, B., Cova, M., Gilbert, B., Kemmerer, R., Kruegel, C., Vigna, G.: Analysis of a botnet takeover. IEEE Secur. Priv. **9**(1), 64–72 (2010)
23. Shin, S., Gu, G., Reddy, N., Lee, C.P.: A large-scale empirical study of Conflicker. IEEE Trans. Inf. Forensics Secur. **7**(2), 676–690 (2012)
24. Konovalov, A.M., Kotenko, I.V., Shorov, A.V.: Simulation-based study of botnets and defense mechanisms against them. J. Comput. Syst. Sci. Int. **52**(1), 43–65 (2013). https://doi.org/10.1134/S1064230712060044
25. Bekeneva, Y., Shipilov, N., Borisenko, K., Shorov, A.: Simulation of DDoS-attacks and protection mechanisms against them. In: IEEE NW Russia Young Researchers in Electrical and Electronic Engineering Conference (ElConRusNW), 2–4 February 2015, pp. 49–55. IEEE, St. Petersburg (2015)
26. Dong, Y., Dai, J., Sun, X.: A mobile botnet that meets up at Twitter. In: Beyah, R., Chang, B., Li, Y., Zhu, S. (eds.) SecureComm 2018. LNICSSITE, vol. 255, pp. 3–21. Springer, Cham (2018). https://doi.org/10.1007/978-3-030-01704-0_1

27. Ling, L., Gao, Z., Silas, M.A., Lee, I., le Doeuff, E.A.: An AI-based, multi-stage detection system of banking botnets. In: 32nd Conference on Neural Information Processing Systems (NIPS), Montréal, Canada, pp. 1–9 (2019)
28. Grant, G.: Botnet mitigation and international law. Columbia J. Transnatl. Law **58**, 189–231 (2019)
29. Sfakianakis, A., Douligeris, C., Marinos, L., Lourenço, M., Raghimi, O.: ENISA Threat Landscape Report 2018, ENISA, pp. 1–139, January 2019
30. Hatzivasilis, G., Fysarakis, K., Askoxylakis, I., Bilanakos, A.: CloudNet anti-malware engine: GPU-accelerated network monitoring for cloud services. In: Fournaris, A.P., Lampropoulos, K., Marín Tordera, E. (eds.) IOSec 2018. LNCS, vol. 11398, pp. 122–133. Springer, Cham (2019). https://doi.org/10.1007/978-3-030-12085-6_11
31. Papaefstathiou, I., Bilanakos, A., Fysarakis, K., Hatzivasilis, G., Manifavas, C.: An efficient anti-malware intrusion detection system implementation, exploiting GPUs. In: International Conference on Advanced Technology & Sciences (ICAT 2014), Antalya, Turkey, 12–15 August 2014, pp. 1–9 (2014)
32. Hatzivasilis, G., Papadakis, N., Hatzakis, I., Ioannidis, S., Vardakis, G.: AI-driven composition and security validation of an IoT ecosystem. Appl. Sci. **10**(14), 1–31 (2020). Special Issue on Smart City and Multi-Agent Systems, MDPI Open Access Journal
33. Berger-Sabbatel, G., Duda, A.: Four years of botnet hunting: an assessment. In: Dziech, A., Czyżewski, A. (eds.) MCSS 2014. CCIS, vol. 429, pp. 29–42. Springer, Cham (2014). https://doi.org/10.1007/978-3-319-07569-3_3
34. Cooke, E., Jahanian, F., Mc Pherson, D.: The zombie roundup: understanding, detecting, and disrupting botnets. In: Usenix Workshop on Steps to Reducing Unwanted Traffic on the Internet (SRUTI), Cambridge, MA, USA, 7 July 2005, pp. 1–6 (2005)

Software System Exploration Using Library Call Analysis

Marinos Tsantekidis$^{(\boxtimes)}$ and Vassilis Prevelakis

Institute of Computer and Network Engineering, TU Braunschweig,
Braunschweig , Germany
{tsantekidis,prevelakis}@ida.ing.tu-bs.de

Abstract. The ability to analyze software systems without access to the source code, offers many advantages including the detection of vulnerabilities so that they may be fixed before an adversary can exploit them in a zero day attack. This type of analysis also has an important role in education as it allows students to use their imagination and creativity in the exploration process. In this paper, we use two techniques for black-box testing based on our previous work, where we demonstrated how library calls may be intercepted using wrappers as well as using the kernel to separate the memory of a process into regions, based on the (statically/dynamically) linked libraries that a program uses. By monitoring function calls to libraries or the main executable, we can determine if a high-level execution signature (which depends not only on the occurrence, but also the sequence and number of calls) fits a pattern of a possible attack against a system under test. We can, then, (a) determine whether a call should go ahead, (b) determine whether the arguments are acceptable and (c) ensure that we will be informed when there is suspicion of foul play. We then demonstrate how these techniques may be used in student training sessions to explore the structure of software systems and determine how such systems respond to specific input sequences designed to trigger bugs or demonstrate unexpected behavior.

Keywords: CRA · Library wrappers · Kernel modification · Library call interception · Training

1 Introduction

When analyzing software without having access to the source, we need to carry out a process that is referred to as "black box" testing. Under this regime, we treat the software (program, application, etc.) as an opaque system where we feed in inputs and observe outputs. This analysis is heavily dependent on the specifications of the system under test (SUT) because these will determine the test inputs and also be used to evaluate the observed outputs. Another complimentary approach is to feed random input to the SUT and make sure that it produces reasonable output (Unix utilities that were fed random input

© Springer Nature Switzerland AG 2020
G. Hatzivasilis and S. Ioannidis (Eds.): MSTEC 2020, LNCS 12512, pp. 125–139, 2020.
https://doi.org/10.1007/978-3-030-62433-0_8

crashed). At the Technical University (TU) of Braunschweig, black box analysis is included in our "Software Exploration/Modification" seminar which is aimed at looking at identifying vulnerabilities in software by understanding how the software works rather than by looking at the code.

However, when identifying a potential issue in the SUT, it is often important to be able to determine whether the issue lies in the core software or in one of the libraries that the SUT is using. A trivial example is the use of the obsolete $gets(3)$ C library routine that may lead to buffer overflows. In this case, the vulnerability manifests itself when that particular library call is used on unsanitized input. For this reason use of the $gets(3)$ routine is actively discouraged. However, other, more esoteric instances of abuse of standard library calls are described in the literature.

Our approach is to break up the SUT into its main components (essentially the main program and the libraries it uses) and examine the interactions between the various components. We use two techniques for our analysis, based our previous work [27,29]. The first one [27] uses a wrapper that is inserted between the program and the actual library code. The wrapper then may contain special code that reports on each call and its arguments. This code may also decide whether to actually call the intended library function or emulate it, report an error, or simply ignore it. It can modify the input arguments and/or the results returned by the call. The second one [29] is more elaborate, as it uses the kernel to intercept the transfer from main program to library or from library to library. Special code is run whenever a library is invoked by the main program or another library. This code functions is a similar way as the wrapper code, but it is better protected from interference from potentially malicious code than the wrapper-based alternative. In this paper, we describe how the two techniques mentioned above may be used in a training environment to look for potential issues or vulnerabilities in code that is distributed in binary form.

The remainder of this paper is organized in the following manner: Sect. 2 offers a brief summary of the timeline of CRAs and related defenses. In Sect. 3 we detail the design of our approach. Section 4, describes the implementation specifics. In Sect. 5, we present two training scenarios that can be used to evaluate trainee knowledge gain and performance. In Sect. 6, we conclude our work.

2   Background and Related Work

The use of programming languages that are not type-safe and the widespread use of pointers that do not support bounds checking, created a seemingly infinite series of buffer overflow attacks and resulted in an arms race to eliminate them. Nevertheless, we still see instances of classical buffer overflow attacks against fairly modern systems [e.g the attack against the time measurement Electronic Control Unit (ECU) [15,17] in a vehicle]. By mounting such an attack, an adversary can eventually mislead the Central Processing Unit (CPU) to jump to an address that was not intended by the running program. This may cause the execution of (i) foreign code injected by the attacker into the address space of the program, (ii) code that already exists within the address space of the victim, or (iii) arbitrary code (junk data, middle of instructions, etc.) that is also located within the address space of the process. This is a direct result of the ability of code to jump anywhere within a process's memory area, as well as the absence of policy checks when a transfer is performed. However, compiler and architectural modifications that make a memory page either writable or executable but not both [2,32], preventing the execution of code from the heap or stack, have made code injection attacks (CIA) [20] all but impossible.

Instead of trying to inject custom code, the attackers responded by using code already present in a program's memory space, resulting in a new type of attacks, i.e. Code Reuse Attacks (CRA). One of the most common forms of CRA is return-to-libc. It first appeared in 1997 [13], redirecting the flow of execution in the libc library. However, in this attack the adversary could only execute straight-line code, chaining together one function after another, resulting in attacks that are not Turing-complete. Stack smashing protection [9,16] and randomization techniques such as Address Space Layout Randomization (ASLR) [19], were then introduced to defeat return-to-libc attacks. In response, researchers proposed more sophisticated approaches - namely Return Oriented Programming (ROP) [5,22,23] and Jump Oriented Programming (JOP) [4]. These attack vectors form snippets of code, "gadgets", chaining together legitimate commands already in memory. In ROP, each gadget ends with a "return" instruction. When it is reached, it diverts control to the next gadget, eventually forming a sequence of gadgets that perform the unauthorized action desired by the attacker. The chained execution of gadgets ending in RET, has enabled researchers to develop several anti-ROP defenses (e.g. [7,14,18]) to detect or prevent it. In order to circumvent these methods, JOP was presented. This new attack also uses chained gadgets to execute arbitrary code, but it does not need RET instructions to alter the flow of execution. It is based on indirect branches and a dispatcher gadget to steer and chain them together.

Initially, CRAs were based on the principle that gadgets are located at known addresses in memory. ASLR, however, randomizes the location of data and code regions every time a process is executed. By randomizing code, ASLR makes CRAs more difficult to succeed as they cannot locate already present code, while randomizing data disrupts the redirection of execution flow as CIAs have far less chances to locate potentially injected code. However, Shacham et al. [24] proved that due to low entropy, caused by a small number of bits available for randomization in the 32-bit architecture, a brute-force attack can lead to a memory leak and eventually reveal the location of the randomized segments.

Furthermore, Snow et al. introduced "Just-In-Time" ROP (JIT-ROP) [25], a technique that exploits the ability to repeatedly abuse a memory disclosure vulnerability to map an application's memory layout on-the-fly, thus bypassing ASLR. Next, it identifies and collects gadgets, and then constructs and delivers a ROP payload based on those gadgets.

Later, Bittau et al. presented a new attack, Blind Return Oriented Programming (BROP) [3]. BROP works against modern 64-bit Linux with ASLR, NX memory and stack canaries [31] enabled. It exploits a single stack vulnerability and uses two techniques to succeed: (*a*) generalized stack reading, which is based on a known technique used to leak canaries, to also leak saved return addresses in order to defeat ASLR on x86-64 systems even when Position Independent Executables (PIE) are used, and (*b*) remotely finds enough gadgets to perform the *write*(2) system call, after which the application's binary can be transferred from memory to the attacker's socket.

Over the years, important work has been carried out with respect to defenses against CIAs/CRAs which, in the scope of this paper, consists of techniques that observe the flow of execution of a program, stepping in to take action whenever is deemed necessary.

Abadi et al. proposed Control-Flow Intetegrity (CFI) [1] which monitors the execution of a program and enforces it to adhere to a control flow graph (CFG), which is statically computed at compile time. If the flow of execution does not follow the predetermined CFG, an attack is detected. CRAs such as ROP and JOP by definition divert the program flow, hence they are discovered. This approach, however, suffers from two main disadvantages. First, the implementation is coarse-grained. Computing a complete and accurate CFG is difficult since there are many indirect control flow transfers (jumps, returns, etc.) or libraries dynamically linked at run-time. Furthermore, the interception and checking of all the control transfers incur substantial performance overhead.

Tian et al. [26] propose PHUKO, an on-the-fly buffer overflow prevention system which leverages virtualization technology. This system offers the monitored program a fully transparent environment and easy deployment without restarting the program. PHUKO combines static analysis and online patching provided by the hypervisor to instrument buffer accesses in the running program. Specifically, it first uses static binary analysis to identify the interesting instructions that are related to buffer overflows and then it replaces them with trap instructions by which the execution of a program will be trapped to the hypervisor. Then, when the monitored program executes these replaced instructions, the built-in bound check mechanism will dynamically take effect to ensure that the buffer access is limited within the scope of the allowed memory area.

Crane et al. [10] identify the interesting technique of booby trapping software. They define booby traps as code providing active defense that is only triggered by an attack. These booby traps do not implement program functionality and do not influence its operation - in fact, the program does not know about its own booby traps and under normal operation cannot trigger them. They propose to automatically insert booby traps into the original program code during compilation or program loading. Whenever an attack triggers one of the booby traps within the program, the trap instantly knows that an attack is underway and is in a position to adequately react to the threat.

Chen et al. [6] propose a kernel-based security testing tool, named ARMORY, for software engineers to detect Program Buffer Overflow Defects (PBODs) automatically when applying testing, without increasing the testing workload. Whenever a developer provides an input string to a program to test its functionality,

ARMORY automatically forks a child process, called PBOD test process, and utilizes it to test whether the code used to handle the input string has any PBOD. The parent and the child processes work independently; thus, they do not influence each other. The original process only handles the original input string to test the functionality.

Volckaert et al. [30] present disjoint code layouts (DCL), a technique that complements multi-variant execution and DEP protection to immunize programs against control flow hijacking exploits, such as ROP and return-to-libc attacks. This technique relies on the execution and replication of multiple runtime variants of the same application under the control of a monitor, with the guarantee that no code segments in the variants' address spaces overlap. Lacking overlapping code segments, no code gadgets co-exist in the different variants to be executed during ROP attacks. Hence no ROP attack can alter the behavior of all variants in the same way. By monitoring the I/O of the variants and halting their execution when any divergent I/O operation is requested, the monitor effectively blocks any ROP attack before it can cause harm.

Zeng et al. [33] propose HeapTherapy, a solution against heap buffer overflows that integrates exploit detection, defense generation and overflow prevention in a single system. During program execution it conducts on-the-fly trace collection and exploit detection and initiates automated diagnosis upon detection to generate defenses in real-time. It can handle both over-write and over-read attacks. It employs techniques to identify vulnerable heap buffers based on the intrinsic characteristics of an exploit, as opposed to filtering out malicious inputs based on signatures.

3   Design

As previously introduced, ours is a two-phase approach. First, we leverage our previous work in [27] by creating a wrapper library that is inserted between the program and the original library code. The wrapper can identify and report each call and its arguments before allowing it to continue to the originally intended function as well as perform some other action if properly configured (e.g., emulate it, ignore it, modify the arguments/return value, report an error, etc.). Figure 1 depicts a high level overview of the steps taken when an untrusted application calls a protected function.

In step (1), the application tries to call a function $foo()$ inside the original library. This call is intercepted and instead of the intended function, the secure wrapper version of it is executed, in step (2). Instrumented inside the wrapper, there is code that reports on the call and its arguments, which is first run before any other steps are taken (step 3). Then, the call continues normally (step 4).

In the second phase, the kernel intercepts the continued call after step (4). Here, we leverage our previous work in [29] by introducing a modified Linux kernel that leverages the Memory Management Unit (MMU) in order to separate the memory of a process into regions, based on the statically/dynamically linked libraries that a program uses. When an untrusted, userspace application issues a

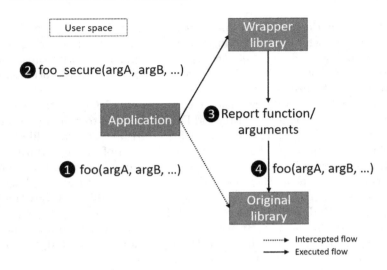

Fig. 1. Overview of the call sequence

call to a protected function, our custom kernel intercepts it, before allowing it to continue to the intended library. This is similar to the library wrapper presented before, with the main difference that it is better protected from interference from potentially malicious code, since the redirection is performed on the secure kernel side.

In order to intercept the library call, our system loops through all the memory regions of a running process and marks all the executable ones (e.g *.text*/code region) as non-executable. These regions are where the actual executable code of the program or of a shared object (external library) is found. At each point in time, only the currently executing region remains executable, while all the others are non-executable. When the flow of execution is transferred to a different region, a page fault is caused since all the functions that are there are located in non-executable memory. This intentional page fault allows us to intercept all the calls to the libraries, analyze them and possibly take some other form of action before handling the fault and continuing execution. Next, the currently executable region is marked as non-executable and this whole procedure is repeated from the beginning. Figure 2 shows this sequence of events.

4   Implementation

Our technique aims to monitor calls to external functions inside a protected library, both on the user as well as the kernel side. On the user side, we create the wrapper by extracting all the relevant functions from an instrumented library (e.g., OpenSSL) and adding code that, before calling the originally intended function, verifies that the wrapper indeed captured the call and that we operate from within it. We, then, visualize the interception by producing a report

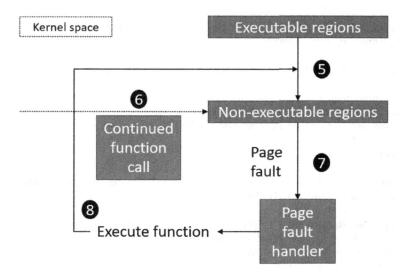

Fig. 2. Page fault sequence

that displays text-based information about the call (e.g., name of the function, parameters, etc.). This way we can provide a forensic trail to identify the functions executed. For example, when starting an OpenSSL server, an initialization phase takes place, where we can see information about the sequence of function calls along with their arguments (Fig. 3) and pinpoint where a potential vulnerability is triggered (e.g., CVE-2016–7054 [11,12]). After reporting the interception, the flow progresses to the original path and onward to the next phase of the implementation.

On the kernel side, we go through the list of processes that the kernel has in store and for each process identify the regions of contiguous virtual memory (Virtual Memory Areas - VMA) that are executable and mark them as non-executable (Fig. 2 (5)) by changing their access rights. After this point, when a process tries to execute a function from a library, it will land on an address in a non-executable area (Fig. 2 (6)), which will result in a page fault. Before the system handles the fault, we interject our customized code in order to monitor the call and report on its occurrence. Next, we mark the previous memory area as non-executable and the current one as executable as long as they are different, in order to adhere to the library-level granularity of our mechanism.

Let's consider an example where an instance of the NGINX HTTP server is running. From the excerpt of the output of our approach in Fig. 4, we can distinguish both cases where the current executable/library is both different and the same compared to the previous one. We can see that in lines 5–9 the flow of execution is inside the main executable. In line 6 we can see that when the fault occurs, the VMA is non-executable ($r - -p$). Continuing, we mark the current VMA as executable in line 7 ($r - xp$, x indicates whether the VMA is

....

Intercepted call to function CRYPTO_strdup ← Allocate memory for **s_server** app
String parameter: apps/s_server.c.

....

Intercepted call to function BIO_new_file ← Read private key file
String parameter 1: cert.key
String parameter 2: r

....

Intercepted call to function BIO_new_file ← Read certificate file
String parameter 1: cert.crt
String parameter 2: r

....

Intercepted call to function EVP_add_cipher ← Push ciphers to cipher stack
Intercepted call to function EVP_aes_256_ccm

....

Intercepted call to function EVP_md5 ← Push digests to digest stack
Intercepted call to function EVP_add_digest
Intercepted call to function OBJ_NAME_add
String parameter 1: ssl3-md5
String parameter 2: MD5

....

Intercepted call to function OBJ_nid2sn
Intercepted call to function EVP_get_cipherbyname
String parameter: DES-EDE3-CBC

....

Fig. 3. Excerpt from our user-side wrapper

executable or not). Since previously (lines 1–4) the flow was inside a different library (*libpthread*), that library is now marked as non-executable (line 8). However, in the next iteration (lines 10–13), the VMA doesn't change, so it remains executable as before (lines 11 and 12, $r - xp$).

Applications

Our monitoring platform can be applied in several real-life scenarios and is addressed to a diverse set of interested parties. However, it is not for the everyday user, but rather for security experts/system administrators/students in the information security domain.

Under our scheme, invoked functions can be intercepted in a controlled manner. When an attacker tries to manipulate a library, the malicious efforts will be made public and the user will be able to identify the attempt to exploit the vulnerability.

In the case of a library that requires heavy resources from the host system, the administrator may wish to better understand how the library behaves and what it asks from the system.

In the case of misuse of a critical component in a secure infrastructure that leads to an attack that jeopardizes the system, our framework can be used as

```
 1  [88.812529]  ===[2578] start __do_page_fault 7f358be3e890===
 2  [88.812531]  7f358be38000-7f358be50000 r-xp /lib/x86_64-linux-gnu/libpthread-2.23.so
 3  [88.812539]  7f358be38000-7f358be50000 r-xp /lib/x86_64-linux-gnu/libpthread-2.23.so
 4  [88.812540]  ===[2578] end__do_page_fault 7f358be3e890===
 5  [88.812556]  ===[2578] start __do_page_fault 41d2d0===
 6  [88.812558]  400000-495000 r--p /usr/local/nginx/sbin/nginx
 7  [88.812561]  400000-495000 r-xp /usr/local/nginx/sbin/nginx
 8  [88.812564]  7f358be38000-7f358be50000 r--p /lib/x86_64-linux-gnu/libpthread-2.23.so
 9  [88.812568]  ===[2578] end__do_page_fault 41d2d0===
10  [88.812579]  ===[2578] start __do_page_fault 41ea5e===
11  [88.812580]  400000-495000 r-xp /usr/local/nginx/sbin/nginx
12  [88.812584]  400000-495000 r-xp /usr/local/nginx/sbin/nginx
13  [88.812585]  ===[2578] end__do_page_fault 41ea5e===
```

Fig. 4. Custom kernel output

a logging mechanism. The inner workings of a protected library will be traced, which will follow the flow of execution of functions held within the library. Forensic actions (after the fact) can, then, be taken to analyze in a more detailed view the events that led to the compromise and identify the culprits responsible.

Furthermore, our monitoring platform can be leveraged in black-box testing applications. Typically when testing in black-box mode, we are not concerned with how a software system works internally. Testing is based on providing some input to the system and observing the output it produces. However, if testing is performed at the overall system level, there is little room for identifying how a specific program behaves. What is a program's interaction with its libraries? What is its interaction with the system resources? Does it read/write from/to a file? Does it open sensitive files (e.g., /etc/passwd)? Does it communicate with a remote end through a socket? We provide answers to these and similar questions by performing black box testing at a lower level, closer to the execution of an application by monitoring its interaction with the underlying system/OS. To demonstrate the applicability of our approach, we used our platform to produce two internal reports, at TU Braunschweig [21,28], which analyze the structure of the Sophos anti-virus product used by our University. The reports highlight potential weaknesses such as the use of *http* for the download of updates. TU Braunschweig (TUBS) has an agreement with Sophos to be supplied with their antivirus product (and updates) to the TUBS academic community. As part of this effort, TUBS has set up a local repository to distribute Sophos software and updates. The repository is accessible over *http* from both inside and outside the TUBS network.

In [21], we demonstrate that since the connection is over *http* and not *https* (i.e. not private), when we trace calls to internal functions we can produce an output of the arguments used. From that trace we see that the local computer connects to *antivirus.tu-bs.de* (whose canonical name is *rznbd3.rz.tu-bs.de*) and then selects *Basic Authorization* which consists of sending a (username, password) pair encoded in BASE64 format. This means that the authorization information is not encrypted but merely encoded using a well known function, which allows us to decode the string giving us the username and password in clear text.

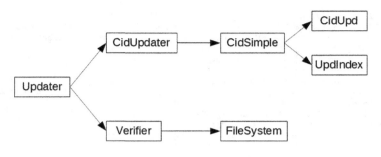

Fig. 5. Overall sequence

In [28], by submitting the credentials identified before, we can download the entire TUBS antivirus website and mirror it locally, in order to set up a fake server from where the user can download fake files customized by us. By leveraging our platform, we identify the flow of execution when the update procedure starts. Figure 5 depicts the overall sequence, while Fig. 6 shows the flow of execution within each module. Furthermore, we are able to modify several key files that we have identified, bypass the signature verification step and perform an unauthorized action (e.g., create a file), which under normal circumstances we should not be able to do.

Additionally, as we are a teaching institution, we have included our monitoring platform in the "Software Exploration/Modification" seminar where students have the opportunity to utilize it in order to explore a software system based on the library calls it performs, identify how it behaves when an attack is underway and take steps to mitigate the attack.

5   Training Scenarios

In this section, we present two scenarios that are included as exercises in a seminar program at TU Braunschweig. These scenarios can, nevertheless, be applied to different domains in the context of training and evaluating trainees on their actions and response when an attack is performed. The first scenario ("Software Exploration") represents the beginner-level course of the seminar, while the second one ("Run-time analysis and modification") corresponds to the more advanced course.

5.1   Software Exploration

In the first scenario, a user that is trained on using our system must observe the occurrence, the number and the sequence of calls and try to identify if and when an attack happens. In this case, a vulnerability of an application is exploited to affect the underlying system. We use a vulnerable version of NGINX HTTP server, where a buffer overflow (CVE-2013–2028 [8]) is triggered under

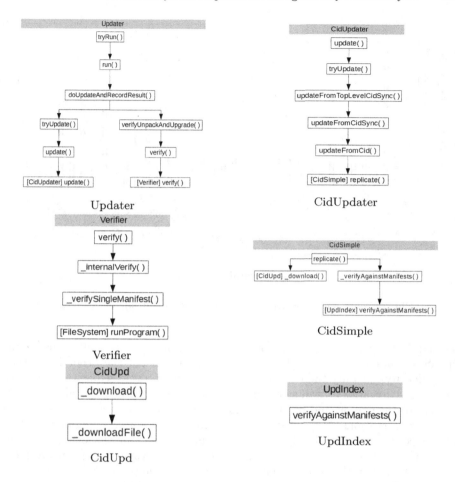

Fig. 6. Flow of execution when updating Sophos

specific circumstances to launch a Denial-of-Service (DoS)/arbitrary code execution attack, in order to compromise the application. By using our monitoring framework to observe the calls the server issues to external library functions (and the subsequent internal library calls), the trainee can better understand the behavior of the attack and provide a signature of the way it works. Hence, they can recognize it when it happens and report it.

Although the specific vulnerability was addressed in versions later than 1.4.0, the trainee can use our approach to examine the chain of calls that NGINX makes to its external libraries (as well as the internal library calls), which result in a crash or remote shell when the vulnerability is exploited.

As the exploitation unfolds, our platform updates two files with the output results of both user- (similarly to Fig. 3) and kernel-side (similarly to Fig. 4) mechanisms. At first, the trainee must monitor the contents of both files. On

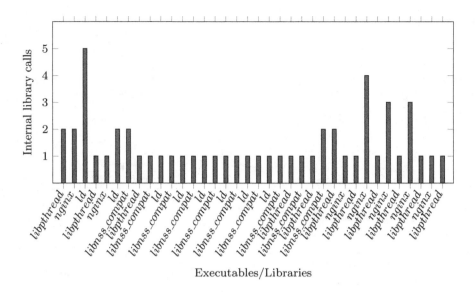

Fig. 7. Sequence of libraries and number of calls inside each library

one hand they are expected to identify which functions are called inside the
OpenSSL library and what these functions perform. On the other hand they
must identify not only the occurrence, but a characteristic sequence of calls to
executables/libraries as well as the number of consecutive internal calls that correspond to the exploit and produce a trail of it (similarly to Fig. 7). Next, based
on their observations, they must develop a small program in a language of their
preference that monitors the files as they are updated by our platform and whenever it intercepts the characteristic signature from the previous steps, it produces
an alarm to notify the trainee that an attack was attempted. Consequently, the
next time that the trainee will run the scenario, they will be expected to report
the alarm to the trainer.

5.2   Run-Time Analysis and Modification

After the initial introduction to software exploration, the trainee is given the
opportunity to continue to the more advanced level. Initially, they are presented
with a piece of software and allowed to install it, read available documentation
and run some examples of its use. Then the trainee is shown the block diagram
of the program and related libraries and is asked to create a call graph showing
the control flow paths between elements of the system. Further analysis may
be used to identify items of interest (IoI) in the design (e.g., the transfer of an
encryption key to a routine, the creation of a network connection, access to a
file, etc.). For each identified IoI, a decision needs to be made as to whether it
is worth monitoring and if so to which extent (just the invocation of a function,
examination of one or more of its arguments, and so on).

After running the program a couple of times under our framework to collect invocation data and possibly confirm some of the initial hypotheses related to the design of the program, the trainee can start the process of active interference in the execution of the program by modifying arguments to functions, or return values etc. Further runs of the program will demonstrate the impact of the modifications, and hopefully shed light to its internal design.

Finally, the trainee must produce a report with their findings, on which they are evaluated at the end of the scenario.

6 Conclusion

In this paper, we present a monitoring framework that uses two techniques based on our previous work: (a) a library wrapper that is inserted between a program and the original library code and (b) a kernel modification that intercepts all calls to libraries/executables. This framework can be applied to multiple real-life scenarios in order to monitor/alter the execution of a program and report any suspicious/malicious activity. We present two training exercises where we give the trainee the opportunity to explore how a program behaves and modify its execution when under attack.

Acknowledgments. This work is supported by the European Commission through the following H2020 projects: THREAT-ARREST under Grant Agreement No. 786890 and CONCORDIA under Grant Agreement No. 830927.

References

1. Abadi, M., Budiu, M., Erlingsson, U., Ligatti, J.: Control-flow integrity. In: Proceedings of the 12th ACM Conference on Computer and Communications Security, CCS 2005, pp. 340–353. ACM, New York (2005). https://doi.org/10.1145/1102120. 1102165. http://doi.acm.org/10.1145/1102120.1102165
2. Andersen, S., Abella, V.: Data Execution Prevention (2004). https://technet. microsoft.com/en-us/library/bb457155.aspx
3. Bittau, A., Belay, A., Mashtizadeh, A., Mazières, D., Boneh, D.: Hacking blind. In: 2014 IEEE Symposium on Security and Privacy, pp. 227–242, May 2014. https:// doi.org/10.1109/SP.2014.22
4. Bletsch, T., Jiang, X., Freeh, V.W., Liang, Z.: Jump-oriented programming: a new class of code-reuse attack. In: Proceedings of the 6th ACM Symposium on Information, Computer and Communications Security, ASIACCS 2011, pp. 30– 40. ACM, New York (2011). https://doi.org/10.1145/1966913.1966919. http://doi. acm.org/10.1145/1966913.1966919
5. Checkoway, S., Davi, L., Dmitrienko, A., Sadeghi, A.R., Shacham, H., Winandy, M.: Return-oriented programming without returns. In: Proceedings of the 17th ACM Conference on Computer and Communications Security, CCS 2010, pp. 559– 572. ACM, New York (2010). https://doi.org/10.1145/1866307.1866370. http:// doi.acm.org/10.1145/1866307.1866370

6. Chen, L.H., Hsu, F.H., Hwang, Y., Su, M.C., Ku, W.S., Chang, C.H.: Armory: an automatic security testing tool for buffer overflow defect detection. Comput. Electr. Eng. **39**(7), 2233–2242 (2013). https://doi.org/10.1016/j.compeleceng.2012.07.005

7. Cheng, Y., Zhou, Z., Miao, Y., Ding, X., Deng, H.R.: ROPecker: a generic and practical approach for defending against ROP attacks. In: Symposium on Network and Distributed System Security (NDSS) (2014)

8. Common Vulnerabilities and Exposures: CVE-2013-2028, February 2013. https://www.cvedetails.com/cve/CVE-2013-2028/

9. Cowan, C., et al.: StackGuard: automatic adaptive detection and prevention of buffer-overflow attacks. In: Proceedings of the 7th Conference on USENIX Security Symposium - Volume 7, SSYM 1998, p. 5. USENIX Association, Berkeley (1998). http://dl.acm.org/citation.cfm?id=1267549.1267554

10. Crane, S., Larsen, P., Brunthaler, S., Franz, M.: Booby trapping software. In: Proceedings of the 2013 Workshop on New Security Paradigms Workshop, NSPW 2013, pp. 95–106. ACM, New York (2013). https://doi.org/10.1145/2535813.2535824

11. CVE-2016-7054: Chacha20/poly1305 heap-buffer-overflow (2016). https://www.openssl.org/news/secadv/20161110.txt

12. CVE-2016-7054: Chacha20/poly1305 heap-buffer-overflow (2016). https://cve.mitre.org/cgi-bin/cvename.cgi?name=CVE-2016-7054

13. Designer, S.: Getting around non-executable stack (and fix) (1997). http://seclists.org/bugtraq/1997/Aug/63

14. Fratric, I.: ROPGuard: runtime prevention of return-oriented programming attacks (2012). http://www.ieee.hr/_download/repository/Ivan_Fratric.pdf

15. Hamad, M., Hammadeh, Z.A.H., Saidi, S., Prevelakis, V., Ernst, R.: Prediction of abnormal temporal behavior in real-time systems. In: The 33rd ACM/SIGAPP Symposium On Applied Computing (SAC 2018) (2018). https://dl.acm.org/citation.cfm?id=3167172

16. Hiroaki, E.: ProPolice: GCC extension for protecting applications from stack-smashing attacks, January 2003

17. Lu, S., Seo, M., Lysecky, R.: Timing-based anomaly detection in embedded systems. In: 20th Asia and South Pacific Design Automation Conference, ASP-DAC 2015, January 2015. https://doi.org/10.1109/ASPDAC.2015.7059110

18. Pappas, V., Polychronakis, M., Keromytis, A.D.: Transparent ROP exploit mitigation using indirect branch tracing. In: Proceedings of the 22Nd USENIX Conference on Security, SEC 2013, pp. 447–462. USENIX Association, Berkeley (2013). http://dl.acm.org/citation.cfm?id=2534766.2534805

19. PaX, T.: Address Space Layout Randomization (2001). https://pax.grsecurity.net/docs/aslr.txt

20. Pincus, J., Baker, B.: Beyond stack smashing: recent advances in exploiting buffer overruns. IEEE Secur. Privacy **2**(4), 20–27 (2004). https://doi.org/10.1109/MSP.2004.36

21. Prevelakis, V.: Use of HTTP protocol by the TU-BS Sophos Repository. Technical report, TU Braunschweig (2017)

22. Roemer, R., Buchanan, E., Shacham, H., Savage, S.: Return-oriented programming: systems, languages, and applications. ACM Trans. Inf. Syst. Secur. **15**(1), 2:1–2:34 (2012). https://doi.org/10.1145/2133375.2133377. http://doi.acm.org/10.1145/2133375.2133377

23. Shacham, H.: The geometry of innocent flesh on the bone: return-into-libc without function calls (on the x86). In: Proceedings of the 14th ACM Conference on Computer and Communications Security, CCS 2007, pp. 552–561. ACM, New York (2007). https://doi.org/10.1145/1315245.1315313. http://doi.acm.org/10.1145/1315245.1315313

24. Shacham, H., Page, M., Pfaff, B., Goh, E.J., Modadugu, N., Boneh, D.: On the effectiveness of address-space randomization. In: Proceedings of the 11th ACM Conference on Computer and Communications Security, CCS 2004, pp. 298–307. ACM, New York (2004). https://doi.org/10.1145/1030083.1030124. http://doi.acm.org/10.1145/1030083.1030124

25. Snow, K.Z., Monrose, F., Davi, L., Dmitrienko, A., Liebchen, C., Sadeghi, A.R.: Just-in-time code reuse: on the effectiveness of fine-grained address space layout randomization. In: Proceedings of the 2013 IEEE Symposium on Security and Privacy, SP 2013, pp. 574–588. IEEE Computer Society, Washington, DC (2013). https://doi.org/10.1109/SP.2013.45. http://dx.doi.org/10.1109/SP.2013.45

26. Tian, D., Xiong, X., Hu, C., Liu, P.: Defeating buffer overflow attacks viavirtualization. Comput. Electr. Eng. **40**(6), 1940–1950 (2014). http://dx.doi.org/10.1016/j.compeleceng.2013.11.032. http://www.sciencedirect.com/science/article/pii/S0045790613003145

27. Tsantekidis, M., Prevelakis, V.: Library-level policy enforcement. In: SECURWARE 2017, The Eleventh International Conference on Emerging Security Information, Systems and Technologies. Rome, Italy (2017). http://www.thinkmind.org/index.php?view=article&articleid=securware_2017_2_20_30034

28. Tsantekidis, M., Prevelakis, V.: Sophos bogus update report. Technical report, TU Braunschweig (2017)

29. Tsantekidis, M., Prevelakis, V.: Efficient Monitoring of Library Call Invocation. In: Sixth International Conference on Internet of Things: Systems, Management and Security (IOTSMS). pp. 387–392. Granada, Spain (2019). DOI: 10.1109/IOTSMS48152.2019.8939203

30. Volckaert, S., Coppens, B., Sutter, B.D.: Cloning your gadgets: complete rop attack immunity with multi-variant execution. IEEE Trans. Dependable Secure Comput. **13**(4), 437–450 (2016). https://doi.org/10.1109/TDSC.2015.2411254

31. Wagle, P., Cowan, C.: Stackguard: simple stack smash protection for GCC. In: Proceedings of the GCC Developers Summit, pp. 243–255 (2003)

32. i386 WX, O.: (2003). http://marc.info/?l=openbsd-misc&m=105056000801065

33. Zeng, Q., Zhao, M., Liu, P.: HeapTherapy: an efficient end-to-end solution against heap buffer overflows. In: 2015 45th Annual IEEE/IFIP International Conference on Dependable Systems and Networks, pp. 485–496, June 2015. https://doi.org/10.1109/DSN.2015.54

Security Policies

A Pattern–Driven Adaptation in IoT Orchestrations to Guarantee SPDI Properties

Papoutsakis Manos[1,2]([⊠]) [ID], Fysarakis Konstantinos[3] [ID],
Michalodimitrakis Emmanouil[1] [ID], Lakka Eftychia[1] [ID], Petroulakis Nikolaos[1] [ID],
Spanoudakis George[2,3] [ID], and Ioannidis Sotiris[1] [ID]

[1] Institute of Computer Science, Foundation for Research and Technology – Hellas,
Heraklion, Greece
{paputsak,manmix,elakka,npetro,sotiris}@ics.forth.gr
[2] Department of Computer Science, City University of London, London, UK
{Emmanouil.Papoutsakis,g.e.spanoudakis}@city.ac.uk
[3] Sphynx Technology Solutions AG, Zug, Switzerland
{fysarakis,spanoudakis}@sphynx.ch

Abstract. The orchestration of heterogeneous IoT devices to enable the provision of IoT applications and services poses numerous challenges, especially in contexts where end-to-end security and privacy guarantees are needed. To tackle these challenges, this paper presents a pattern–driven approach for interacting with IoT systems, whereby the required properties are guaranteed. Patterns are leveraged to represent the relationship between security, privacy, dependability and interoperability (SPDI) properties of specific smart objects and corresponding properties of orchestrations that include said objects. In this way, patterns allow the verification that certain SPDI properties hold for an IoT orchestration, while also enabling the adaptation of IoT orchestrations in ways that allow the given properties to hold.

Keywords: Security patterns · IoT orchestrations · SPDI properties · Adaptation · Node–RED · Drools rule engine

1 Introduction

The term "Internet-of-Things" (IoT) has been introduced by the expansion of the Internet from the usual devices such as desktop pc, laptops etc, to different machines and smart objects, in an effort to describe the new environment which represents new ways of working, interacting entertainment and living by enabling the creation of new applications [1]. Admittedly, there are numerous challenges of IoT orchestrations due to their heterogeneity of the IoT devices including end-to-end security and privacy and that is evident from various studies in the field [2–4].

© Springer Nature Switzerland AG 2020
G. Hatzivasilis and S. Ioannidis (Eds.): MSTEC 2020, LNCS 12512, pp. 143–156, 2020.
https://doi.org/10.1007/978-3-030-62433-0_9

Motivated by the above, this paper presents a pattern driven approach for composing IoT systems where security properties are guaranteed. Security patterns are intended to capture security expertise in the form of worked solutions to recurring problems. Consequently the security patterns provide the developers a comprehensive tool that enables them to utilise security concepts without having to be a security professional [5].

The role of patterns into our approach is to represent the relationship between Security, Privacy, Dependability, and Interoperability (SPDI) properties of specific smart objects and corresponding properties of orchestrations that include said objects. The adoption of patterns allows for (i) the verification that a smart object orchestration satisfies certain SPDI properties, and (ii) the generation (and adaptation) of orchestrations in ways that are guaranteed to satisfy required SPDI properties. The proposed approach is based on the development and the architecture that is carried out in SEMIoTICS[1], a horizon 2020 project.

The remainder of this paper is organized as follows. In Sect. 2 an overview of related work is presented. Section 3 presents a background to the underlying technologies and concepts used. Section 4 outlines the architecture of our approach. In Sect. 5 we present an implementation of our approach where the mechanisms of an IoT orchestration adaptation are detailed. Finally, Sect. 6 provides concluding remarks.

2   Related Work

It is common knowledge that the IoT is consisted by physical or virtual object/devices (Things), equipped with sensing, accumulating and transferring data over the internet automatically. In parallel, billions of sensors and actuators have been already deployed and should be combined into a number of domain-specific platforms. Taking to account said issues, a widespread interest of both industry and academy was increased to overcome several challenges such as the dynamicity, scalability, heterogeneity and end-to-end security and privacy requirements of such environments. This implies that the system should have the ability to adapt (semi)-itself in order to continue offering the above requirements. Dynamic proactive adaptation in particular is demanded to provide adjustments at runtime [6].

The huge number of dimensions over which such a big arena spans, makes the investigation of the adaptation domain in IoT very hard and subject to entropy [7]. Thus, the first attempts that are presented in this section, are focused on the description of IoT service compositions [8–10] taking to account the energy consumption of the involved IoT devices; the latter pays attention to Quality of Service (QoS) properties reducing the services search space and the composition time. Although these works are interesting, none of them takes into consideration possible security properties of the individual IoT services or the whole composition.

---

[1] https://www.semiotics-project.eu/.

Additionally, there is the work of [11], in which a contExt Aware web Service dEscription Language (wEASEL) is introduced. wEASEL is an abstract service model to represent services and user tasks in Ambient Assisted Living[2] (AAL) environments. Attention is paid to data-ow and context-ow constraints for the service composition but the authors do not mention any security properties. A work that includes security aspects is that of [12]. BPMN 2.0[3] is used for the description of the service choreographies that the built platform can synthesize and execute. Regarding the security aspect, the enforcement of security properties is exclusively done by the existing communication protocols since the security filter component is able to filter these protocols and keep only those that conform to the specified security requirements.

Finally, [13] provide a mechanism that manages IoT choreographies at runtime dynamically. According to their approach IoT service compositions are described by templates called Recipes, which consist of Ingredients and their Interactions. Furthermore, there are more requirements described by Offering Selection Rules (OSRs) that make the reconfiguration of the system possible during runtime. The authors' service composition approach is semi-automated to avoid the complexity of the semantic models and the inefficiency of the reasoner due to the large number of available devices and services. We consider this approach closer to the way we envision a pattern language. Their way of IoT representation with the notions of Ingredients and Interactions, and the fact that the OSRs allow for requirement description inspired the creation of the language described in the next section.

3 Background

The core of our approach is pattern based reasoning that can deliver verification of SPDI properties or adaptation of IoT orchestrations in a way that guarantees such properties. In the next subsections innovative building blocks of the pattern based reasoning concept are presented.

3.1 Pattern Language

The proposed approach infers the development of a framework for managing IoT applications based on patterns. A language for specifying the components that constitute such applications along with their interfaces and interactions has been created. Moreover, the said language is able to encode various functional and non-functional properties of such components and their orchestrations. The corresponding model was derived using the Eclipse Modeling Framework[4] (EMF), visualizing the Ecore part of the EMF metamodel, which contains the information about the defined classes. The defined model in conjunction with patterns

---

[2] http://www.aal-europe.eu//.
[3] http://www.bpmn.org/.
[4] https://www.eclipse.org/modeling/emf/.

allows for the verification of SPDI patterns in IoT applications and possibly enables different adaptation actions.

The main classes of the model, which are used in the pattern specification, include Placeholders, Orchestrations, OrchestrationActivities and Properties. An orchestration of activities may be of different types depending on the order in which the different activities involved in it must be executed. As a result, an orchestration can be defined as Sequence, Merge, Choice or Split. An orchestration involves OrchestrationActivities. The implementation of an activity in an IoT application orchestration may be provided by: i) a software component, ii) a software service, iii) a network component, iv) an IoT sensor, v) an IoT actuator or vi) an IoT gateway. Orchestrations and OrchestrationActivities are grouped under the general concept (class) of a Placeholder. Placeholders may be characterized by SPDI properties. A Property can be verified at runtime, through the verification process, which can be done through monitoring, testing, a certificate or via a pattern. The first two cases require the existence of a monitoring service or a testing tool allows the verification of the SPDI property of a placeholder activity. The third case refers to a service allowing the verification of validity of certificates verifying that a placeholder satisfies a certain property. Thus, while in the case of a pattern, the verification points to a specific pattern rule, in all the other cases the verification must point to the interface of a monitoring tool, testing service or certificate repository. Moving on, a category is assigned to each Property. A category can refer to confidentiality, integrity, availability (covering the Security property), privacy, dependability, interoperability or even QoS. In this way a classification of the properties is achieved.

Finally, the set of all the SPDI properties that are inferred for the different placeholders of an orchestration by a pattern are aggregated into a PropertyPlan object. A detailed representation of the pattern language and model is presented in our previous work [14].

3.2   Pattern Definition

SPDI patterns encode proven dependencies between SPDI properties of individual placeholders implementing activities in IoT applications orchestrations (i.e. activity-level SPDI properties) and SPDI properties of these orchestrations (i.e. workflow-level SPDI properties). The specification of an SPDI pattern consists of the following parts:

1. **Activity Properties (AP)** part, which defines the SPDI properties required of the activity placeholders present in the workflow of the pattern, to allow for the guarantee of the OP properties detailed in the corresponding part of the pattern.
2. **Orchestration (ORCH)** part, which defines the abstract form of the orchestration that the pattern applies to.
3. **Conditions** part, which defines the functional requirements, the states or the constraints that a system should define, or what a system must do, and how it reacts on specific inputs or situations.

4. **Orchestration Properties (OP)** part, which defines the SPDI properties that the pattern guarantees for the orchestration that is specified in its ORCH part.

The semantic interpretation of an SPDI pattern, as described above, is that if the AP properties that have been specified for the activity placeholders, part of the orchestration of the pattern, and the Conditions of the pattern hold (verified as True), then the specified OP property also holds for the whole ORCH. Formally, this can be expressed as:

$$APs \wedge ORCH \wedge Conditions \models OP \tag{1}$$

where APs are materialized using the Property class described above. Each Property is uniquely identified by its name, while the attribute PropertySubject the orchestration component for which the property verifiable. ORCH is an Orchestration object including Placeholders. Finally, OP is an orchestration-wide Property object.

3.3 Pattern Rule

Towards the automated processing of the SPDI patterns, the latter are expressed as Drools [15] business production rules, and the associated rule engine. A Drools production rule has the following generic structure:

```
rulename
    <attributes>*
when
    <conditional element>*
then
    <action>*
end
```

In the *when* part of the rule the ORCH part of the pattern, the conditions regarding the inputs and outputs of orchestration placeholders, and the OP property guaranteed by the pattern for the specific ORCH are described. Additionally, in the *then* part, the AP properties are described, which will guarantee the OP property, if they are satisfied by the orchestration placeholders. The above can be expressed formally as:

$$ORCH \wedge Conditions \wedge OP \Rightarrow APi \quad (i = 1, ..., n) \tag{2}$$

where APi are the AP properties required by the orchestration placeholders of the SPDI pattern. As we can see, this is the opposite of the dependency relation proven in the equation (1) defined above. Thus, this encoding allows the inference of the APi properties which, if satisfied, guarantee the satisfaction of the ORCH-level SPDI property of it, as encoded in the pattern. In this way, Drools Rules can be used to allow the automated design or adaptation of the ORCH in order to preserve the ORCH-level SPDI property defined in the pattern.

4   Architecture and Core Building Blocks

In this section we describe the components that constitute our architecture which are depicted in Fig. 1 The main build blocks are (i) Node–RED, (ii) Pattern Orchestrator and (iii) Pattern Engine instances. The interaction between these blocks is achieved through Representational State Transfer Application Program Interface (REST API).

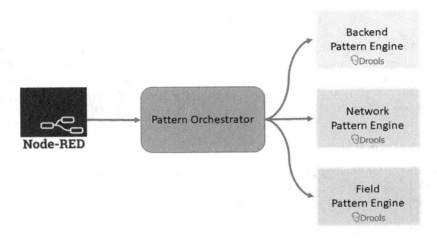

Fig. 1. Architecture

4.1   Node–RED

Node–RED[5] is a tool that helps programmers to visually create their applications, inspired by the flow-based programming paradigm [16]. The underlying framework is NodeJS[6] which enables the programmer to develop an IoT system with concepts such as nodes and flows. A node reflects a service offered by the system. When nodes are used in cooperation, constitute a flow that is able to perform a task and provide functionalities to the system while creating most of the code automatically.

Due to the fact that Node–RED is open source with an active community, new nodes with up-to-date technologies are constantly available, thus making it feasible to complete a variety of tasks like storing values to database, encrypting traffic between nodes, establish communication using the Message Queuing Telemetry Transport[7] (MQTT) protocol and more.

---

[5] https://nodered.org/.
[6] https://nodejs.org/en/.
[7] https://mqtt.org/.

4.2   Pattern Orchestrator

The Pattern Orchestrator module features an underlying semantic reasoner able to understand the internal components of IoT Service orchestrations expressed using the pattern language, received from the Node–RED module and transform them into architectural patterns. The Pattern Orchestrator is then responsible to pass said patterns to the corresponding Pattern Engines (as defined in the Backend, Network, and Field layers), after translating them to a machine-processable format (in Drools), selecting for each of them the subset of patterns that refer to components under their control (e.g. passing Network-specific patterns to the Pattern Engine present in the Software Defined Network (SDN) controller). Through the above functions, the module achieves automated configuration, coordination, and management of the patterns across different layers and service orchestrations.

4.3   Pattern Engine

The Pattern Engine (PE) module enables the capability to insert, modify, execute and retract patterns at design or at run-time. PE is based on a rule engine which is able to express design patterns as production rules. Enabling reasoning, driven by production rules, appeared to be an efficient way to represent patterns. For that reason, a rule engine is required to support backward and forward chaining inference and verification. Drools rule engine [17] appeared to be a suitable solution to support design patterns by applying and extending the Rete algorithm [18] and later the Phreak algorithm [19]. Finally, the PE integrates different sub-components required by the rule engine such as the knowledge base, the core engine and the compiler.

The Drools Engine in the PE is not running continuously. On the contrary, it is started only when needed, i.e. when a Fact or a Rule is added/updated/removed. To prevent the loss of the facts when the Drools Engine stops, they are also saved in the memory of the PE. Additionally they are stored locally in the file system where the PE is installed for debugging purposes. The PE also has the Rules stored locally and loads them every time the engine is required to run. These Rules may be pre-installed, but they can also be added during run-time through the corresponding endpoint "insertRule". Facts are inserted from the Pattern Orchestrator by using the "addFact" endpoint as well as from internal monitoring mechanism.

5   Implementation Details

We have described in previous work [21] the way an SPDI property is verified in orchestration-level, using our pattern-driven approach. In this section, we focus on describing the mechanisms that will be engaged in the form of adaptation actions, when a given SPDI property referring to an orchestration, does not hold. The result of the said adaptation actions is an updated orchestration, that is communicated back to Node–RED in order to be deployed again. This updated version of orchestration may differ from the original in terms of adding new components and/or replacing others. The said adaptation actions are driven by a specific pattern, chosen from the literature and in our case it is the Encrypted Storage Pattern [20]. The next two sub-sections describe in detail the chosen pattern and the information flow among the components of our architecture.

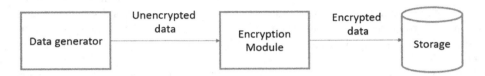

Fig. 2. Encrypted storage pattern

Encrypted Storage Pattern: This pattern constitutes a second layer line of defense against the theft of data on systems. Even if the data is stolen, the most sensitive data will remain safe, since it cannot be decrypted.

Well-known examples of the Encrypted Storage Pattern usage include: a) the UNIX password file that hashes each user's password and stores only the hashed form and b) web sites that use encryption to protect the most sensitive data that are stored on the website server.

An implementation of the pattern is depicted in Fig. 2. As it can be seen, the specific implementation imposes the existence of an encryption module between the data generator and the storage unit. Our implementation is based on this pattern, therefore the absence of the said module will trigger adaptation actions that will result in the addition of the encryption module where it is needed.

Information Flow: Node–RED is used to describe the functionality of the IoT system which will later on will be distributed to the Pattern Orchestrator in a translated version of the flow. This translation will encode the flow from Node–RED to pattern language thus enabling the Pattern Orchestrator to create a Drools fact, i.e. an instance of the corresponding Java class of the IoT application model, for every orchestration activity, control flow operation or property. For a more detailed view regarding the creation of a Drools Fact inside Pattern Orchestrator please refer to our previous work [21,22].

As soon as the Pattern Orchestrator receives the translated flow, has to decide based on each of the orchestration components involved, which Pattern Engine will be the recipient of the said components. Not all components may arrive at the same Pattern Engine as it may refer to different layers e.g. components that represent services will be forward to the Pattern Engine residing at the Backend Layer, whereas components that represent field devices will be forwarded to the Pattern Engine residing at the Field Layer.

Upon arrival at the corresponding Pattern Engine, each orchestration component is inserted into knowledge session of Drools Engine as Drools facts. These Drools facts are used by Drools rules, which are fired when their conditions are met. A Pattern Engine equipped with the said rules, is capable to verify whether an SPDI property holds for a given orchestration. Additionally when such a property does not hold, appropriate rules can be used to trigger adaptation actions which will result to the satisfaction of the property.

The adaptation actions that are presented in the current implementation include the addition of a new component in the original orchestration, which corresponds to a new node in the Node–RED editor. The said addition means that new connections between the latter and the pre-existing nodes will be created. Node–RED exposes an API that allows such flow updates and in this particular case a PUT method request is used at the following URL: http://"nodeRedIP":"nodeRedPort"/flow/"ID". The updated flow is passed to the request body in JavaScript Object Notation[8] (JSON) format which represents a single flow configuration object in Node–RED. Upon successful consumption of the said request, the status code returned from Node–RED is 204 combined with the id of the new flow.

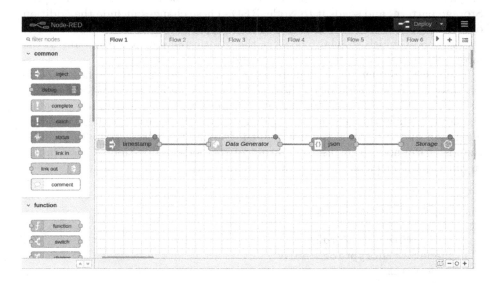

Fig. 3. Service orchestration depicted as Node–RED flow

The orchestration that has been used in the current implementation is depicted in Fig. 3, in the Node–RED editor. Its main components are a data generator and a storage unit where the data are driven. The former is depicted as a node named Data Generator, which makes an Hypertext Transfer Protocol

---

[8] https://www.json.org/json-en.html.

(HTTP) request whenever triggered by the timestamp node. The output of the Data Generator is essentially the response of the HTTP request, which is in JSON format and parsed by a simple JSON node.

The storage unit is represented by a node named Storage, which sends data to an InfluxDB, a time-series database, to be stored. The described orchestration along with the SPDI property (Encrypted Storage Property) to be verified, is translated in the pattern language and sent to Pattern Orchestrator. Having such a property hold for a certain orchestration component, it states that the said component stores data in an encrypted format. All the orchestration components and the desired SDPI property are sent to Pattern Engine and added to Drools working memory as Drools Facts.

Since no encryption takes place between the two main components of our orchestration, the corresponding adaptation Drools rule that will be triggered will respond that the Encrypted Storage Property is not satisfied and adaptation actions will be initiated.

The Pattern Engine will send a request to an appropriate API of the Pattern Orchestrator with the SPDI Property that is not satisfied. As soon as, the Pattern Orchestrator receives the said request, adapts the JSON representation of the original orchestration, based on the presented implementation of the Encrypted Storage pattern, and sends it to Node–RED. These changes include the addition of an EncryptionModule node along with the appropriate connections, in front of Storage node, which is able to encrypt the transferred message using any of the most well-known encryption algorithms and a provided secret key.

The code snippet below depicts what is added by Pattern Orchestrator to the JSON representation of the flow in particular the EncryptionModule node. As we can see, its id, name and type are defined and the z attribute represents the flow to which this new node is added. Moreover, we see that the encryption algorithm and the secret key are defined. Finally, the wires attribute includes the ids of the nodes that use the output of the node in question as their input. In our case, it includes the id of the Storage node.

```
{
    "id": "6757fce7.108a94",
    "type": "encrypt",
    "z": "99783291.272d2",
    "name": "EncryptionModule",
    "algorithm": "AES",
    "key": "semiotics",
    "x": 720,
    "y": 260,
    "wires": [
        [
            "eae7b2ac.b98fc"
        ]
    ]
}
```

The new, updated orchestration, after the adaptation actions, is depicted in the form of a flow inside the editor of Node–RED, in Fig. 4.

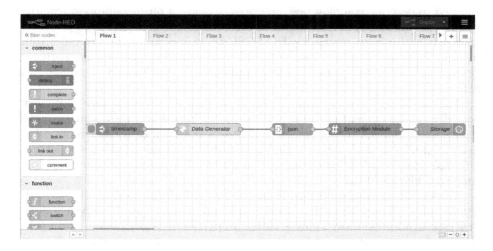

Fig. 4. Updated service orchestration depicted as Node–RED flow

Performance Measurements: As a preliminary implementation of the feasibility of the proposed approach, a virtual environment has been setup housing an instance of the Pattern Orchestrator, Node-RED and Influx-DB to simulate the cloud deployment. Additionally we chose to take our measurements twice based on the location of the Pattern Engine instance. In the first iteration the Pattern Engine was hosted in a different location from the rest of the components simulating that different components may reside in different providers/locations. On the other hand, in the second iteration the Pattern Engine was hosted in the same virtual environment with the rest of the involved components.

The results showed that when the components are distributed, that is when the Pattern Engine is separated from the other components, the required adaptation time was approximately 2,57 s. On the other hand when all the involved components were hosted in the same environment the required adaptation time was decreased to 1,02 s. As adaptation time we consider the amount of time measured from the realization of the security requirement by the Pattern Orchestrator, to the successful deployment of the updated flow by the Node-RED instance.

6   Comparison with Alternative Approaches

In this section we present other approaches to adapting a process-based application or a system and highlight the differences between these approaches and ours.

The authors in [23] propose a pattern-based approach for adapting process-based applications. They correlate Cloud patterns to green business process patterns and organize them within a classication. Green business process patterns are used to describe common best practices to adapt a business process towards a more eco-efcient one in an abstract manner. The main concept of the proposed approach is a business process model (TOSCA[9]) that is adapted based on certain criteria. They mention that although they used green business process patterns in this work other use-cases such as compliance or security may be applied as well.

Authors in [24] present a maintenance service delivery use case and show how hierarchical context rules tailor the workow. In that way they actually make use of adaptation patterns that are realized in the form of jBoss Drools rules. According to this work the proposed approach can be extended with a pattern catalogue that is able to capture event-based adaptation semantics for modeling languages like BPMN2.

The work presented by the previous two papers lacks any automation regarding the adaptation process thus needing manual intervention. Also even though their work can potentially apply security properties, it is not presented. In contrast, our work tackles the adaptation process in an automatic way such that, as soon as, the corresponding security requirement is inserted to the system the adaptation actions are triggered automatically.

In [25] a security adaptation Framework for wireless environments called Security Adaptation Reference Monitor (SARM) is proposed. The said Framework is based on the concept of adaptation security and autonomic system. However, this work addresses security issues related to a specific wireless network application under certain constraints, including performance or/and minimizing energy consumption. Our approach makes use of security patterns which potentially allows for tackling security issues regardless of the context of the application by creating new security patterns.

7   Conclusion

This work presented a pattern–driven approach able to rectify an IoT orchestration in a way that an SDPI property to hold. A proof of concept is presented including an exemplary IoT orchestration that is consisted of mainly two components, a data generator and a data storage. The SPDI property that needs to be enforced to this orchestration requires the addition of an encryption node between them, according to the Encrypted Storage pattern.

Currently, only a small number of patterns has been used for verification of SPDI properties and adaptation of IoT orchestrations. Our plans for the future are to incorporate even more patterns that will allow a wider range of adaptation actions that will enable the application of a plethora of SPDI properties.

---

[9] http://www.tosca-open.org/.

Acknowledgments. This work has received funding from the European Union's Horizon 2020 research and innovation programme under grant agreements No. 780315 (SEMIoTICS).

References

1. Miorandi, D., Sicari, S., De Pellegrini, F., Chlamtac, I.: Internet of things: vision, applications and research challenges. Ad Hoc Netw. **10**(7), 1497–1516 (2012)
2. Čolaković, A., Hadžialić, M.: Internet of Things (IoT): a review of enabling technologies, challenges, and open research issues. Comput. Networks **144**, 17–39 (2018)
3. Singh, S., Singh, N.: Internet of Things (IoT): security challenges, business opportunities & reference architecture for E-commerce. In: 2015 International Conference on Green Computing and Internet of Things (ICGCIoT), Noida, pp. 1577–1581. IEEE, (2015). https://doi.org/10.1109/ICGCIoT.2015.7380718
4. Xu, T., Wendt, J.B., Potkonjak, M.: Security of IoT systems: design challenges and opportunities. In: 2014 IEEE/ACM International Conference on Computer-Aided Design (ICCAD), San Jose, CA, pp. 417–423, IEEE (2014). https://doi.org/10.1109/ICCAD.2014.7001385
5. Kienzle, D.M., Elder, M.C.: Final Technical Report: Security Patterns for web Application Development. DARPA, Washington DC (2005)
6. Achtaich, A., Souissi, N., Mazo, R., Salinesi, C., Roudies, O.: Designing a framework for smart IoT adaptations. In: Belqasmi, F., Harroud, H., Agueh, M., Dssouli, R., Kamoun, F. (eds.) AFRICATEK 2017. LNICST, vol. 206, pp. 57–66. Springer, Cham (2018). https://doi.org/10.1007/978-3-319-67837-5_6
7. Arcelli, D.: Exploiting queuing networks to model and assess the performance of self-adaptive software systems: a survey. Procedia Comput. Sci. **170**, 498–505 (2020)
8. Baker, T., Asim, M., Tawfik, H., Aldawsari, B., Buyya, R.: An energy-aware service composition algorithm for multiple cloud-based IoT applications. J. Network Comput. Appl. **89**, 96–108 (2017)
9. Zhou, Z., Zhao, D., Liu, L., Hung, P.C.: Energy-aware composition for wireless sensor networks as a service. Future Gener. Comput. Syst. **80**, 299–310 (2018)
10. Alsaryrah, O., Mashal, I., Chung, T.Y.: Energy-aware services composition for Internet of Things. In: 2018 IEEE 4th World Forum on Internet of Things (WF-IoT), pp. 604–608. IEEE (2018)
11. Urbieta, A., González-Beltrán, A., Mokhtar, S.B., Hossain, M.A., Capra, L.: Adaptive and context-aware service composition for IoT-based smart cities. Future Gener. Comput. Syst. **76**, 262–274 (2017)
12. Chen, L., Englund, C.: Choreographing services for smart cities: smart traffic demonstration. In: 2017 IEEE 85th Vehicular Technology Conference (VTC Spring), pp. 1–5. IEEE (2017)
13. Seeger, J., Deshmukh, R.A., Broring, A.: Running distributed and dynamic IOT choreographies. In: 2018 Global Internet of Things Summit (GIoTS), pp. 1–6. IEEE (2018)
14. Fysarakis, K., Papoutsakis, M., Petroulakis, N., Spanoudakis, G.: Towards IoT orchestrations with security, privacy, dependability and interoperability guarantees. In: Conference: 2019 IEEE Global Communications Conference (GLOBECOM), At Waikoloa, HI, USA (2019). https://doi.org/10.1109/GLOBECOM38437.2019.9013275

15. Business Rules Management System (BRMS). https://www.drools.org. Accessed 5 Aug 2020
16. Morrison, J. Paul.: Flow-Based Programming: A new approach to application development. CreateSpace, (2010)
17. Drools - Business Rules Management System (Java^{TM}, Open Source). https://www.drools.org. Accessed 5 Aug 2020
18. Forgy, C.L.: Rete: a fast algorithm for the many pattern/many object pattern match problem. In: Readings in Artificial Intelligence and Databases, pp. 547–559. Morgan Kaufmann (1989)
19. Chapter 5. Hybrid Reasoning. https://docs.jboss.org/drools/release/6.4.0.Final/drools-docs/html/ch05.html. Accessed 5 Aug 2020
20. Kienzle, D.M., Elder, M.C., Tyree, D., Edwards-Hewitt, J.: Security patterns repository version 1.0. DARPA, Washington DC (2002)
21. Bröring, A., Seeger, J., Papoutsakis, M., Fysarakis, K.: Networking-aware IoT application development. Sensors **20**, 897 (2020). https://doi.org/10.3390/s20030897
22. Soultatos, O., et al.: Pattern-driven security, privacy, dependability and interoperability management of IoT environments. In: 2019 IEEE 24th International Workshop on Computer Aided Modeling and Design of Communication Links and Networks (CAMAD), Limassol, Cyprus, pp. 1–6 (2019). https://doi.org/10.1109/CAMAD.2019.8858429
23. Nowak, A., Binz, T., Fehling, C., Kopp, O., Leymann, F., Wagner, S.: Pattern-driven green adaptation of process-based applications and their runtime infrastructure. Computing **94**(6), 463–487 (2012)
24. Döhring, M., Zimmermann, B., Godehardt, E.: Extended workflow flexibility using rule-based adaptation patterns with eventing semantics. INFORMATIK 2010. Service Science–Neue Perspektiven für die Informatik, Band 1 (2010)
25. El-Maliki, T., Seigne, J.: Efficient security adaptation framework for internet of things. In: 2016 International Conference on Computational Science and Computational Intelligence (CSCI), Las Vegas, NV, pp. 206–211 (2016). https://doi.org/10.1109/CSCI.2016.0046

Password Management: How Secure Is Your Login Process?

George Hatzivasilis[1,2]([⊠]) [iD]

[1] Foundation for Research and Technology, Heraklion, Greece
hatzivas@ics.forth.gr
[2] Department of Electrical and Computer Engineering,
Hellenic Mediterranean University (HMU), Heraklion, Greece
hatzivas@hmu.gr

Abstract. Pairs of usernames and passwords are widely used nowadays by mobile and web applications to identify users. The exposure of this data harms both users and vendors. The client-server model is the most common. The provided services implement front-end interfaces that run on the client's side and back-end interfaces that run on the server side. A proper password management policy administrates the password creation, storage, processing, and transmission in both ends. This article overviews the theory and provides a practical guide for password management and implementation of a safe login process for mobile and web application developers, and IT organizations. An empirical research and several case studies are surveyed for the password habits of three universities, an army school, an IT company, and two accounting offices in the province of Crete in Greece. Moreover, a software benchmark analysis is conducted for the computational demanding primitives of the secure login operations.

Keywords: Login · Password management · Password hashing · Empirical study · PHC · BYOD · OAuth

1 Introduction

Usernames and passwords continue to form the main mean of user authentication in computers (e.g. [1–3]). Mobile and web applications process high volumes of them every day in order to manage and facilitate the provided personalized functionality to their users.

However, poor password protection practices [4, 5] expose high mounts of user accounts. Such disclosure operations harm the software vendor's market value [6, 7] and the confidence of the legitimate user, like in the cases of LinkedIn [8] and Sony PlayStation [9].

Every user nowadays holds dozens of electronic accounts with relevant username/password pairs that are hard to get remembered. Thus, the typical user applies easily memorable ways to create this information [10]. This fact results in low-entropy secrets and enables fast on-line guessing attacks or off-line cracking.

© Springer Nature Switzerland AG 2020
G. Hatzivasilis and S. Ioannidis (Eds.): MSTEC 2020, LNCS 12512, pp. 157–177, 2020.
https://doi.org/10.1007/978-3-030-62433-0_10

On-line guessing attacks takes advantage of the login or password alter/reset services. The attacker tries to guess the user information, consulting the people's habits in forming these secrets. The problem is generally circumscribed by policies that enforce users to create high entropy passwords and robust password processing operations.

Moreover, many vulnerabilities are usually located at the service provider side. Attackers may infiltrate the system and gain access to the stored data. Analysis discloses the username/password pairs, exposing the account information (e.g. [11–13]). Password hashing techniques constitute the main mean for concealing the stored user-related information. However, the evolution of parallel computing enables several attacks in password hashing cracking [14]. The Password Hashing Competition (PHC), held in 2013–2015, proposed state-of-the-art solutions with memory-hard structures or other operations that provide protection [15, 16].

In this article, real case studies are reported from an empirical study in the public, private, and military sectors, revealing practical and essential problems of establishing secure password management services. Thus, a guide of password management for developers is recommended to enhance the provided protection of feature applications and login operations. A software benchmark analysis is also conducted for the 5 PHC finalists and the 3 mainstream password hashing solutions. The state-of-the-art solutions in terms of security and performance are then indicated and mapped for mobile, web, or other applications.

The rest of the paper is structured as follows: Sect. 2 overviews the details of the empirical study. Section 3 presents the information theory concerning the entropy of passwords. Section 4 describes the process for storing password-related information as well as the password hashing primitives. Section 5 discusses the implication of mobile applications and the necessity for BYOD policies. Section 6 summarizes the operation of OAuth 2.0. Section 7 summarizes a benchmark for related technologies and Sect. 8 concludes this work. Appendix I mentions the specific question sets that were used for the empirical study, evaluating the password-related habits of simple users and administrators.

2 Empirical Study

The anonymous empirical study includes 200 university students and staff, 50 military personnel, and 40 IT and accounting employees. The respondents were asked relevant questions during an oral interview. All participants answer questions regarding their password habits as users. Moreover, 20 of them who are working on the relevant IT help desks as administrators are also asked about the password management policies that are applied by the organizations. The question sets and the answers are detailed in the Appendix I and Table 2 and Table 3 for users and administrators, respectively.

The empirical study reveals that an average user nowadays possesses around 50–70 accounts. As most people do not realize this high volume of information that they owned, they utilize simple and convenient ways to administrate it. The high majority of 98% ignores the password management software solutions and does not use any.

Moreover, users do not update their passwords in a regular basis. If a default password is assigned by the service provider when a new account is established (e.g. university e-mails), the user does not change it unless it is forced to (e.g. change the password during the first login). In general, a user may alter the password by his own will when security incidents on popular services become known.

To create a password, the user complies with the least requirements that are enforced by the service. On average, the user utilizes three username/password pairs, with low deviation among them. One of them is the favourite one and is tried to get assigned in all cases. When the relevant username is already registered in the service by another user, one of the other pairs is inputted. The infiltration of social media in our ordinary lives led to the creation of fake or clone cyber-identities. The *73%* of the users creates around *2–3* redundant identities with relevant username/password pairs.

More specialized results, real case studies or failed policies, and other useful conclusions are reported in the following sections, discussing specific issues of password management and login processes.

3   Entropy

Passwords are user-memorable secrets that consist of several printable characters [10]. A pair of the user's identity with a relevant secret password, authenticates each active account during the login process.

An exhaustive search attack tries out all character combinations until the right password for a username is found. Then, the attacker owns the account as the legitimate user does. The ordinary option for safe user-login services is passwords of *8* characters long (*8* bytes with ASCII encoding). Even a password with *6* random digits would be sufficient for many attacks, as it would take $2^{(6*8)} = 2^{48}$ tries, resulting in about *8890* years with *1000* guesses per second. However, the user-originated secrets might exhibit low entropy. This fact facilitates attacks with lower computational complexity than the exhaustive search.

The ordinary policy of creating safe passwords with adequate entropy imposes that the secret must contain at least three of the following character sets: lower- and uppercase letters (i.e. *a-z*, *A-Z*), numbers (i.e. *0–9*), and symbols (e.g. *$, @, !*). Although this policy seems sufficient for many applications, weak passwords can still be produced [17].

The empirical study reveals such weaknesses. The case of the on-line tax and custom services system of Greece, called Taxisnet, is such an example. The system was implemented with high security and privacy standards, and was supported by the European commission's eGoverment initiatives. A serious problem regarding password entropy occurred during the establishment of the users' records. Most citizens bestow their tax ministration on accounting offices. The accountants deal with the bureaucracy and create the Taxisnet accounts for their customers. However, instead of following a password safe policy, they perform an archiving strategy to accelerate the process and easy their later accounting operation of accessing the system in regard of their clients.

For this study, the password establishment of two accounting offices in Greece are evaluated. For the username, the first office uses the prefix *user*, the customers last name, and the initial letter of the first name (with English characters), while the second office concatenates the last name with the *3–5* first letters of the first name. For the password, the first office applies the client's initials with the tax identification number (ten digits long) appended with *0* and the second office inputs the tax ID, the *2* first letters of the last name, and the initial letter of the first name. Although the passwords are *13* characters long and comply with the safe password policy, the passwords exhibit quite low entropy and can be even reproduced in a deterministic manner along with the relevant username. However, the aforementioned policies of the two evaluated accounting offices are not exceptional but indicative for many accounting offices, as such simple and easily-understood examples where utilized during the demonstration and training sessions by several regional economic champers. In 2012, the Greek police arrested a hacker for possessing and selling around *9* million Taxisnet accounts (Greece's population is *11* million) in the black market [18]. The accounts could have been disclosed by on-line guessing attacks that exploit such low-entropy passwords.

According to best practices and security experts' suggestions, the avoid-list for building secure passwords includes:

- The default passwords that are automatically produced by the service provide during the account creation, like *admin*, *user*, *guest*, *default*, and *password*
- The dictionary words, such as *dragon*, *sandbags!*, and *AppleTree*, including words of non-English languages
- Words with appended numbers: *password1*, *secteam2017*, *George85*, etc., as they are easily tested automatically with little effort
- Words with simple obfuscation: *p@ssw0rd*, *r@bb1t*, *@dm1n* etc., are also tested automatically with little additional effort
- Repeated words or characters: *useruser*, *passpass*, *aaaabbbb* etc
- Common sequences from a keyboard or mobile device's virtual-keyboard row: *qwerty*, *asdfgh*, *abcdef*, *12345*, etc
- Numeric sequences based on well-known numbers such as *314159* and *27182* (for pi and e respectively) or dates like *9/11/2011*
- Identifiers like *computer123*, *01/08/2017*, or the account's username
- Any personal information that is related with the account owner: relatives or pets (e.g. names, nicknames, initials, birthdays), student or other IDs, birthday or anniversary dates, Birthplace or favourite holiday, sports team, addresses, telephone numbers, vehicle or license plate numbers, and social security number which can be easily deduced automatically after a simple investigation of person's public information.

Most of these examples utilize simple patterns which exhibit low entropy, enabling efficient automatic attacks.

The main security property of a safe password is high entropy, similarly to a complete random one, along with the exclusion of patterns that are related with the user. When high security is the target, the application must additionally measure the entropy of the account credentials and reject weak passwords. As suggested by many security experts, the guidelines for strong passwords include:

- At least *12-14* characters long secrets
- At least on digit of the four character sets: lower and upper case letters, numbers, and symbols

- Prevent biographical information, user-related information, dictionary words, digit repetition, keyboard patterns, letter or number sequences
- Prevent combinations of the above-mentioned restrictions
- Prevent element patterns that might become associated with the user via information that is either publicly known or known to other acquaintances
- and if possible, generate random passwords and avoid using a password more than once

Newer trends of user-drawn graphical passwords [19–21] also exhibit low-entropy properties, offering an average security of 4-5 bytes [22]. Map-based passwords could produce better results [23, 24].

4 Storage and Password Hashing

4.1 Stored Information

In many occasions the account-related information is stored in plaintext without any protection at the service provider side. Thus, an attacker that gains access to the back-end infrastructure obtains the credentials of all users without further effort.

Key stretching is the typical method for protecting against cracking attacks. Cryptographic hash functions constitute a cryptographic primitive type that parses input of arbitrary size and produces a fixed-length digest. In the password hashing domain, hash functions process the password and produce a fixed-length output, which now acts as the password. The result is longer than the original password (e.g. *32* or *64* bytes), making the attacks less feasible. The hashed password is further fortified by iterating the hash function several times. Thus, the attacker is slowed down by a factor of 2^{n+m}, where n is the number of the iterations and m is the number of the output bits. However, the user is also slowed down. The parameters of key stretching are bounded by the user's tolerance to compute a robust hash password.

If two or more users have the same password, they will result the same hashed password too. The disclosure of this information for one of these users could raise security issues for the rest ones. The problem is exponentially evolved as many users utilize the same password in many different services. To prevent the correlation of hashed passwords that are created by the same password, a small parameter of random bytes, called *salt*, is utilized. Thus, the same password produces different hashes for different users or services. The salt hardens attacks with precomputed data. The attacker tries hundreds of possible matches (dictionary attacks) or uses tables with precomputed hashes (rainbow table attacks) in order to guess or correlate the legitimate password information [11, 12]. The typical sizes for salt are *8–16* bytes. It is generated when the user account is created and is concatenated with the password during hashing. Normally, it is stored in plaintext along with the hashed password. The authentication procedure uses the salt to validate the password of a login request.

Except from the salt, an additional random parameter, called *pepper*, can be used. The pepper takes a value from a constrained and small set, like a number from *0* to *5*, but in contrast to the salt, it is not stored anywhere. Ordinary, the pepper is one-byte long. When a password-hashing operation is performed, a randomly selected value from the set is appended to the hashed data. During the login phase, the process validates the user in different verification attempts, where the input data are examined along with all pepper values, checked one-by-one while trying to figure out the correct setting. If all attempts fail, the login information is incorrect. The computational complexity of the account verification is increased in the server side according to the number of the different pepper values. The user login operation is delayed, but similarly, the attacker's cracking capabilities are further slowed down.

The simple use of cryptographic functions, where the passwords are hashed before being stored, is considered outdated. The hash functions are susceptible to cryptanalysis attacks, which in the password management field, results in aforementioned attacks that utilize precomputed data.

Thus, more advanced password hashing schemes (PHS) are proposed, like the PBKDF2, Bcrypt, and Scrypt, that derive the ordinary attacks computational infeasible. A study in mobile application security [25] (i.e. on iOS and BlackBerry) reveals that most popular applications provide low password protection. The high majority of them simply hash the user data with SHA2 or MD5 while only a small number of them utilizes PBKDF2. Similar practices can be observed for web applications. An analysis in *150* sites [26] shows that *29%* of them store the password in plaintext and do not hash the passwords at all.

This empirical study exhibits similar results. The university emails now provide adequate security as they constitute popular target for attackers. The private companies focus on the main functionality of a service, with the limited budget on security resulting in low protection. The military services provide high protection, following NATO [27] design guidelines.

However, the modern parallel computing architectures and the dedicated hardware platforms, enhance the cracking capabilities and enable more efficient attacks [11, 12]. Password crackers try out several attempts in parallel on GPUs, FPGAs, and ASICs, gaining a significant boost in disclosing the user information. PBKDF2 and Bcrypt are vulnerable to such attacks due to their low memory requirements.

The newer trend are memory-hard PHSs. The parallel platforms have limited memory resources and on dedicated hardware the memory is considered expensive. Thus, for a PHS with high memory requirements, the cracker makes significantly less parallel attempts as every parallel element must have access to the platform's memory.

The defender adjusts the memory and computational requirements of the PHS to design secure and usable schemes. The goal is to render the password scrambling on parallel cores not much faster than it is on a single core. Scrypt implements this approach. It is estimated that the cost of a hardware brute force attack is around *20000* and *4000* times larger than in PBKDF2 and Bcrypt respectively [28]. However, Scrypt and other memory-hard PHSs may be vulnerable to cache memory attacks. A spy process that runs on the same machine can gather memory-access patterns by measuring cache-timings [11]. The analysis empowers attacks with low memory for each parallel core. The huge memory block that is allocated during the password hash computation, is later ends up as a *garbage*. In garbage-collector attacks [12] the attacker correlates an obtained secret hash with the memory content that is collected after the PHS termination.

The Password Hashing Competition (PHC) conducted in 2013 to counter these issues and deploy modern and secure schemes for password hashing [15]. In 2015, the winner and other 4 finalists with special recognition were promoted, based on security, efficiency, and the extra deployed features. They will be further examined by NIST and other organizations in order to become the new standards in the field. Figure 1 illustrates the winning PHC scheme Argon2. The other finalists are the Catena, Lyra2, MAKWA, and Yescrypt. Moreover, poly password hashing schemes with k-threshold encryption are proposed for constrained embedded systems to balance performance and security [29].

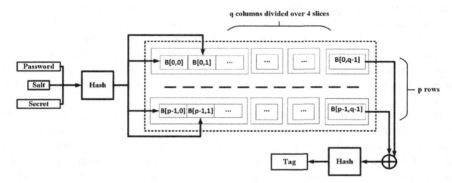

Fig. 1. The single-pass Argon2 PHS

4.2 Login Process

Web and mobile applications serve thousands of users. The server maintains the authentication data for all users and must respond to high volumes of simultaneous login requests from clients. In every transaction, the password must not be transmitted in plaintext (e.g. transmission of the password from the user's browser to the application's server or confirmation e-mail with the new password from the server to the user), otherwise the security may be lost. The Transport Layer Security (TLS) protocol is the most common solution for cryptographic communication. The server is authenticated and the password is encrypted. The RFC standard Secure Remote Password (SRP) protocol functions upon TLS and further prevents dictionary attacks by eavesdroppers [26].

However, on-line guessing attacks are applicable here [13]. The guesses that an attacker makes can be bounded, by limiting the total number of failed login attempts. For example, a password is disabled and requires a reset after some consecutive failed logins (i.e. 3–5 tries). The user may also be enforced to change his password after a large number of failed guesses that are interspersing between the legitimate logins (e.g. 30 bad guesses). However, in both cases, the login-inspection parameters must be securely stored and processed in order to avoid their manipulation by an attacker.

Another defense strategy introduces a delay, a CAPTCHA or another human interaction proof [30] between login submissions to slow down automated-guessing attacks. The exploit time can be increased drastically, rendering on-line attacks inefficient, and as a consequence, improving the lifetime of the legitimate passwords. Moreover, the error message of a failed login attempt must not reveal if the problem was in the username, the password, or both.

The user may need to alter a password, either because it is compromised or as a precautionary measure. The system must provide a safe way to change it. To prevent attackers from arbitrarily changing passwords, the reset-password services must verify the user's identity, for example, by requesting the current password. Similar restrictive strategies as for the bad login guesses can be applied here.

Due to the automatic-login capabilities of the modern web and mobile applications, it has become very common nowadays for the users to forget their passwords and not being able to enter the system. The typical method to authenticate such users is by asking questions and comparing the answers to ones previously stored (i.e., when the account was created) [31]. However, some question sets ask for personal information that may be public (e.g. favourite movie, best teacher) or account usage data that can be inferred by social networks analysis (e.g. frequent or last contacts). Thus, it is recommended the users to give false answers and the developers to permit users making up their own questions.

Password-ageing policies impose that the password must be altered in a periodic basis (i.e. monthly or annually) to conceal security against adversaries that have obtain a subset of the currently legitimate passwords. The process is mainly implemented for organizations that process classified information, like military and embassy agencies. The associated office informs the employees to change the passwords when the active period expires. The safe-reset functionality can be utilized for this purpose by the service provider [32].

The different examined organizations of this empirical study exhibit diverse password-ageing policies. For the academic society, the computing center office informs all partners via e-mail about changing their account secrets in an annual basis. The alternation is optional. In the private sector, no specific policy is enforced and the passwords are modified in an arbitrary manner. In the military school, the passwords are altered every three months. A massage is prompted automatically five days before the expiration date.

The aging policies result in different entropy and password-correlation properties. Around 80% of the university interviewees ignore the optional recommendation. Nonetheless, the universities inform users to create safe passwords immediately when their account is created. Thus, the high entropy passwords remain safe for long-term use even if they are not changed regularly. In the private sector, the clerks create memorable secrets with low or moderate entropy. The passwords are changed mostly when security incidents on large IT companies are announced and become popular. The military policy on the other hand produces in practice highly correlated passwords. A user would require at least four passwords per year for each service (the permanent personnel possess at least two accounts for a PC in the intranet and the military email). Although the individual passwords comply with the typical secure password strategies, the common choice is a memorable prefix appended with some additional characters [33]. The problem is dominant in the case of conscript privates. Around 90% of the examined passwords include a variation of the school name and the year, resulting in high correlated secrets.

However, in all cases, the most correlated passwords are produced by the system administrators. These employees must maintain administrative passwords for almost every computer or service. In general, the secrets exhibit high entropy but the administrative teams establish the same password for all accounts. The burden to comply with the aging policy results in correlated passwords with low variation and password re-use. Moreover, the passwords are hard to change when employees leave the organization, exposing the confidential information.

In order to avoid these issues, an organization should acquire security awareness programs [34–36]. Thus, the personnel learn about the implications of low security practices and the potential threats for the organization, while the administrative staff fully complies with the organization's policies in order not to get reported by external audit.

5 Mobile Applications and BYOD Policy

The physics of the mobile ecosystem are different from the web [37, 38]. A mobile application runs on movable devices, like laptops, smart phones or tablets. Regarding password management, they also utilize the client-server model. In contrast to web applications, great attention must be paid in the storage process of private information in the device end. If the device gets lost, confidential data can be exposed.

Mobile applications' security is not only a problem of individual users. Bring Your Own Device (BYOD) is the IT policy for permitting employees to use their own personal mobile devices in the workplace. Organizations support this action as BYOD increases personnel productivity and decreases equipment investments. However, BYOD has resulted in data breaches [39, 40].

The empirical study of this article reveals the diverse status of different operational sectors. In the academic community, it is the norm to use personal devices and access the universities' infrastructure. All professors, personnel, and students use in daily base their personal movable devices. A few security incidents include phishing e-mails requesting login data, DoS attacks on the servers, and infected computers in the public libraries. For the private sector, the provided infrastructure is considered sufficient for each job position. Nevertheless, the employees may use own equipment for their convenience, mostly for outdoor tasks. No serious security issues are countered as the computers are solely used for business purposes. In the military sector, the computer access is restricted. However, the staff uses portable storage devices to transfer data from standalone computers to the confidential Intranet. In some cases, personal equipment (e.g. USB sticks, SD cards, and smart phones) may be utilized against the rules. The small number of security events that are detected, like malware software, is originated by such infected devices. Around the 82% of the owners of all these devices do not apply any additional security than what is already installed by the manufacturer.

Several related studies have examined the security implications of BYOD (e.g. [41, 42]). Businesses are unable to stop employees from bringing personal devices into the workplace, with 41% of employees (among 2100 individuals) having used at least one personal device at work [42]. The 70% of these devices apply no additional security than what is installed by the owner. As employees may access privileged organization information and applications, security concerns arise. For example, a smartphone that contains confidential data may be lost or stolen, with untrusted parties retrieving any unsecured data. A device may also be sold or given to a family member without erasing the sensitive information. As employees leave the organization and take their personal devices, valuable data and applications can still be retained in them. Such devices can be also used by various family members, who may accidentally share the content to unauthorized entities (e.g. via email or Dropbox). The *39%* of the organizations have a data breach due to employees' personal devices that are either lost or stolen. Thus, many companies, like CISCO and IBM, are adopting BYOD policies to regulate the usage of such devices and secure their data. The typical policy must:

- Formally register the personal devices that are used
- Specify the usage period (e.g. office working hours)
- Regulate the device's camera and video capabilities when on-line
- Regulate the recorded capabilities of the device
- Block/Permit access to specific sites or applications
- Specify the organization resources that can be accessed (email, contacts, documents, etc.)
- Constrain usage when driving (i.e. no use or with hands-free)
- Report a set of specific devices/programs that are allowed and can be supported by the organization's IT support. No problems regarding connectivity or malfunctioning must be send to the manufacturer. Only the organization's IT support must resolve these issues.
- The organization's IT support must install the security software and configure the relevant parameters.
- Prevent unauthorized access by using the password protection features of the device and a strong password policy to access the organization's networks
- Establish device self-lock policies for idle periods with password or PIN
- Remotely wiped the device in cases of lost, policy or security breaches, and employment termination

6   OAuth 2.0

OAuth 2.0 [43] is an IETF open standard for authentication that allows users to log in to applications with their existing accounts from a trusted third party, like Google, Facebook, Microsoft, and Yahoo. The web or mobile application utilizes the provider's OAuth API to implement the login service. When the user accesses the application data, he inputs the username and password of his account in the OAuth-provider's site. After authenticating the user, the OAuth service sends an authentication token to the application along with the authorization settings of the specific account. Figure 2 illustrates a reference OAuth protocol.

After signing in, the application detects the authorization access rights of the user (e.g. viewer, editor, owner or administrator, and App Engine App Admin in case of mobile applications). The application's developer easily implements protected pieces of code that process admin-only functionality.

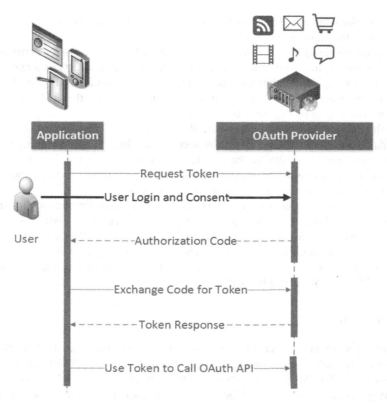

Fig. 2. OAuth sequence diagram. The application requests an authentication token from the trusted third party. The user logins the account. An authorization code is sent to the application as the result of the correct authentication. The application requests an authentication token for the specific authorization code. The token enables the usage of the OAuth API.

OAuth is provided for free and can be easily integrated in existing applications. It is efficient and enhances security and scalability. The registration friction for the user is low, as he does not have to create a new account for each application.

Moreover, it decreases the infrastructure and operational costs of an application while facilitating and attracting the OAuth provider's users (e.g. billions of users from Amazon, PayPal, Twitter or LinkedIn). Amazon is the largest Internet-based retailer in USA with more than *200* million customers [44]. The on-line shoe retailer Zappos.com adopts the Amazon OAuth [44]. Around the *30%* of the customers use the Amazon login to accommodate payments and product advertisements. The OAuth services of the leading social network Facebook were utilized by *470* billion users in 2014, reaching the *660* billion in 2015 [45]. League of Legends, a multi-player team video game by Riot, cooperates with Facebook [45]. Riot launches the Facebook Friend Discovery – a login-integrated feature where the game makes a recommendation list of potential on-line co-players based on the Facebook friends. This paper focuses in the password management aspects of OAuth, thus the authorization capabilities are out of the scope.

Nonetheless, the selection of the proper OAuth provider should comply with the targeted user groups of the application.

The main vulnerability of OAuth are phishing attacks. The user is prompted to input his identifiers in a bogus site belonging to the attacker that acts as a man-in-the-middle between the application and the OAuth provider. The adversary discloses the relevant information and gains access to the account. However, the application's own login process can also be exploited by such attacks.

OAuth is also vulnerable to Cross-Site Request Forgery (CSRF) [46]. A currently authenticated user is forced to perform unwanted actions, like changing the email address or transferring funds. To counter the attack, the session cookie that is seeded for the generation of the access token should be hashed. The state must match the session cookies and be verified prior accepting the access tokens.

The empirical study concludes that the OAuth login usage is limited only for specific reputable sites and applications (e.g. Booking.com, TripAdvisor). For new and less known services, users do not trust OAuth login (i.e. *72%*), as they consider that the provider will obtain their account credentials, raising privacy considerations [47,48]. Interviewees prefer to create new accounts, even if they input data that are the same as the denied OAuth requested information.

7 Benchmark

A comparison study is conducted for the PBKDF2, Bcrypt, Scrypt, and 5 PHC finalists. All PHSs are evaluated on an Intel Core i7 at 2.10 GHz CPU with 8 GB RAM, running 64-bit Windows 8.1 Pro over a common benchmark suite. The PHSs process *1000* randomly generated passwords and the average results are detailed in Table 1, using the default values for password, salt, and output sizes. The t_cost and m_cost parameters tune time and space-memory requirements respectively. No specific norm is proposed for establishing the two parameters and the benchmark reports the relevant settings, as reported by each scheme.

Table 1. Software implementation of PBKDF2, Bcrypt, Scrypt and the 5 PHC finalists. The cost t_cost and m_cost tune time and space-memory requirements respectively

PHS	Password (bytes)	Salt (bytes)	Output (bytes)	t_cost	m_cost	ROM (KB)	RAM (KB)	CPU (secs)
PBKDF2	24	8	64	1000	0	30	0	0.002024
PBKDF2	24	8	64	2048	0	30	0	0.004150
PBKDF2	24	8	64	4096	0	30	0	0.008141
Bcrypt	12	16	54	12	0	27	492	2.668653
Scrypt	8	32	64	5	0	182	450656	2.837654
Argon2d	32	32	32	3	2	110	44	0.000524

(continued)

Table 1. (*continued*)

PHS	Password (bytes)	Salt (bytes)	Output (bytes)	t_cost	m_cost	ROM (KB)	RAM (KB)	CPU (secs)
Argon2d	32	32	32	56	100	110	136	0.077891
Argon2d	32	32	32	3	10000	110	10112	0.434536
Argon2i	32	32	32	3	2	111	40	0.000522
Argon2i	32	32	32	56	100	111	136	0.080158
Argon2i	32	32	32	3	10000	111	10112	0.431438
Catena-Dragonfly	8	16	64	3	18	34	16496	0.093241
Catena-Dragonfly	8	16	64	3	20	34	65764	0.379892
Catena-Butterfly	8	16	64	3	18	35	24668	1.450987
Catena-Butterfly	8	16	64	3	20	35	98448	6.402041
Lyra2	8	16	64	5	100	98	696	0.001463
Lyra2	8	16	64	5	1000	98	6104	0.015104
Lyra2	8	16	64	5	10000	98	60128	0.159651
MAKWA	8	16	64	0	0	95	335	0.000096
MAKWA	8	16	64	1000	0	95	335	0.002035
MAKWA	8	16	64	8192	0	95	335	0.015621
Yescrypt	8	16	64	0	8	44	2124	0.005796
Yescrypt	8	16	64	3	8	44	2124	0.011544
Yescrypt	8	16	64	0	11	44	16460	0.046733

Figure 3 illustrates the best speed to RAM-consumption settings. The most efficient implementations are reported based on the execution time that is required for similar amounts of memory. PBKDF2, Lyra2, Yescrypt, Catena-BRG, Argon2i, and Argon2d are the most efficient ones, followed by Catena-DRG, Bcrypt, Scrypt, and MAKWA.

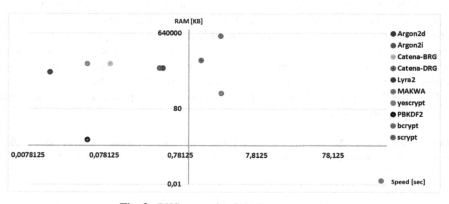

Fig. 3. PHS – speed to RAM measurement

As aforementioned, PBKDF2, Bcrypt, and Scrypt are vulnerable to attacks. For typical RAM-hard schemes, Argon2 is the best choice as the PHC winner and the state-of-the-art scheme. Lyra2 fits well in general applications and can process high amounts of memory, as Scrypt. Catena produces low code and RAM consumption, and is designed with embedded system constraints in mind [49]. All three schemes function well on the web and mobile domain. MAKWA can safely substitute Bcrypt as it consumes similar amounts of RAM for two to four magnitudes lower CPU time. Yescrypt supports a mode of operation that is compatible with Scrypt and can easily replace the scheme to existing systems, enhancing security.

Moreover, the Argon2 PHS is integrated with the WRAP OAuth API to protect the session cookie for a login service that confirms Facebook or Twitter accounts. The computational overhead is low in both cases and the communication delay ranges from *0.0012* ms to *0.8* ms for low and high PHS memory cost respectively.

For secure transmission, it requires *6.5* KB on average to establish a TLS session. Then, *40* additional bytes are needed for encrypted data, in contrast to the unprotected communication channel, with low processing overhead.

As a case study in this article, the state-of-the-art Argon2 PHS is integrated with the WRAP OAuth API to protect the session cookies. Two demo login services are implemented in C++. The first one confirms Facebook accounts. The second service authenticates Twitter users and authorizes show-tweet requests. The computational overhead is low in both cases and the communication delay ranges from *0.0012* ms to *0.8* ms for low and high PHS memory cost respectively.

8 Conclusions

The secure management of passwords is hard. Security breaches on famous applications have revealed massive amounts of user data, harming the reliability of their providers. The OAuth feature can leverage security and attract targeted users, if it is used properly. Small companies that are not able to invest a significant amount of their budgets for security, could utilize OAuth services. Thus, the login process and the stored password data are safeguarded by a larger IT organization that has advanced computer security knowledge and infrastructures, and keeps up to dated its security policies and products. The developer must adopt the state-of-the-art solutions for storing, processing, and transmitting user-related credentials. Despite of these technical solutions, the user behavior remains dominant. A proper IT policy should face the low-entropy or easily-guessed secrets, and the rising challenges of BYOD reality. Security awareness programs could inform personnel about the security risks and the potential damage, enhancing protection. The overall analysis could be extended in other settings where passwords are applied, like Wi-Fi passwords (inserted by the user or default password generation) and cryptographic session keys.

Acknowledgements. This work has received funding from the European Union Horizon's 2020 research and innovation programme under the grant agreements No. 786890 (THREAT-ARREST) and No. 830927 (CONCORDIA).

Appendix I – Question Sets for Users and Administrators

This appendix details the two question sets that were used for simple users (Table 2) and service administrators (Table 3), respectively.

Table 2. Password management question set and answers for users

Questions	Answers
Q1	
Question	How many electronic accounts do you possess?
Answer set	Specify a number
Result	The users possess 50–70 accounts on average
Q2.1	
Question	Do you use any password management tool?
Answer set	Yes or No
Result	98% of the users answer that the do not use any tool
Q2.2	
Question	If yes, which one?
Answer set	Specify the tool or tools
Result	The most common answers include KeePass2, Password Safe, LastPass, and browser's build-in tools
Q3.1	
Question	How many times do you update your passwords in the last year?
Answer set	None, 1–4 times, 5–8 times, or more than 9 times
Result	58% answers none, 39% answers 1–4 times, 2% answers 5–8 times, 1% answers more than 9 times.
Q3.2.1	
Question	If yes, why you update the passwords?
Answer set	Own habit, working organization policy, site/service recommendation, or other
Result	From the initial 42% that change the password: 3% answers own habit, 17% answers working organization policy, 13% answers site/service recommendation, 9% answers other
Q3.2.2	
Question	If other, give more details?
Answer set	Specify the reason why you change the passwords
Result	Other reasons for changing the password include the announcement of large hacking operations, hacking of an own account of device, or because the user had forgotten the current password

(continued)

Table 2. (*continued*)

Questions	Answers
Q4	
Question	Which policy do you use for creating a password?
Answer set	The service's recommendations or the security experts' recommendations for creating strong passwords
Result	The 64% answers that they apply the service's recommendations and the 36% answers that they apply the security strategies that are recommended the security experts
Q5.1	
Question	Do you reuse username/password pairs in different services?
Answer set	Yes or No
Result	The 90% answers that they reuse username/password and 10% answers that they use different password for different services
Q5.2	
Question	If yes, give more details?
Answer set	Specify your policy
Result	The average user possesses 1–3 favourite pairs that he/she tries to use in all cases.
Q6.1	
Question	Do you create fake or clone identities in services where you already possess an active account?
Answer set	Yes or No
Result	The 73% answers yes.
Q6.2.1	
Question	If yes, how many?
Answer set	Specify a number
Result	The average user possesses 2–3 redundant accounts in social media.
Q6.2.2	
Question	Which policy do you apply for creating the password of a redundant account?
Answer set	Specify the policy for selecting the used username/password pair
Result	The average user possesses 1–3 favourite pairs (different from the relevant pairs that are used in the original accounts) that he/she uses for the redundant accounts
Q7.1	
Question	Do you use OAUTH?
Answer set	Yes or No
Result	The 90% answers yes.

(continued)

Table 2. (*continued*)

Questions	Answers
Q7.2.1	
Question	If yes, which OAUTH providers do you prefer?
Answer set	Specify a number
Result	The highest majority prefers Facebook and Google
Q7.2.2	
Question	If no, why?
Answer set	Specify the reasons why you avoid using OAUTH
Result	The average user that does not utilize OAUTH, does not trust that his/her OAUTH credentials will be safe
Q8.1	
Question	Does your organization support BYOD?
Answer set	No, informal and voluntary policy, formal policy, strict monitoring of formal policy compliance
Result	The answers vary based on the organization: the small private companies apply no or informal policies, the universities have formal policies for fair use, and the army school enforces the last option
Q8.2	
Question	Do you apply any additional security mechanisms except from those that are imposed by the BYOD?
Answer set	Yes or no
Result	The 82% of applies no additional protection mechanisms and 18% installs additional free anti-virus and anti-malware applications

Table 3. Password management question set and answers for administrators

Questions	Answers
Q1.1	
Question	What password-creation policy does your organization recommends to the users?
Answer set	Specify a the policy
Result	The private companies do not apply a specific policy and the employees create memorable passwords. The military school impose the creation of typically safe or strong passwords that contain at least 3 or 4 items (depending on the service) from the basic character sets. The universities impose the creation of strong and random passwords as students must take an initial course when enrolling the faculty where they are taught how to create their institutional accounts

(*continued*)

Table 3. (*continued*)

Questions	Answers
Q1.2	
Question	How do you create the administration accounts?
Answer set	Specify the applied policy
Result	In cases, the administrators create at least typically safe passwords. However, as they have to maintain several administrative accounts for different services, there may be correlation among the admin accounts or the services'/departments' name (e.g. a lab's or a division's name may be included in the password)
Q2	
Question	Which password-hashing technique is implemented by the provided services?
Answer set	None, simple hashing with a generic hash function, or hashing with a PHS
Result	The private companies apply no or simple hashing, the universities hash the passwords with a generic hash function or a PHS, and the military school utilizes PHSs
Q3.1	
Question	Which password-update policy does your organization apply?
Answer set	None, periodically messages to users for changing their passwords in a voluntary basis, imposed change of the passwords in a periodic basis
Result	The private companies apply no specific password update policy. The universities send periodical messages, but as reported by the administrators, the messages are in general ignored by the high majority of the students and the personnel (80%). The military sector imposes that the passwords must be updated every three months
Q3.2	
Question	Do the administrators comply with the password-update policy?
Answer set	Yes, partially, or no
Result	In all cases, the administrators comply partially with the update policy and they do not change the passwords as frequent as they should
Q4	
Question	Do the provided services support OAUTH?
Answer set	Yes or No
Result	The universities, the military school, and most of the two accounting offices do not support OAUTH. Only the IT company support the functionality for customer related services
Q5.1	
Question	Do you impose a specific BYOD?

(*continued*)

Table 3. (*continued*)

Questions	Answers
Answer set	No, informal and voluntary policy, formal policy, strict monitoring of formal policy compliance
Result	The universities apply no BYOD or advertise a general announcement for fair use. The most of the private companies also apply no specific policies or have an informal BYOD, while only one of them impose a formal regulation after a security incident that was caused by an external college. The military sector applies a formal and strict BYOD which is imposed by the responsible security personnel
Q5.2	
Question	Do the administrators comply with the BYOD?
Answer set	Yes, partially, or no
Result	In general, the administrators comply with the BYOD policies, however, in all cases, they admit that they have violated them in specific occasions

References

1. Herley, C., Oorschot, P.V.: A research agenda acknowledging the persistence of passwords. IEEE Secur. Priv. **10**(1), 28–36 (2012)
2. Snow, C.R. Whitfield, H.: Simple authentication. Softw. Practice Exp. **24**(5), 437–447 (2015)
3. Miltchev, S., Smith, J.M., Prevelakis, V., Prevelakis, A., Ioannidis, S.: Decentralized access control in distributed file systems, ACM Comput. Surv. (CSUR) **40**(3), Article no. 10 (2008)
4. Farcasin, M., Chan-tin, E.: Why we hate IT: two surveys on pre-generated and expiring passwords in an academic setting. Secur. Commun. Netw. **8**, 2361–2373 (2015)
5. Furnell, S.: An assessment of website password practices. Comput. Secur. **26**(7–8), 445–451 (2007)
6. Telang, R., Wattal, S.: An Empirical analysis of the impact of software vulnerability announcements on firm stock price. IEEE Trans. Softw. Eng. (TSE) **33**(8), 544–557 (2007)
7. Cavusoglu, H., Cavusoglu, H., Raghunathan, S.: Efficiency of vulnerability disclosure mechanisms to disseminate vulnerability knowledge. IEEE Trans. Softw. Eng. (TSE) **33**(3), 171–185 (2007)
8. Finkle, J., Saba, J.: LinkedIn suffers data breach - security experts, Reuters, June 2012
9. Richmond, S., Williams, C.: Millions of internet users hit by massive Sony PlayStation data theft, The Telegraph, London, 26 April 2011
10. Yan, J., et al.: Password memorability and security: empirical results. IEEE Secur. Priv. **2**(5), 25–31 (2004)
11. Forler, C., Lucks, S., Wenzel, J.: Memory-demanding password scrambling. In: Sarkar, P., Iwata, T. (eds.) ASIACRYPT 2014. LNCS, vol. 8874, pp. 289–305. Springer, Heidelberg (2014). https://doi.org/10.1007/978-3-662-45608-8_16
12. Forler, C., Lucks, S., Wenzel, J.: The Catena Password Scrambler, PHC submission, 15 May (2014)
13. Van Oorschot, P.C., Stubblebine, S.: On countering online dictionary attacks with login histories and humans-in-the-loop. ACM Trans. Inf. Syst. Secur. (TISSEC) **9**(3), 235–258 (2006)

14. Kim, J.W., et al.: High-speed parallel implementations of the rainbow method based on perfect tables in a heterogeneous system, Softw. Practice Exp. **45**(6), 837–855 (2015)
15. Hatzivasilis, G.: Password-hashing status, cryptography. MDPI Open Access J. **1**(2), 10 (2017)
16. Hatzivasilis, G., Papaefstathiou, I., Manifavas, C.: Password hashing competition – survey and benchmark. Cryptology ePrint Archive, IACR **2015**(265), 1–30 (2015)
17. Yu, X., Liao, Q.: User password repetitive patterns analysis and visualization. Inf. Comput. Secur. **24**(1), 93–115 (2016)
18. REUTERS: Man arrested in Athens over ID theft of most Greek population, 2012, 20 November 2012
19. Catuogno, L., Galdi, C.: Analysis of a two-factor graphical password scheme. Int. J. Inf. Secur. **13**(5), 421–437 (2014). https://doi.org/10.1007/s10207-014-0228-y
20. Liu, X.-Y., Gao, H.-C., Wang, L.-M., Chang, X.-L.: An enhanced drawing reproduction graphical password strategy. J. Comput. Sci. Technol. **26**(6), 988–999 (2011)
21. Carter, N., et al.: Graphical passwords for older computer users. Int. J. Secur. Netw. **13**(4), 211–227 (2018)
22. Van Oorschot, P.C., Thorpe, J.: On predictive models and user-drawn graphical passwords. ACM TISSEC **10**(4), Article No. 5, January 2008
23. Shin, J., et al.: SmartPass: a smarter geolocation-based authentication scheme. Secur. Commun. Netw. **8**(18), 3927–3938 (2015)
24. Al-Salloum, Z.S.: GeoGraphical passwords. Int. J. Secur. Netw. **9**(1), 56–62 (2014)
25. Belenko, A., Sklyarov, D.: "Secure Password Managers" and "Military-Grade Encryption" on Smartphones: Oh, Really? Hack to Ergo Sum (HES), 3rd edn., February 2012
26. Bonneau, J., Preibusch, S.: The password thicket: technical and market failures in human authentication on the web. In: 9th WEIS (2010)
27. National Atlantic Treaty Organization: NATO Cyber Defence (2017). http://www.nato.int/cps/en/natohq/topics_78170.htm
28. Percival, C.: Stronger key derivation via sequential memory-hard functions. In: BSDCan 2009, May 2009
29. Hatzivasilis, G., Papaefstathiou, I., Manifavas, C., Askoxylakis, I.: Lightweight password hashing scheme for embedded systems. In: Akram, R.N., Jajodia, S. (eds.) WISTP 2015. LNCS, vol. 9311, pp. 260–270. Springer, Cham (2015). https://doi.org/10.1007/978-3-319-24018-3_17
30. Nayeem, M.T., et al.: Design of a Human Interaction Proof (HIP) using human cognition in contextual natural conversation, IEEE ICCI*CC, pp. 146–154. London, UK (2014)
31. Just, M.: Designing and evaluating challenge-question systems. IEEE Secur. Priv. **2**(5), 32–39 (2004)
32. Farcasin, M., Guli, A., Chan-Tin, E.: Fluid passwords – mitigating the effects of password leaks at the user level, Cornell University Library, arXiv:1708.09333, pp. 1–11, August 2017
33. Zhang, J., Luo, X., Akkaladevi, S., Ziegelmayer, J.: Improving multiple-password recall: an empirical study. Eur. J. Inf. Syst. **18**(2), 165–176 (2009)
34. Tsohou, A., Karyda, M., Kokolakis, S.: Analyzing the role of cognitive and cultural biases in the internalization of information security policies. Comput. Secur. **52**(2015), 128–141 (2015)
35. Tsohou, A., et al.: Investigating information security awareness: research and practice gaps. Inf. Secur. J. Glob. Perspect. **17**(5–6), 207–227 (2008)
36. Manifavas, C., Fysarakis, K., Rantos, K., Hatzivasilis, G.: DSAPE – dynamic security awareness program evaluation. In: Tryfonas, T., Askoxylakis, I. (eds.) HAS 2014. LNCS, vol. 8533, pp. 258–269. Springer, Cham (2014). https://doi.org/10.1007/978-3-319-07620-1_23
37. Chang, B., Li, Y., Wang, Q., Zhu, W.-T., Deng, R.H.: Making a good thing better: enhancing password/PIN-based user authentication with smartwatch. Cybersecurity **1**(1), 1–13 (2018). https://doi.org/10.1186/s42400-018-0009-4

38. Hatzivasilis, G., et al.: MobileTrust: Secure Knowledge Integration in VANETs. ACM Trans. Cyber-Phys. Syst. Spec. Issue User-Centric Secur. Saf. Cyber-Phys. Syst. **4**(3), 1–25 (2020), Article no. 33
39. Miller, K.W., Voas, J., Hurlburt, G.F.: BYOD: security and privacy considerations. IEEE IT Prof. **14**(5), 53–55 (2012)
40. Hatzivasilis, G., et al.: Review of security and privacy for the internet of medical things (IoMT). In: 1st International Workshop on Smart Circular Economy (SmaCE), Santorini Island, Greece, pp. 457–464, IEEE, 30 May
41. Harris, M.A., Patten, K.P.: Mobile device security considerations for small- and medium-sized enterprise business mobility. Inf. Manage. Comput. Secur. **22**(1), 97–114 (2014)
42. Chang, J.M., Ho, P.-C., Chang, T.-C.: Securing BYOD. IEEE IT Prof. **16**(5), 9–11 (2014)
43. Kaur, E.G., Aggarwal, E.D.: A survey òf social sign-on protocol OAuth 2.0. J. Eng. Comput. Appl. Sci. (JEC&AS), Blue Ocean Res. J. **2**(6), 93–96 (2013)
44. Amazon Developer Center: Securely connect with millions of Amazon customers and personalize their experience, Amazon (2017)
45. Facebook for developers: Success story: Riot Games' League of Legends, Facebook (2017)
46. Li, W., Mitchell, C.J.: Security issues in OAuth 2.0 SSO implementations. In: Chow, S.S.M., Camenisch, J., Hui, L.C.K., Yiu, S.M. (eds.) ISC 2014. LNCS, vol. 8783, pp. 529–541. Springer, Cham (2014). https://doi.org/10.1007/978-3-319-13257-0_34
47. James, T., Nottingham, Q. J., Ziegelmayer, J.: Determining an individual's concept of privacy. In: 39th Annual Meeting of the Decision Sciences Institute, DSI, pp. 5011–5016 (2008)
48. James, T.L., Nottingham, Q., Collignon, S.E., Warkentin, M., Ziegelmayer, J.L.: The interpersonal privacy identity (IPI): development of a privacy as control model. Inf. Technol. Manage. **17**(4), 341–360 (2015). https://doi.org/10.1007/s10799-015-0246-0
49. Manifavas, C., et al.: Lightweight cryptography for embedded systems – a comparative analysis. In: Garcia-Alfaro, J., Lioudakis, G., Cuppens-Boulahia, N., Foley, S., Fitzgerald, W. (eds.) DPM 2013. LNCS, vol. 8247, pp. 333–349. Springer, Cham (2013). https://doi.org/10.1007/978-3-642-54568-9_21

Author Index

Astaneh, Sadegh   79

Beckers, Kristian   61
Bierwirth, Tore   3
Braghin, Chiara   79

Chung, Tek Kan   92
Cimato, Stelvio   79

Damiani, Ernesto   79
Drury, Vincent   41

Eftychia, Lakka   143
Emmanouil, Michalodimitrakis   143

Frati, Fulvio   79
Fysarakis, Konstantinos   22

George, Spanoudakis   143
Goeke, Ludger   61

Hatzivasilis, George   22, 111, 157
Hillmann, Peter   3

Knüpfer, Marcus   3
Koehler, Klemens   41
Konstantinos, Fysarakis   143
Kunc, Martin   111

Manos, Papoutsakis   143
Meyer, Ulrike   41

Nikolaos, Petroulakis   143

Pape, Sebastian   61
Pöhn, Daniela   3
Prevelakis, Vassilis   125

Quintanar, Alejandro   61

Riccobene, Elvinia   79
Roepke, Rene   41

Schopp, Matthias   3
Schroeder, Ulrik   41
Seeber, Sebastian   3
Smyrlis, Michail   22
Sotiris, Ioannidis   143
Spanoudakis, George   22
Stiemert, Lars   3

Tsantekidis, Marinos   125

Wang, Xiao-Si   92
Welding, Jessica   92
Wolf, Martin R.   41

Printed in the United States
By Bookmasters